WHAT REMAINS

WHAT REMAINS

Bringing America's Missing
Home from the Vietnam War

SARAH E. WAGNER

Harvard University Press

Cambridge, Massachusetts
London, England
2019

First printing

Library of Congress Cataloging-in-Publication Data
Names: Wagner, Sarah E., author.
Title: What remains : bringing America's missing home from the Vietnam War/
Sarah E. Wagner.
Description: Cambridge, Massachusetts : Harvard University Press, 2019. |
Includes bibliographical references and index.
Identifiers: LCCN 2019014450 | ISBN 9780674988347 (alk. paper)
Subjects: LCSH: Vietnam War, 1961–1975—Missing in action—United States. |
Missing in action—Vietnam—Identification. | Vietnam War, 1961–1975—
Repatriation of war dead—United States. | Vietnam War, 1961–1975—Search
and rescue operations—United States. | Grief—United States.
Classification: LCC DS559.8.M5 W34 2019 | DDC 959.704 / 38—dc23
LC record available at https://lccn.loc.gov/2019014450

♦ TO THOSE WHO CAME HOME RIGHT AWAY

♦ TO THOSE WHO CAME HOME YEARS LATER

+ TO THOSE WHO MAY NEVER COME HOME

Contents

Abbreviations

ABMC	American Battle Monuments Commission
AFDIL	Armed Forces DNA Identification Laboratory
AFRSSIR	Armed Forces Repository of Specimen Samples for the Identification of Remains
ARVN	Army of the Republic of Vietnam
ASCLD/LAB	American Society of Crime Laboratory Directors/Laboratory Accreditation Board
ASGRO	Armed Services Graves Registration Office
AWOL	absent without leave
BNR	body not recovered
BTB	believed to be
CIL	Central Identification Laboratory
CILHI	Central Identification Laboratory Hawaii
DMZ	demilitarized zone
DNA	deoxyribonucleic acid
DOD	Department of Defense
DPAA	Defense POW/MIA Accounting Agency
DPMO	Defense Prisoner of War/Missing Personnel Office
EOD	explosive ordnance disposal
GAO	Government Accountability Office
IED	improvised explosive device
JCRC	Joint Casualty Resolution Center
JFA	Joint Field Activity
JPAC	Joint POW/MIA Accounting Command

JPRC	Joint Personnel Recovery Center
JTF-FA	Joint Task Force-Full Accounting
KIA	killed in action
LPDR	Lao People's Democratic Republic
LSEL	Life Sciences Equipment Laboratory
MACV	Military Assistance Command, Vietnam
MIA	missing in action
mtDNA	mitochondrial DNA
NGS	next generation sequencing
NPR	National Public Radio
PACT	Personnel Accounting Consolidation Task Force
POW	prisoner of war
PSYOP	psychological operations
PTSD	posttraumatic stress disorder
REFNO	reference number
SEA	Southeast Asia
SOP	standard operating procedure
SRV	Socialist Republic of Vietnam
STR	short tandem repeat
USPACOM	United States Pacific Command
UXO	unexploded ordnance
VFW	The Veterans of Foreign Wars of the United States
VNO	Vietnamese Office for Seeking Missing Persons (VNOSMP)
WWI	World War I
WWII	World War II
Y-STR	STR on the Y-chromosome

WHAT REMAINS

· HOMECOMING ·

After forty-six years, Lance Corporal Merlin Raye Allen came home. To fanfare and flags, he returned to the little town on the shores of Lake Superior in northern Wisconsin where, as a child, he had spent his summer vacations and later, when his family moved north, he finished out his high school years. He loved the lake and its sandy beaches; he made good friends and felt at home on the water.

But, in 1965, he also felt a duty to serve his country. A few months after his graduation from Bayfield High School, Allen enlisted in the Marine Corps to fight in Vietnam.

For almost half a century, Merlin Allen was one of Bayfield, Wisconsin's missing in action from the war in Southeast Asia, and on June 28, 2013, the town readied itself for his homecoming.[1] Too small to have its own funeral parlor, Bayfield would wait an extra day to host the memorial service for him in its local high school. In the meantime, Allen's remains would be shepherded to the Bratley Funeral Home in nearby Washburn, just a few miles south on Route 13, the two-lane highway that traces the lake's southern shoreline and the promontory leading to the one of region's prized landscapes, the Apostle Islands National Lakeshore.

It was a beautiful day, the kind when all of the glory of the Canadian Shield is on display, and the sweet scent of the woods, cut with wild flowers and the cool breeze from the lake, fills the air. A perfect day to greet a fallen hero.

Well before he arrived in Washburn, Allen had already returned to the fold of the military and the care of the nation. He flew from the United States military's forensic facility in Hawaii, where his remains had been identified, to the Minneapolis/St. Paul airport, where his family and an honor guard waited planeside for the arrival of the urn—a compact wooden chest—nested inside a flag-draped coffin. Soon afterward, members of the Minnesota and Wisconsin Patriot Guard Riders, many of them Vietnam War veterans, with their signature leather vests and rumbling Harleys, joined the official escort. As the column of vehicles moved northward, squad cars from towns and counties along the way led the procession. When they hit the Wisconsin border, state troopers took over.

In Washburn, people of all ages lined the main street in anticipation. Local television crews set up to capture the convoy's arrival. Flags were given out for children to wave at the cars passing by.

It was a return more symbolic than material. Little of Lance Corporal (LCpl) "Merl" Allen remained—just a single tooth unearthed from a mountainside in the jungles of central Vietnam one year before as part of the US military's efforts to account for its missing service members from the war in Southeast Asia. If the crowd that had assembled to welcome him home knew what a small fraction of LCpl Allen had returned, they didn't let on. Or it didn't matter. What mattered was that after so many years of uncertainty, his family, friends, schoolmates, fellow veterans, and the Bayfield community could finally reclaim him. They could welcome him back and give him the marked resting place that he deserved. And so when the motorcade rolled down Highway 13 and into Washburn, past the local diners, the grocery store, the auto shop, and the memorial park, they stood at attention, many waving flags and wiping away tears. It was, as one vet told me, the only homecoming of its kind that people in northern Wisconsin could remember.

Bayfield is both singular and common in its story of a lost son returned. With a population of 487, it's a sleepy town despite the influx of tourism and lakeshore development. But on this occasion, as it received that tiny fragment of a once vibrant human life, Bayfield became something larger. The remains of LCpl Allen did more than just put Bayfield on the map for a few days. It created a powerful, if ephemeral, community of mourners—kith and kin and strangers alike.[2] Around that single tooth, a temporary assembly memorialized a lost life and recalled a war long past. The gathered mourners imagined, if only for an instant, their connection to the young man, a US Marine, and to the nation that sent him off to die and that decades later labored to find his body and to bring him home.

Lance Corporal Merlin Raye Allen.

This book is about the Bayfields and LCpl Allens of this country, about the efforts to recover and name the Vietnam War's missing in action, and about how science is changing the way American war dead are remembered and honored. It's about what happens when missing service members are identified and what happens when they remain missing. It's about war, its tolls, and its legacies.

Introduction

THE FIRST TIME I WATCHED a military burial at Arlington National Cemetery, I was riveted by the hands. The hands of the honor guard detail had all the mesmerizing otherworldly energy of a burning fire. White gloves glided along clean edges, pulling taut the fabric of the flag suspended just above the wooden casket in a delicately choreographed motion. Fold after fold, the red, white, and blue receded into itself until all that remained was a tight triangular package, a gift from the nation presented on bended knee to the bereaved.

Burials, as a form of ritual, shed light on what a community or society values—not only what it holds dear or deems essential, but also what obligations arise and what rites are required. The famous sociologist Émile Durkheim, whose own son died in combat during World War I, once said that through rituals, "society never stops creating new sacred things."[1] Rituals consecrate objects, ideas, individuals, even nations. They guard against transgressions, defining how we orient and comport ourselves in the presence of sacred things.[2] Rituals also help make sense of the unfathomable, like aberrant or untimely death. In such circumstances, they do important work for both the living and the dead. In the words of Durkheim's student Robert Hertz, rituals help the mourning society return to a "state of peace," and thus "triumph over death."[3]

But what rituals suffice when there is nothing of the dead to bury or to care for—when there are no bodies to "ritual about" or "ritual with?" Rituals often turn on material objects, and in the case of the dead, the body itself becomes that focal point. Think of the cult of the saints in early

Christianity: their relic bones serve as powerful, tangible symbols for their supplicants, consecrating the spaces and artifacts around them. But what happens when those powerful symbols are missing? Our story, the story of the Vietnam War and its aftermath, begins with that fundamental conundrum—when the remains of war dead go unrecovered and their fates unaccounted for—and explores its consequences. By no means the first or even the most extreme instance of armed conflict to introduce such a conundrum, the war in Southeast Asia, at least within the American experience, inaugurated a new way of confronting war's destruction: through science, in its capacity to recognize the sacred and to enable rituals of remembrance and mourning.[4] The forensic science of accounting for the missing in action (MIA) presented the nation, the state, and its military, local communities, veterans, and, most important of all, surviving kin with a new means by which to respond to mass death and counter the sting of the war's defeat.

It's a jarring notion; we tend to think of science as grounded in the traditions of empiricism and objectivity, not as the stuff of social rites and sacred objects.[5] And of course, science is, indeed, empirical and objective. But it is also deeply social; reflecting the values of the society in which it exists, scientific inquiry produces knowledge and baseline facts, and in doing so, shapes the way people approach problems and seek their resolution. Science can help render the unfathomable less so, including the devastating effects of war. This was the case—though belatedly—for the Vietnam War. The forensic efforts of recovering and identifying remains of service members missing in action or killed in action/body not recovered—since 1973 collectively known as the "unaccounted for"—gave rise to new rituals, creating "new sacred things" in the wake of violent rupture.[6] Chief among those new things is a different way of talking about and thus apprehending war's human tolls; forensic science has given families of the unaccounted for a new language of remembrance, one that seeks to address the ambiguities of unknown fates and unreturned remains through the promise of accuracy, calculability, and efficiency.[7] In this novel lexicon of individuated loss and sacrifice, the science of MIA accounting has also affected how this country remembers its war dead, raising expectations for what is possible and what is necessary in honoring those who died fighting on its behalf.

Why Vietnam?

"Missing in action" is a deceptively neat phrase for the messy category of remains unrecovered and fates unaccounted for in any modern war. The ambiguity surrounding their physical remains and the facts of their absence elude easy resolution. But with the Vietnam War and, in particular, its postwar politics, the disjuncture between language and experience was especially sharp. To begin with, the MIA category represented merely one column within a larger account book of destruction—from ravaged land and property to decimated communities, families, lives, and bodies. Some five million tons of bombs were dropped on Vietnam, another two million on Laos, and an estimated half a million on Cambodia—in total, three times the amount dropped over both Europe and the Pacific during World War II.[8] The United States and its South Vietnamese allies spread seventy-three million liters of chemical agents, 62 percent of it Agent Orange, an herbicide whose full impact, particularly with its deadly dioxin, is not yet known, even three and four generations later.[9] In Vietnam alone, an estimated three million people were killed between 1954 and 1975, most of them by the United States and its allies, while 58,220 US forces are counted as killed in action (KIA) or as non-combat deaths.[10] At the signing of the Paris Peace Accords in 1973, the United States listed 2,646 Americans as unaccounted for from the war, "with roughly equal numbers of those missing in action, or killed in action/body not recovered";[11] of those, 1,589 US service members are still missing.[12] The number for Vietnamese missing, estimated at three hundred thousand, is harder to tabulate as the postwar country confronts not only a significantly greater scale of loss, but also the question of which lives and what forms of sacrifice merit remembering.[13]

With its number of unaccounted for less than 4 percent of the total listed fatalities (2,646 of 58,220), the Vietnam War was by no means exceptional in the history of US military engagement.[14] On the contrary, the percentage paled in comparison to that of the missing and unknown American war dead from World War II—19 percent (79,000 of 400,000 dead)—and the Korean War—22 percent (8,000 of 36,500).[15] The Civil War's carnage dwarfed those numbers, as "hundreds of thousands of men—more than 40 percent of deceased Yankees and a far greater proportion of Confederates—perished without names, identified only, as Walt Whitman put it, 'by the significant word UNKNOWN.'"[16] But in the postwar politics of reckoning with defeat, the unaccounted for from the war in Southeast Asia assumed a qualitatively different force than their antecedents. In part, that force derived from how closely connected the categories of POW and MIA became during and after the war.[17] Uncertainty bred hope and anxiety; wartime contentions bred postwar frustrations. For example, in the early years, for some surviving relatives, the status of "missing in action" left the door of survival cracked open. It meant an entirely different order of knowledge, or more precisely, the lack thereof, than that of "killed in action but body not recovered," where an individual was known to have died but whose remains were not located and repatriated, owing to the circumstances of the loss. "Missing means you don't know what happened to them. . . . Missing means you have uncertainty about what happened to them."[18] Given that uncertainty, might the MIA someday reappear—alive—as a POW released or escaped from captivity? On the national stage, both during the war and after the signing of the peace accords, voices within the POW/MIA advocacy movement sought to preserve this connection, stoking the fires of hope, for political purposes as well as for personal needs.[19] But away from that spotlight, in households across the United States, MIA status often introduced a delicate, strained position of dependence that compounded the uncertainty, as spouses and children continued to receive benefits of an active-duty service member. Whether remains came home, an official finding of death had profound material and social consequences.[20] In these trying circumstances, Vietnam War POW/MIA families and returned veterans waged their own private battles of hope, fear, anger, and resignation. More often than not, they were left to navigate the murky waters of MIA status, of uncertain fate and absent remains, with little help from the government.

"You are not forgotten." Even as the POW/MIA movement's slogan insisted that the country hold the war's unaccounted for in the clear light of memory, on some level, not forgetting was not enough. National attention focused on fates of the living and remains of the dead—a different kind of "body count" from the one evoked by Secretary of Defense Robert McNamara's statistical measure of enemy attrition.[21] Vietnam War veterans issued their own challenge: "Bring them home or send us back!" They argued that the missing deserved to be located and repatriated; indeed, their sacrifice required it. In pushing for the "fullest possible accounting"—the phrase first adopted by the National League of POW/MIA Families (arguably the most politically powerful such organization in the country) and used by President Nixon when he announced the Paris Peace Accords in 1973 and again in his State of the Union Address in 1974—both the

POW/MIA families and the Vietnam vets were demanding that the US government fulfill its obligation to those sacrificed in its service.[22]

Yet accounting, especially for the missing and presumed dead, wasn't merely about tabulating and documenting. It was about care, a system of social value and practice that understood those dead as more than just organic remnants, bones subject to decay; rather, they were "social beings" in need of posthumous care.[23] For historian Thomas Laqueur, that sensibility is inherently human: "We as a species care for the dead; we live among them; we make of them ciphers of memory."[24] The living have ethical obligations to the dead, "creatures who need to be eased out of this world and settled safely into the next and into memory."[25] But what to do when there is nothing tangible to "ease out," or to "settle safely?" And what to do when those "creatures" are young men and women who died fighting on behalf of the abstraction that is the nation? Though joining a much longer lineage of American unknowns and unrecovered from past conflicts stretching back to the Civil War, the unaccounted for from the Vietnam War prompted new rituals of meaning making. For in its ambiguity, the missing-in-action label proved both too vast and too empty to contain the hopes, anxieties, and demands of surviving kin. A different response to their absence had to be devised, one that centered on caring for the physical remains of the missing through scientific means—recovering, repatriating, identifying, and returning them to their families and their communities of mourning.

Rituals for the Missing

I didn't start out thinking of science as a source of ritual. On the contrary, from the beginning I was struck by much more obvious forms of ritual activity in American military life. Perhaps because I came to the story of the missing in action as an uninitiated observer—only one person in my family, my mother's brother, had served in the Vietnam War, and of my generation, only two older cousins had joined the military, one the air force and the other the navy. To my eye, there seemed a symbol, or symbolic act, for everything; one just needed to know how to recognize and translate it. Part of the task of anthropological research is to undertake a long-term, fine-grained analysis, what we call ethnographic study—of a community, a social practice or institution, a set of beliefs, and so on—and attempt to understand it according to the internal logics of that society, for example, to tease out the meanings of symbols and rituals, how they've come to be, and how, why, and by whom they're employed. It takes time and requires patience; it depends on people's willingness to share their insights and experiences and the anthropologist's ability to aggregate and juxtapose those views until a clearer picture emerges.

Thus, only later did I begin to appreciate that the surfeit of ritual surrounding the MIA's ambiguous fate stemmed from the context of the war itself: in the absence of military funeral honors with the three volleys of rifle fire, folded flag, and marked headstone, the missing in action from the prolonged and contentious war in Southeast Asia have generated their own repertoire of symbols and rituals. Take, for example, the Missing Man Table ceremony. In Veterans of Foreign Wars posts, at Memorial Day gatherings and MIA commemorative events across the country, a table is set and chairs arrayed to honor those still absent. While it's now used to commemorate the unaccounted for from other conflicts—World War II, the Korean War, the Cold War, the First Gulf War—the ritual originated in response to the Vietnam War. Little is left to the imagination, as the accompanying script, often read aloud at commemorative events, explains each symbol, its meaning, and the audience's expected response:

> The table is round—to show our everlasting concern.
>
> The cloth is white—symbolizing the purity of their motives when answering the call to serve.
>
> The single red rose reminds us of the lives of these Americans . . . and their loved ones and friends who keep the faith, while seeking answers.
>
> The yellow ribbon symbolizes our continued uncertainty, hope for their return and determination to account for them.
>
> A slice of lemon reminds us of their bitter fate, captured and missing in a foreign land.
>
> A pinch of salt symbolizes the tears of our missing and their families—who long for answers after decades of uncertainty.
>
> The lighted candle reflects our hope for their return—alive or dead.
>
> The Bible represents the strength gained through faith to sustain us and those lost from our country, founded as one nation under God.
>
> The glass is inverted—to symbolize their inability to share a toast.
>
> The chairs are empty—they are missing.[26]

With its symbolic elements subsuming individual experience into collective categories—draftees and enlistees are leveled in purity of motive; faith is explicitly Judeo-Christian; families are uniformly unwavering in their hope and grief—the ceremony sets apart both the missing and their surviving kin as sacred. It lets us know how to think and feel and act in the face of one of war's most destructive ends: to be still missing; or, more to the point, not yet home, indefinitely.

The Missing Man Table ceremony itself incorporates another important symbol of the war in Southeast Asia—the iconic image from the POW/MIA flag. Conceived and commissioned by an MIA wife in 1970, the flag is black and white, with the silhouette of a service member.[27] Behind him, one sees a prison watchtower; in front of him there is a strand of barbed wire. Atop flagpoles in small towns and big cities across the United States, decorating pickups and stitched on leather jackets, the flag has become a recognized national symbol. Most Americans old enough to remember the war understand the consciously yoked categories of POW and MIA, even if they don't know the individual stories behind the flag or the specifics of the policies that enshrined it at municipal buildings, fire stations and police stations, rest stops and toll plazas.[28] For many, the silhouette of the bowed head recalls the era's fractious politics that reverberate to this day in public debates about foreign policy and entanglements abroad. However they choose to acknowledge or embrace it, Americans young and old recognize the flag's call to action: the printed pledge "You are not forgotten" that defies time's threat (and the threat of a potentially indifferent society) to blur, even to erase, memories of absent service members and of war's tolls.

Next to these more obvious ceremonies and symbols of the Vietnam War's POW/MIA movement, science seems an unlikely source or catalyst for ritual. But its role in generating "new sacred things" becomes clearer in light of the conundrum of the war's missing service members and the thorny questions invited by their absence. Beyond raising flags and setting tables, how should a nation, a surviving parent, sibling, or child, a veteran or a current military member commemorate a combatant whose fate has yet to be known with certainty? On a more abstract level, how does one remember a person who is neither definitively dead nor positively alive? What works to ease such absence? What brings about an end to uncertainty? While almost every war waged sooner or later provides its own, if partial, answers to these questions, for the United States, the Vietnam War heightened and expanded a national tradition of individuated recovery, repatriation, and identification that stretched back to the Civil War, one in which "bringing them home" trumped "burying them where they fell." Sharpened by the postwar politics of duty and debt, the cultural demand of repatriating and identifying remains from the conflict in Southeast Asia required more advanced technologies and different forms of expertise. That demand in turn has given rise to a forensic enterprise, which, in its attempts to order facts and bodies, has spanned decades, cost hundreds of millions of dollars, and returned thousands of absent American war dead to their surviving families and to the nation.

In this shifting set of practice and ideals, the named individual come home has become the expected end, the final act in the nation's proper response to its missing fallen. The forensic work of MIA accounting has helped create a "new sacred thing": an ethos of exceptional care. The point about this exceptionalism isn't that the United States is, in fact, the only country that goes to such lengths and spends such resources (approximately $130 million annually) to recover, repatriate, and scientifically individuate its war dead.[29] Rather, it is about what that ethos of promised, indeed obliged, care—the fullest possible accounting for every possible case—itself enables. On an ideological plane, this notion of exceptional care provides the state an expedient narrative to push past the Vietnam War's embittering divisiveness and instead train attention on its unparalleled efforts to bring its fallen home. Named and returned missing war dead become powerful symbols to rehabilitate or reanimate the memory of past wars for present and future use, buttressing claims of contemporary military valor. Seen in this light, science offers a potent response to defeat and death.

Yet the ethos of exceptional care also exposes the fragmented and unstable nature of memory itself. The state may go to extraordinary lengths to bring fallen service members home, but their memory belongs to more than the nation in the abstract. Homecomings are just that—highly localized and personalized—not merely fodder for national celebration. Here, the exceptional exists in the unusual and unexpected, with the commonplace itself suddenly transformed into the sacred. For as sites of collective burial and commemoration have gradually given way to opportunities and spaces for individuated remembrance, memory takes shape idiosyncratically and according to local traditions. Sometimes, those traditions challenge narrow understandings of national belonging.

Regardless of the tradition invoked, with returned and named remains come stories, and with stories come the possibility to reconnect a life to a family and friends, to classmates, neighbors, and communities, and even to strangers in acts of local (rather than exclusively national) remembrance. This last point is perhaps the most important: the return of scientifically identified remains—their physical homecoming—allow the living to participate in the rituals of exceptional care otherwise afforded to the state. Sometimes that care and those stories fray the edges of the tightly woven script of national sacrifice, insisting on recounting a life lived before and beyond the flattening biography of military service. Moreover, for Victnam War families and veterans especially, the return of remains also offers a chance to correct past injury; forty and fifty years later, long-absent war dead are welcomed home in ways never thought possible by those who survived and returned to their country during the war. Geography matters, but not always in a directly correlating sense. These homecomings are public, yet intimate, affairs, as individual families and communities reconstitute themselves, if only temporarily, around the event of return; home may be the missing service member's birthplace, or the place where surviving kin now reside, or even military burial grounds such as Arlington National Cemetery. Whatever the final destination, homecomings enabled by forensic scientific innovations entwine the living with the dead in the project of national belonging, but they do so on local terms and according to the particular histories of loss and remembrance.

Things Carried and Left

The shards of memory acquired greater status, greater resonance, because they were *remains;* fragmentation made trivial things seem like symbols, and the mundane acquired numinous qualities.

—SALMAN RUSHDIE, "Imaginary Homelands"[30]

War and memory, missing persons and social repair. Before turning to the MIA accounting mission here in the United States, I had already spent years exploring these themes in a very different place—Bosnia and Herzegovina. For almost a decade, I studied the forensic scientific efforts to identify the victims of the Srebrenica genocide, working with families of the more than eight thousand missing men and boys, the majority of whom were killed in groups and their bodies dumped into mass graves, and the forensic practitioners who labored to recover and return those remains. Though civilian victims of state-sponsored violence and members of a nation's armed forces—whether draftees, enlistees, or officers—occupy inherently estranged positions vis-à-vis the experience of violent conflict, there are nevertheless commonalities across incidents of prolonged absence, the memory politics that seeps into its crevices, and the tools forensic science brings to bear in its wake. And so my anthropological sensibilities were already attuned to the potential overlaps among absence, memory, and science when I shifted my ethnographic gaze homeward.

As strange as it may sound, Bosnia helped make sense of what I was observing not just of the science of MIA accounting, but also of the war's material legacy of commemoration. When I first began researching the topic in the spring of 2008, I visited a museum exhibit at the Department of the Interior, a display about the Vietnam Veterans Memorial and objects left at the monument. The memorial's stone panels with their chronicle of etched names pay tribute to the Americans killed and missing from the war. It's a popular site on the National Mall, drawing an estimated four million visitors annually. For years, the Vietnam Veterans Memorial Fund and the National Park Service, which jointly oversee the monument, had been collecting, cataloging, and storing the items, everything from letters and photos to Zippos and dog tags, that accumulated each day at the base of the monument. To mark the twenty-fifth anniversary of the memorial's dedication, the organizations decided to put together an exhibition.

The idea of a curated selection of mementos left for the war's dead and the missing immediately called to mind a different, though connected, set of mundane and exceptional wartime items. In his collection of short stories, *The Things They Carried,* author Tim O'Brien, himself a Vietnam War veteran, opens with an essay about the various burdens, physical and psychological, that soldiers "humped" across the foreign terrain. Unfolding sporadically and evoked by the essay's different characters, his lists mix specificity and metaphor:

> Mitchell Sanders, the RTO, carried condoms. Norman Bowker carried a diary. Rat Kiley carried comic books. . . .
>
> They carried all they could bear, and then some, including a silent awe for the terrible power of the things they carried. . . .
>
> They carried the land itself—Vietnam, the place, the soil—a powdery orange-red dust that covered their boots and fatigues and faces. . . .
>
> They carried all the emotional baggage of men who might die.[31]

As I approached the building, I wondered how the material artifacts on display at the museum might echo or add to O'Brien's compendium.

The exhibit filled a single room. To the left, a textual and photographic display laid out the war in compact narratives and timelines and then turned to the memorial itself (what has come to be known as the Wall)—its genesis, the design competition, twenty-one-year-old Maya Lin's winning entry, its construction, and finally its reception. For all the descriptions and quotations, images and maps, it was the right-hand side of the room that conveyed the human side of the war most powerfully. Badges, buttons, patches, metals, bracelets, coins, lighters, caps, photographs, letters, a single stiletto heel, a pair of lace panties, a tube sock, dog tags, cigars, helmets—objects of war, of camaraderie, of love and lives cut short, of habit and ritual—all told the story not of the war per se but of the people who fought it, of those who survived it, those who died in it, and those left behind to remember it.[32] These were not mere artifacts. They were encapsulated biographies, "objects," as Stephen Greenblatt explains, "of resonance and wonder."[33]

The centerpiece of the display was the so-called Hero Bike, a custom-built, 1960s-era chopper fashioned from Harley Davidson parts. It stood on a platform set off from all the other objects, an artwork of polished chrome, leather, and detailing. Like O'Brien's description of Vietnam's soil, "a powdery orange-red dust," the bike's hand-painted panoramas evoked the wartime landscape through color. On the gas tank, two dark HU-1A helicopters—the "Hueys" that became so emblematic of the Vietnam War era—emerged against the orange glow of a setting sun, the horizon merging with a jungle scene of "a GI in distress in front of a crumbling wall, inscribed with the names of Wisconsin's MIAs."[34] Dog tags stamped with the names of those same thirty-seven missing service members hung at the front of the bike, and a hand-stitched leather seat cover bore the signature veteran's slogan, "POW/MIAs—Bring 'em home or send us back." A placard nearby explained that the bike, which had been built by several Vietnam vets from Wisconsin, was dedicated to that state's missing on the condition that each of its MIAs would have the chance to ride it when he returned, but it "was not to be ridden until the last one comes home."

In that simple equation, the dedication captured the ambiguity of the missing-in-action status and the obligations owed the individuals who shared its uncertain fate. At the same time, it acknowledged the sad truth of that fate, so many years later. Conceived and assembled in

1994, driven from Wisconsin to Washington, DC, as part of the Rolling Thunder commemorative motorcycle ride through the capital on Memorial Day, 1995, the bike appeared at the Wall over two decades after the last living POWs came home from Vietnam. For its creators, little if any doubt remained about whether the thirty-seven men from Wisconsin were still alive. Yet the dedication staked its claim to an imagined, impossible future in which the long-absent men come home; until then, the bike would only ever exist as homage to their absence and the certain sacrifice that stood behind it.

The Arc of MIA Accounting

The Vietnam War MIA experience in the United States is anything but black and white, and families' and veterans' ways of responding to the unaccounted for are anything but monolithic. Nevertheless, there are themes that emerge in the contemporary practice of accounting for the war's missing and commemorating their return—from scientific advances to shifting modes of remembrance. Often we look to the pageantry of national holidays to gauge how a nation recalls and honors those who fought and died for it, but this book invites a view onto places of the average and the everyday, of small-town America, alongside more frequented sites of memory and mourning.[35] Through their examples, we glimpse not only the unstable, fragmented nature of memory itself, but also the possibilities for ethical or just memory within the bounded efforts to remember national sacrifice on a local scale and within a particular community.[36] It is a different kind of memory work taking place in those tight circles of grief—and sometimes laughter—that seek to recall the absent through seemingly mundane, even trivial, gestures. But those too, I discovered, are acts of exceptional care.

One place where such memory work unfolds is in the neighboring communities of Bayfield and Red Cliff, Wisconsin. It's a region that has its own unique story of loss from the Vietnam War, with a significant Native American population and history of military service, but also one that reflects the broader experience of MIA accounting, from prolonged absence to eventual resolution. I first visited the area, the Bayfield Peninsula, in July 2014, two years after having participated in a US military-led excavation in central Vietnam that had recovered the remains of Lance Corporal Merlin Allen, one of the town's two missing in action from that war.

In Bayfield, I wanted to follow the accounting process to its logical end, the official homecoming and burial of the identified service member. I had arranged to meet a few people who had welcomed LCpl Allen home the previous year and helped bury him next to his parents on York Island in Lake Superior. I hoped to learn more about Merlin Allen himself and what his return had meant to his surviving family, friends, fellow service members, and veterans of the community.

On the morning of the appointed day, I set out on the 150-mile drive west through the North Woods and along the Lake Superior shore to reach Bayfield and the nearby town of Red Cliff, which is the administrative center for the Red Cliff Band of Lake Superior Chippewa. My first meeting was with one of Merl Allen's high school friends, Dan. It was his last day working at the local casino's gift shop in Red Cliff, and so we agreed to meet at 9:30 a.m. for a coffee before his shift began.

The early-morning drive along Highway 2 was quiet, with few cars on the road and long stretches of woodlands between towns and the occasional traffic light. "Friday Fish Fry" signs appeared in almost every town, German Catholic roots still firmly in place, along with other emblems of of life in northern Wisconsin and Upper Peninsula Michigan—pasty stands, diners and bars, Miller Lite signs, and Green Bay Packers satellite dishes; National Park entrances; a small house boasting a Museum of Finland. On the radio, a Swedish restaurant advertised between NPR shows. The Bad River Casino (owned by the Bad River Band of the Lake Superior Chippewa) had a half-full parking lot. The highway cut its narrow strip through this segment of the Upper Midwest, revealing a history of immigration, forest conservation, and Native American territorial rights, all of which played a role in Bayfield's own past.

At 9:25 a.m., I panicked a bit, still a few miles shy of Red Cliff and the casino. I called Dan's number and got his wife. "He'll just get some coffee and wait," she assured me. When I arrived in Bayfield several minutes later, there was little time for more than a quick glance at the shops that lined the main street. Even from that snapshot, Bayfield stood out from the other small towns I had passed on my way there, including Washburn just a few miles back. It looked a lot wealthier. Later I would learn of the Twin City weekenders who come up to enjoy the lake, with their sailboats and yachts docked in the marina.

That first meeting was at the heart of another important site within the local economy, the Legendary Waters Resort and Casino, run by the Red Cliff Band. A large complex that boasts 240 slot machines, blackjack and

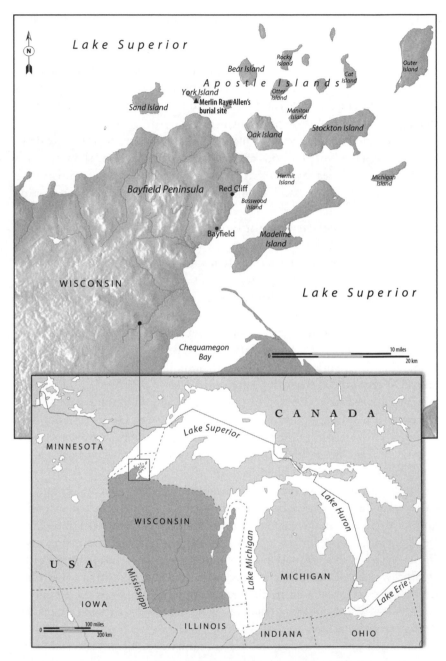

Map of Northern Wisconsin.

poker games, a marina, and a campground, the casino is a recent addition, built in 2011. Once there and the car parked, I hustled through the main entrance and into the scene of dim lights and dark carpet. Above me, signs pointed right, down the foyer that led to the adjacent hotel and restaurant. I was fifteen minutes late. My heart sank a little; it seemed a bad way to start the day's meetings.

Seated at a table several yards away were two men who looked to be in their mid-sixties, each wearing a black baseball cap with patches, the kind you'd see at Rolling Thunder or Veterans Day parades. They had spotted me already. One had to be Dan. I took a deep breath as he called out, "Are you Sarah?" We shook hands and he immediately introduced me to Bootin (Larry), the brother of Duwayne Soulier, the other MIA/KIA from the Red Cliff community. I apologized for keeping them, and they kindly brushed it off.

More than anything in those first few minutes, I remember Dan and Bootin's willingness to sit and wait for a stranger on a bright summer morning in the foyer of a casino. If they were wary, they didn't let on, though nerves seemed to have us all a bit tongue tied. Just as we were grasping for the right direction, Bootin pulled out a thin copper bracelet and handed it to me. Printed in black lettering were the names of all the MIAs (or more precisely, unaccounted for) from the state. My eyes snapped up toward him. "Are these the thirty-seven?" At first, he didn't quite understand what I meant. I tried to explain. "The thirty-seven MIAs from Wisconsin?"[37] Yes, he nodded, yes, it was. His brother's name was on it, as was Merlin Allen's. I rushed to say that I had a story to tell them, about this number, about the first time I learned of the thirty-seven missing men from their state.

For anthropologists, there are invariably scenes from our fieldwork, our research in particular places and with particular communities, that tend to stick with us, encounters whose force lingers in our memory long after the study has ended. I can remember sitting in the back room of the Women of Srebrenica's office in Tuzla, Bosnia and Herzegovina, poring over a book of photographs of clothing exhumed with remains, leafing through page after page of tattered T-shirts and jackets, pondering the wretchedness of the mass graves, the bodies they contained, and those pieces of cloth. I can remember the sound of the earth falling on the coffins, the hollow thump of dirt on the pine boxes, as a whole community of mourners labored under the hot July sun to bury their slain, once missing but now identified fathers, sons, husbands, and brothers.

The encounter at the casino that morning was one such scene. After Bootin left, Dan let me pick our spot in the restaurant, and I found a booth in the corner, next to the wall of glass windows that opened out onto the bay, the expanse of Lake Superior's cool silver water. The booth itself was classic diner decor: burnished yellow vinyl seats and a faux-wood tabletop. Silverware lay tightly bundled in thin paper napkins, cream and sugar packets to the side. We both ordered coffee, almost apologizing to the waitress for our meager tab.

And then we began. The conversation that ensued was far ranging, almost peripatetic in its course, leapfrogging sporadically from Dan's life and career, to Bayfield, to the nearby Chippewa Reservation, to the Allen family, to the past summer's burial, to Merl himself. Merl was the touchstone, the subject we would return to if it seemed to Dan that we might have strayed too far afield, into his own life ("but that's just a little about me"). I took occasional notes, but it was not that kind of conversation.

Duwayne and Merl had been good friends, students in the same class at Bayfield High School, just one year below Dan. Dan had brought his yearbook and tried to find photos of Merl and Merl's older sister to show me. He flipped through pages, sliding the book toward me to point out faces among the black-and-white portraits. It was a small high school with maybe two hundred students in total. The two boys had graduated in 1965, and by 1966, both were enlisted in the marines. In those days, as a vet explained to me later, "Either you enlisted, or the army would get you." Enlisting at least gave you a choice from among the other branches, maybe a better shot at surviving. Otherwise, the army would draft you, and in Vietnam, he continued, it was the army that saw the most combat. But the two friends' choice didn't spare them. Both Duwayne and Merl were killed within weeks of each other, in the spring and summer of 1967.

At one point, when we circled back to Merl, I asked him, too abruptly, too nonchalantly, "So what was he like?" The question hung in the air for a split second before Dan looked away. His eyes watering, he replied in a choked-up voice, "He was nice." As he fought back the tears and wiped away at his eyes, we sat in silence for a few moments. It was such a simple utterance, yet it had such tremendous weight. For all the fanfare the year before, all the news coverage of a fallen hero recovered and returned, Dan remembered Merl as he knew him from his own youth—as a high school friend, a nice boy with a wide grin and a mischievous streak. In that instant, he mourned the loss of a person, not a symbol. Collecting himself,

Dan apologized, and we spoke about how powerful some memories are, their pull, even so many years later.

After we finished up our conversation and he left for his last shift at the casino, I made my way to the next meeting. It was at the local Veterans of Foreign Wars of the United States (VFW) post down the road. There, just inside the screen door in the main room, Bootin and the post's quartermaster, Randy Bresette, had been busy pulling material from the post's archive about Merlin Allen's memorial service. Newspaper clippings, photos, and assorted documents were spread out on a table for me to look through. In a few short minutes, they chronicled the area's unique and yet all-too-common history of military service and wartime losses, including Merl's death. They pointed to the wall covered with framed photos of the post's current and deceased members. In the center, three pictures marked the threshold between the living and the dead: the three young men sent off to fight the war in Southeast Asia, whose fates represented the span of the missing and killed in action. Randy summed it up: "One came home right away. One came home forty-six years later. One will never come home."

Red Cliff's VFW Post 8239 is named the Duwayne Soulier Memorial Post after Bootin's brother. While Merl Allen returned home in 2013, Duwayne "Wotsy" Soulier will remain an MIA (in fact, killed in action / body not recovered) for years to come. Lost at sea when the helicopter transporting him to a hospital ship crashed into the water, his mortal remains, whatever bones now rest at the bottom of the South China Sea, are unlikely ever to be recovered. Having both joined the marine corps and died within weeks of each other, the two friends shared the ambiguous "unaccounted for" status for over four decades, until Merl's identification the year before. Their stories, their intertwined lives and ends, make vivid the Wisconsin "Hero Bike" dedication. Among one of the few recovered of the thirty-seven missing, Merl can't ride the bike until his high school friend Wotsy comes home too.

Duties and Debts

For the American men and women who take up arms on behalf of a nation, as conscripts or volunteers, to die in that service and yet be forgotten represents a sacrilege of an extraordinary kind. Influenced by the Civil

War, the two world wars, and the Korean War, the conflict in Southeast Asia produced a new sensibility among members of the US military and their families. More than just memories, bodies too need to be tended—the nation that sent them off to do its bidding had an obligation to care for their remains, with a forensic precision, to help "ease them into the next world." And if the state wouldn't do it, veterans challenged, at least it should send them back to get the job done.

Lance Corporal Allen, the single tooth that constituted his mortal remains forty-six years after his death, came home in the end because the state faced a new cultural demand. The cost of leaving MIAs unaccounted for from the Vietnam War (and, later, other wars and conflicts, as the MIA accounting mandate gradually expanded) was too great. Though born of a longer tradition of repatriation, since the early 1990s, this cultural imperative to return individually identified remains of missing war dead has mobilized a vast technological apparatus and enormous human and financial resources. That apparatus now seeks to locate, repatriate, and identify as many of the missing and unknown service members from conflicts of the past century as possible. The Vietnam War was the impetus. As Ann Mills-Griffiths, one of the leading figures of the POW/MIA movement, once argued before a congressional hearing, "It all started with the Vietnam War. If it wasn't for the Vietnam War, we wouldn't have the organization, the personnel, the assets and resources devoted that are today."[38] Beyond dedicated resources, many of the innovations in knowledge and practice have flowed from the contentious politics of the state's unmet obligations to that specific group of missing war dead.

Over the past decade, I have traced the arc of Vietnam War MIA accounting along the line of science and its social import, paying particular attention to how its advances have influenced, indeed changed, the way the United States as a nation remembers and honors its fallen service members. I have come to appreciate science as another "language of memory"—it too frames how we see and understand war's human tolls and shapes what recovery efforts and identifications mean to families of the missing and veterans, most of them far removed from the inner circles of Beltway policy making.[39] In that regard, forensic science offers a partial view onto the complex enterprise and infrastructure of the US government's MIA accounting mission. There are other components integral to making homecomings possible—the operational and policy-oriented wings of the mission, the service casualty offices, intelligence gathering, and archival and historical analysis. Though my research touched on these different realms within the government's accounting branches, I focused most heavily on the science of the mission. This choice was driven partly by my own interests and expertise, partly by what I see as a broader public intrigue with forensic science, and partly by the state's own choice to develop such a vast forensic scientific program to account for its missing war dead. Yet even in an era of popular fascination with forensic science—with television hits such as *Bones, CSI, Forensic Files,* and *NCIS*—its expertise has also come under fire, increasingly challenged in national conversations about the military's care for its absent dead. Like the burials they enable, the scientific pursuit of locating and naming the unaccounted for reveals the values the United States as a nation holds most dear—a moral commitment to reunite the individual and the homeland, and faith in what Walt Whitman called "real science," that is, "the science of the soul and science of the body."[40] At the same time, the work of recovery and identification reminds us of the limits of knowledge and practice. The forensic efforts at MIA accounting continually bump up against the messy realities of war's destruction and thus frequently invites outsized expectations of what science can and cannot achieve.

"Science," renowned paleontologist and evolutionary biologist Stephen Jay Gould once argued, "is a socially embedded activity."[41] Given that science never exists in a vacuum (rather that people make it happen and people feel its force), this story travels beyond the laboratory and into the social spaces where the war and its absent war dead are recalled.[42] It moves from excavation sites in Southeast Asia to US military forensic facilities in Hawaii, Maryland, and Delaware, from small-town memorials to national cemeteries, from MIA family updates to spontaneous and scripted gatherings at the Vietnam Veterans Memorial on the National Mall. The stories that arise across these diverse sites help explain why, in the pursuit and performance of exceptional care, the United States goes to such efforts and spends such resources to recover its missing service members. Collectively, they show how the nation seeks to remember its past debts and strives to honor its current obligations, how communities welcome home long-absent fallen, and how powerful war dead remain in our national and local imagination, even decades later.

Obligations of Care

1st Lt. Michael Blassie
Beloved Son,
Brother and Hero

THE MODEST INSCRIPTION ON THE WOODEN BENCH lets you know you've reached the spot. A few feet away is the resting place of the former Unknown Soldier of the Vietnam War—though he is no longer unknown, and he wasn't a soldier but rather an airman. First Lieutenant Michael Joseph Blassie is buried in Section 85 of Jefferson Barracks National Cemetery, just off Circle Drive. It's a peaceful place, Jefferson Barracks, tucked in the leafy suburb of St. Louis County, Missouri, near the banks of the Mississippi River. Deer graze freely among the headstones in such numbers that feeding them has become one of Jefferson Barrack's recent traditions.[1]

But for an extra bit of color from the flowers laid at its base or pennies and pebbles stacked on its curved top, 1st Lt. Blassie's grave looks like the thousands of others there: a simple white headstone with his name etched in block letters beneath a cross, his rank in the air force, the war he helped fight (Vietnam), his dates of birth and death, and the signs of the same dedication of kinship that you see on the bench, "Beloved Son and Brother." In keeping with US military tradition, the back of the tombstone lists his service accolades—Silver Star, Distinguished Flying Cross, Purple Heart, Air Medal with four Oak Leaf Clusters. But inscribed beneath those distinctions are words that no other grave bears, not in Jefferson Barracks, not in any of the American military cemeteries on US soil or abroad: "Unknown Soldier, May 28, 1984/May 14, 1998."

In many ways, that title, and that span of years with its unprecedented end, are where this book first began. In the early to mid-2000s, my research in Bosnia and Herzegovina focused on the innovative forensic response to the Srebrenica genocide. The grim conditions of the mass graves where the victims' bodies had been disposed had frustrated local and international forensic specialists seeking to return remains to grieving families. In the end, DNA testing proved instrumental, becoming the engine that would drive the entire identification process for the Srebrenica missing, matching bone samples from remains to blood samples collected from surviving relatives. In studying the origins of the DNA-led system developed for the Srebrenica cases, I learned that one of the key scientists working in those early years at the International Commission on Missing Persons, the organization that pioneered the front-loaded genetic testing model, was a man named Ed Huffine. Before arriving in Bosnia, Huffine had worked for the US military at the Armed Forces DNA Identification Laboratory (AFDIL). He was eventually succeeded by another American geneticist, Tom Parsons, who likewise had come from AFDIL to Bosnia to lead the scientific efforts of the International Commission on Missing Persons. In addition to their contributions in Bosnia, the two forensic scientists shared another important achievement. Both Huffine and Parsons worked in AFDIL on the identification of the Vietnam War Unknown Soldier. Both had played a role in naming and returning 1st Lt. Blassie to his family and to the marked grave in Jefferson Barracks.[2]

From the start, the story of the Vietnam Unknown intrigued me. On the one hand, the connection between Bosnia and AFDIL illustrated how forensic expertise in this realm of postmortem identification circulated from one context to another. On the other hand, the story underscored the significance of DNA testing, both scientifically and symbolically. Forensic genetics was a powerful tool, capable of dismantling even the most sacred of national monuments. When I finally began researching the case of 1st Lt. Blassie, I visited AFDIL as a guest of its former scientist, Tom Parsons. We toured the facility, then located in Rockville, Maryland—room after room of high-tech equipment operated by staff in lab coats—and afterward sat down with Tom's colleague Jim Canik, the deputy director of the Department of Defense (DOD) DNA Registry. Canik's task was to help run the lab, but where he really excelled was with the families of the missing in action. He explained the science well and convinced families to support the accounting mission through their own DNA by giving a "family reference sample" that could be used to help identify (or rule out the identity of) a missing service member. Though he didn't wear it on his sleeve, Canik's own military service, particularly as a medical evacuation pilot during the Vietnam War, helped build trust among families over the years. With over five hundred "blade hours" to his name, Canik risked his life repeatedly to extract the wounded and dying. In some sense, for the families, he was one of theirs.

That day in his office, Canik spoke briefly about the Blassie case, including a visit he made to Jefferson Barracks a few years after the high-profile identification. Standing at the marked tombstone, he was struck by the profound difference in circumstances. Blassie had gone from having hundreds of thousands, if not millions, of people visit his grave each year at the Tomb of the Unknowns in Arlington National Cemetery, to this quiet, almost unsung existence. Though he now lies where he belongs, Canik explained, there was something poignant about that change.

On the occasions I've visited 1st Lt. Blassie's grave in Jefferson Barracks, Canik's words come to mind. The cemetery, at least Section 85, is tranquil, its silence interrupted occasionally by the drone of lawn mowers or leaf blowers in the distance. Sitting on the bench nearby, you can't help but notice a lack of ceremony. But the seemingly unremarkable masks the extraordinary: a few feet from the curb of Circle Drive, the interred remains of the once Unknown Soldier—now known airman—have traveled a long and circuitous route from the war in Southeast Asia, to a lab shelf in Hawaii, to the hallowed grounds of Arlington National Cemetery, and finally to this simple plot, capped by a marble headstone among a sea of marked graves. For all its present ordinariness, 1st Lt. Michael J. Blassie's grave in Jefferson Barracks remains the touchstone for the Vietnam War MIA accounting efforts.

The Tomb

Welcome to Arlington National Cemetery, Our Nation's Most Sacred Shrine. Please Conduct Yourselves with Dignity and Respect at All Times.

Please Remember These Are Hallowed Grounds.

—*Sign posted at the cemetery's entrance*

We disturb this hallowed ground with profound reluctance. . . .
[but] yield to the promise of science with the hope that the heavy
burden of doubt may be lifted from a family's heart.

—SECRETARY OF DEFENSE WILLIAM S. COHEN, *May 14, 1998*

One of the most popular sites to visit in Arlington National Cemetery is
the Tomb of the Unknowns. On most days, the steps that lead up to the
Memorial Amphitheater, just in front of the tomb, are filled with onlookers,
many with their smartphones and tablets held aloft to capture the perfectly synchronized motions of the sentinels, members of the Third Infantry's Old Guard—the US Army's official and elite ceremonial unit responsible for watching over the monument and the unnamed war dead buried
there. The Tomb of the Unknowns is a prime destination on the Washington, DC, tourist map, these days perhaps more for the pageantry of the
Changing of the Guard ceremony than for its original dedication.[3] In the
aftermath of WWI, the 66th US Congress approved Public Resolution 67
to establish the tomb, and on Armistice Day, November 11, 1921, an unknown soldier from a battlefield in France was buried in Arlington, just
across the Potomac River from the National Mall and the seat of the federal government. With crypts later dedicated to unknowns from World
War II, the Korean War, and the Vietnam War, the inscription on the massive 72-metric-ton memorial above the WWI crypt now announces,
"Here Rests in Honored Glory an American Soldier Known But to God."
Freighted with such sacred anonymity, the tomb was to serve as a monument to notions of sacrifice, duty, and debt. Its form, like that of other
monuments and memorials to unknown war dead, reinforces an impression of fixed and enduring ideals: sarcophagi and cenotaphs hewn from
thick slabs of marble; words of homage etched onto their surface; some
even accompanied by an "eternal" flame.[4]

But monuments to a nation's fallen, known or unknown, are never
static. Instead, they exist for a changing national public amid shifting
political winds and social conditions. The Tomb of the Unknowns at
Arlington National Cemetery has been profoundly transformed by the
nation's evolving efforts to account for its missing in action and its unknown and unidentified service members. Perhaps more than any other
missing US service member from the past century, the story of 1st Lt.
Blassie as the named Unknown Soldier—his selection, disinterment, and
identification—spotlights the national politics that shaped and continue
to shape the accounting mission. But it also makes clear the shift in memory

work—the movement away from aggregated, unnamed war dead to individuated, personalized narratives of recovery and homecoming and localized rituals of remembrance. In many ways, First Lieutenant Michael J. Blassie laid the groundwork for MIA homecomings like that of Lance Corporal Merlin Allen.

Moreover, his naming and return helped recalibrate expectations about what forensic science was capable of and what distinguished the United States from other nations in its obligations to its military members and their families. If identifying the Vietnam War Unknown exposed past deficiencies in the government's care for war dead, it also telegraphed its burgeoning ethos of exceptionalism—the narrative by which the US government could insist that in an unparalleled and unprecedented effort, it spares no expense, no resource, to bring its fallen service members home.[5] In the wake of a war that had dislodged that central tenet of American national identity—exceptionalism—MIA accounting and, specifically, the forensic scientific component of that effort with its ready tools of empirical, objective precision (epitomized by DNA testing) offered the state a means to distance and rehabilitate its memory by locating, repatriating, and identifying its missing fallen.[6] Though unfolding in the late twentieth century, these changes nevertheless have deep roots both in the American tradition of caring for war dead that began with the Civil War and in modern, industrialized warfare, in particular that which defined the death and destruction of World War I. To appreciate the former, we need to start with the latter.

The Unknown and the Named

In its scale of mobilization, novel forms of warfare, and unprecedented slaughter, the Great War transformed the peoples and landscapes caught up in its devastation. With artillery capable of shattering bone and obliterating bodies, 50 percent of those killed—five million of the ten million war dead—were missing.[7] In its trail, the violence also ruptured certain conventions of remembrance. As Jay Winter so eloquently explains, "In the years following the war, in the face of the army of the dead, the effort to commemorate went beyond the conventional shibboleths of patriotism."[8] Among those efforts was the singular writing of the "war poets," who "pointed a way beyond glory, at the very moment the word had lost its purchase in describing the fate and fortune of the men who had fought in the Great War."[9] Wilfred Owen, for example, wrote of how the war's brutality drained the language of sanctity from martial death. In the final stanza of one of his most famous poems, "Dulce et Decorum Est," a searing portrait of the ravages of gas attacks (which he himself had survived), he takes aim at the glory of dying for one's nation:

> If in some smothering dreams you too could pace
> Behind the wagon that we flung him in,
> And watch the white eyes writhing in his face,
> His hanging face, like a devil's sick of sin;
> If you could hear, at every jolt, the blood
> Come gargling from the froth-corrupted lungs
> Obscene as cancer, bitter as the cud
> Of vile, incurable sores on innocent tongues,—
> My friend, you would not tell with such high zest
> To children ardent for some desperate glory,
> The old Lie: *Dulce et decorum est*
> *Pro patria mori.*[10]

How then to apprehend, let alone memorialize, such horrific ends? And how to remember those who had simply vanished in the cloud of combat? The dead, their bodies "blown into the air, pounded into the mud of abandoned trenches and mine craters . . . lost at sea or shot out of the sky," became the epicenter of mourning, both in their lifeless presence and fleshless absence.[11] Taking up the example of the British response, Thomas Laqueur shows that the Great War gave rise to a new era of commemoration that tacked between these two poles of presence and absence: through inscribing names and venerating unknown remains, or in his words, memorializing "the common soldier's name or its self-conscious and sacralized oblivion."[12] For the first time in its history, Britain created a Graves Registration Commission to document the names of the missing and dead and to clean up battlefields and rebury remains and a War Graves Commission to inscribe names onto gravestones and monuments listing the fallen. "Names," Laqueur explains, "are the traces of bones or of the last place where a soldier had been seen," and for the 337,000 British and Imperial unrecovered dead, names were all that was left to attest to their sacrifice and the "carnage of war."[13]

For the European combatants on the Western Front, "the decision to let the dead rest where they had fallen was taken by all participants."[14]

Reburials occurred on or near the battlefields as war cemeteries proliferated in northern France and Flanders. For those who could not be identified, burial practices varied. The French interred their own and German nameless in mass graves and collective ossuaries; the British chose to bury their unidentified under individual headstones marked with a phrase proposed by Rudyard Kipling, mourning his own son who disappeared at the Battle of Loos in 1915: "Known unto God."[15] In response to their absence, communities of mourners in the small towns and cities across England and France erected monuments to the fallen, many adorned with plaques listing their individual names. In this way, the inscriptions not only recognized the dead, but also their grieving families, pointing out "who needed help in the aftermath of the war."[16]

Creating a monument to an unknown, unnamed soldier achieved similar commemorative ends, but from the extreme opposite pole, from the utter collapse of individual identity into an all-encompassing emblem. Laqueur argues that "while the names and markers that gird the battlefields in France and Belgium cry out in their specificity, their one-to-one correspondence with a body, . . . the unknown warrior becomes in his universality the cipher that can mean anything, the bones that represent any and all bones, equally well or badly." "In short, by being so intensely *a* body, it was *all* bodies."[17]

The British were not alone in their desire to address absence and thereby honor all their war dead. To that end, it would be a single symbolic anonymous body that would make the trip "home." In 1920, both England and France decided to bury an unknown soldier in their respective national shrines, Westminster Abbey and the Arc de Triomphe.[18] Selecting and interring an unidentified fallen, whose birth, rank, and service were unknown, "came to symbolize the ideal of the national community as the camaraderie among members of equal status."[19] The symbolically laden unknown did work for the nation because of his very anonymity. In the absence of a concrete name and a personal history invoked by that name, visitors were left to imagine the tie that might bind them to the unknown—that is, the bond of belonging to the same nation for which the unknown soldier fought and died on foreign soil. While not focused on World War I per se, Benedict Anderson writes about the emotional force behind such an object of national veneration, a sensibility he views as particular to modernity:

> No more arresting emblems of the modern culture of nationalism
> exist than cenotaphs and tombs of Unknown Soldiers. The public

ceremonial reverence accorded these monuments precisely *because* they are either deliberately empty or no one knows who lies inside them, has no true precedents in earlier times. To feel the force of this modernity one has only to imagine the general reaction to the busybody who 'discovered' the Unknown Soldier's name or insisted on filling the cenotaph with some real bones. Sacrilege of a strange, contemporary kind! Yet void as these tombs are of identifiable mortal remains or immortal souls, they are nonetheless saturated with ghostly *national* imaginings.[20]

For Anderson, "nationalism, like religion, was rooted in the grave."[21] Death consecrates the bond between the remains within and the onlookers without. Anderson thus invites us to consider the rupture, the shock, that dismantling the national icon would elicit. Implicit in his argument is not just how we imagine our relationship to the unknown soldier, but also what obligations might arise according to that imagined connection.

These notions of obligation and indebtedness, so pressing in the aftermath of the Great War, were also critical to the evolving practice and values surrounding how the United States cares for its missing in action and presumed dead. The American interpretation of that debt is what distinguished its practice from the other combatant nations of the Great War: the obligation to repatriate the fallen—to bring them home—and to identify and name them individually.

Indebtedness and Gratitude

In late autumn of 2011, the Joint POW/MIA Accounting Command (JPAC)—one of the US Department of Defense's entities dedicated to accounting for its missing war dead that now forms part of the Defense POW/MIA Accounting Agency (DPAA)—sent a member of its scientific staff to oversee an exhumation. Most exhumations undertaken by DPAA (and formerly by JPAC) are of the yet unidentified and unknown war dead. But in this particular instance, the forensic experts at JPAC's Central Identification Laboratory were circling back to an old case, to remains that had long since been named and returned to surviving kin. The decision stemmed from a scientific advance. DNA technology had revealed new evidence relating to the case, requiring that the remains, those of a Korean War airman identified in the early 1990s, undergo additional analysis at the forensic anthropology laboratory on Oahu, Hawaii. One of the lab's senior scientists had already visited the family to explain the circumstances and ask for their consent. This second trip was to ensure that the disinterment went smoothly, the chain of custody was secure, and the transfer case would be escorted safely back to the lab.

Marin Pilloud, an anthropologist at the lab, was assigned the job. Having worked on the case at an earlier stage, Pilloud was happy to make the trip to the mainland to assist with this latest development. She was also six months pregnant. On the appointed day, she flew to Florida, where she met the air force casualty officer, the funeral director, and two members of the deceased's family, his brother and his brother's grandson. The family was understanding; though the event was a painful reminder of their loss, they appreciated that other cases, the fate of other unknowns, were tied to the results of the pending examination. The exhumation itself went smoothly, and the remains were soon readied for transport to Hawaii.

With the main task behind her, Marin headed to the airport and boarded her flight as the official military escort for the remains now stored in the belly of the aircraft.

> So I didn't think anything more of it, but then as we land [in Atlanta], they say, "We're escorting remains from a fallen service member." But they didn't say Korean War or anything. They just said that it's a service member. "We need the escort to come up ahead so she can escort the remains." I didn't know that they were going to do this, and of course I'm in the last row, window seat. So, you know, out to here [mimes her pregnant belly] and I get up. Okay, that's fine, I'll get off the plane first, that's great. And people start clapping. They're like, "Thank you for your service," and . . . I can't say anything.[22]

At its headquarters and main hub in Atlanta, Delta Air Lines has assembled its own military-style honor guard to receive and render rites to the in-transit remains of war dead from current and past conflicts. The volunteer unit pulls out all the stops: a chaplain waits planeside; fire trucks are parked on the runway to greet incoming planes with water-cannon salutes; even a Delta honor guard coin is given to the war dead's surviving kin.[23] To her surprise and dismay, Marin was quickly co-opted into the airline's rituals marking heroism and sacrifice:

Then we come off [the plane] and the color guard is there with the flags. . . . It's freezing cold and I don't have a coat because I'm flying to Honolulu and we're standing outside while they take the casket off and cart it away. At the end, the chaplain [explained that] the members of the color guard would like to thank you, and they all shook my hand individually and said, "We're sorry for your loss, ma'am. We're sorry for your loss." Each one. There were five of them.[24]

A pregnant woman escorting remains of a dead service member—the two could only add up to one thing in the minds of the fellow passengers and the honor guard waiting to receive, if only for temporary rites, the coffin of a "fallen hero." Written into the script of the young war widow, carrying the yet unborn child of her husband, killed in the Middle East, in service and defense of the nation, Marin the scientist had little recourse but to acknowledge, however awkwardly, people's words of comfort and support. There was no room to express how discomfiting she found those implicit gendered assumptions or, when people along the route did understand her proper role, the effusive gratitude for what she felt was simply her professional responsibility—nothing like the sacrifice of the men whose remains she sought to locate and identify.

THANK YOU FOR YOUR SERVICE.[25] On one level, the reactions to her pregnant form and the coffin on the tarmac fit the times—that is, they reflect notions of gratitude and obligation that have come to define civil-military relations in post-9/11 America. In his novel (adapted for the screen by director Ang Lee) *Billy Lynn's Long Halftime Walk*, Ben Fountain captures that divide through the irrepressible reverence thrust on the nineteen-year-old protagonist who is part of a nationwide "war hero" publicity tour following a battle in Iraq:

After two solid weeks of public events Billy continues to be amazed at the public response. . . . *We appreciate,* they say, their voices throbbing like a lover's. Sometimes they come right out and say it, *We love you.* We are so grateful. We cherish and bless. We pray, hope, honor-respect-love-and-revere and they *do,* in the act of speaking they experience the mighty words, these verbal arabesques that spark and snap in Billy's ears like bugs impacting an electric bug zapper.[26]

Fountain's portrait may be fictional, but he's getting at something—the compunction, the obligation felt by many Americans to acknowledge perceived debts owed to current (and past) service members. This obligation is part of what former US Army colonel and historian Andrew Bacevich has called the new American militarism, in which "paying homage to those in uniform has become obligatory and the one unforgivable sin is to be found guilty of failing to 'support the troops.'"[27]

The applause and the words of consolation that were pressed on Marin as she escorted the remains back to Hawaii, however, weren't just about paying homage to an abstract notion of military service; they were keyed to the specific phenomenon of the nation's war *dead*. America's fallen service members, especially its nameless and unidentified service members, have long proved rife, useful symbols for the state—bodies, like vessels, that can be loaded up with the ideals of a nation to help shuttle them across gaps of time and space, connecting the nation's past wars with present defense interests and imagined future threats.

Why is this the case? Why are the remains of fallen service members so powerful and authority over those remains so coveted? Scholars have long argued that war dead can both polarize and unite, sometimes surprising us in their simultaneously transgressive and sacred worth. In her seminal book, *The Political Lives of Dead Bodies,* anthropologist Katherine Verdery explains, "Remains are concrete yet protean."[28] One can touch them, hold them, perform rituals of bereavement over them, and yet their meaning—the respect (or revulsion or indifference) they engender—can vary. "What gives a dead body symbolic effectiveness in politics is precisely its ambiguity, its capacity to evoke a variety of understandings."[29] War dead occupy an especially ambiguous position when their unnamed remains become not just forceful emblems of the state, but also barometers of changing political will and repositories of national memory. Consider the very origins of Arlington National Cemetery. It was hewn from war dead politics that enlisted the bodies of Union fallen to lay claim to Robert E. Lee's home, ensuring the Confederate general's family could never return. Lee's wife, Mary Lee, recoiled at the thought of her garden filled with bodies and the graves "planted up to the very door without any regard to common decency."[30] In 1866, a collective tomb for unknowns was erected next to one of her flower gardens near the main house; placed within its vault were the remains of 2,111 unknown soldiers recovered from Bull Run and the road to Rappahannock.[31]

From the Civil War to the more current conflicts of Afghanistan and Iraq, or even special forces operations in West Africa, the symbolic power of war dead derives from an implied social contract between the US government and surviving relatives, the military (veterans and current servicemen and women), and the general public. A military death is cast as the ultimate sacrifice an individual can make on behalf of his or her country, and the social contract between the state and its subject derives from the promise to care for the individual killed in battle. Caring is multifold: having sent the individual to die doing its bidding, the state—more specifically, its government—is responsible for locating, naming, and *returning* his or her remains, and, with its scientific, legislative, and military institutions, that government levies its authority and resources to carry out the obligation of care. In its double indebtedness—first to the war dead, having sacrificed his or her life, and second to the surviving family, burdened with mourning that lost life—the United States has come to define its duty to missing war dead through the acts of repatriation and individuated forensic care.

Repatriation

The terms of this social contract have evolved over the last two centuries, especially regarding repatriation—the return of war dead to American soil. The American act of physical, geographic return stands in stark contrast to that of other nations, like the British and now Commonwealth nations and the French and Germans after World War I.[32] But this American sensibility regarding the need to bring home the fallen dead from foreign soil didn't originate with the Great War; rather, it first emerged amid the devastating losses of the Civil War, with the nation bitterly divided in its sense of belonging and sovereignty. As historian Drew Gilpin Faust so deftly chronicles in *This Republic of Suffering,* from embalming and individuated burial practices to the creation of a comprehensive system of national cemeteries and the compunction to account for the unidentified, the war transformed the nation's sentiment toward caring for the dead. "We still live in the world of the dead the Civil War created," she explains. "We take for granted the obligation of the state to account for the lives it claims in its service," and through that accounting to return remains to surviving kin.[33]

By the Spanish-American War, when US soldiers' remains were sent back from Cuba, Puerto Rico, and the Philippines, the federal government had assumed the explicit charge of repatriating remains of service members who died on foreign soil.[34] That practice would continue to develop in response to the wars of the twentieth century, with advances in transportation technology and, later, forensic expertise, enabling comprehensive efforts of repatriation and identification.[35] The Great War was the first major test of this nascent national tradition.

A conflict the United States belatedly joined with its American Expeditionary Force sent into battle in 1917, World War I made explicit the terms of the social contract between the government and grieving families. While "repatriation of the dead would certainly have to wait until the end of hostilities," surviving relatives were given the choice of leaving their fallen kin interred overseas in a national cemetery or having the remains returned to them for burial at home, work to be carried out by the newly established Graves Registration Service.[36] An estimated 70 percent of families chose to have them repatriated.[37] Others decided against bringing the coffins home, including Theodore Roosevelt, who insisted that his son Quentin "lie where he fell and where the Germans buried him."[38] The domestic debate over repatriation or burial overseas was nested within the time's larger divisive politics regarding America's standing in the world and its obligation to intervene in war. Some urged the removal of the nation's sacred dead from the iniquitous grounds of Europe so that they could not be held hostage in the likely event of another conflict there. Others argued that "the war dead should remain interred overseas as a symbol of US commitment to Europe."[39] In the end, the families' wishes won out. The Great War's pledge to care for the fallen thus "triggered a massive and highly controversial repatriation of war dead from the battlefields of Europe to the United States between 1919 and 1922," a "colossal task" that "set an enduring national precedent for generations."[40]

World War II policies followed suit, with surviving relatives again given ultimate authority over the disposition of loved ones' remains. "Despite the government's pleas against removal"—as in WWI, the military and the American Battle Monuments Commission (ABMC) saw overseas cemeteries as powerful symbols of national unity and reminders to foreign states of American sacrifices made on their behalf—"the majority of widows and parents once again wanted the bodies of their next of kin brought back to the United States."[41] For war dead whose remains would lay in rest overseas as well as the thousands of unknown (unidentified) service members, permanent national cemeteries were established in four-teen locations, ten of them in Europe.[42] They were, in the words of General George C. Marshall, who took over chairmanship of the ABMC in 1949, "still conscripts," with their "primary task . . . to serve national goals and objectives."[43] For those to be repatriated, remains were disinterred from temporary burial sites and sent to one of the various "processing stations" in the respective theaters of conflict, where American Graves Registration Service personnel checked identifications.[44] Unnamed remains were routed to the station's laboratory, including the Central Identification Laboratory at Schofield Barracks on Oahu, Hawaii. There, the pioneering forensic anthropologist Mildred Trotter detailed in one of her reports that "remains are either positively identified or they are not—there is no tentative identification of remains which are about to be delivered to the next of kin."[45]

The Korean War signaled important changes not only in the practice of remains repatriation but also in how war dead entered into the United States' expanding role as a global power. Although that war was waged under the aegis of the United Nations, the United States led the fight and paid a steep price with its casualties. It adopted the practice of "concurrent return"—repatriating remains while the war was still being fought.[46] In fact, though bruited about as a policy before the war began, it took root only after public outcry arose over the preferential treatment of four-star army general Walton Walker, killed in a jeep accident in December 1950 and his remains repatriated immediately.[47] Within a month, a temporary mortuary facility was set up in Kokura, Japan, where the American Graves Registration Services sought to identify and process remains for return to the United States. The departure from procedures during the previous world wars also reflected uncertainties about the war's outcome and "whether future access to a U.S. military cemetery in the Republic of Korea could be guaranteed."[48] At the war's end, the United Nations negotiated the exchange of war dead, an enormous undertaking dubbed Operation Glory. The Kokura lab and the postwar exchange together exposed deep-seated anxieties over foreign, and specifically Asian, enemy control of US remains that had already surfaced in the wake of World War II. While historian G. Kurt Piehler explains that "there is no solid evidence to suggest that the decision not to maintain permanent cemeteries in Asia . . . was motivated by racism," notions of difference stoked concerns: many Americans conceived of the enemy as communist and atheist and therefore more likely to desecrate the sacred remains of US fallen.[49] "Americans had always been reluctant to bury their war dead in Asia, and after 1950 they would never willingly do so again."[50]

Although recovery efforts and forensic practice had changed substantially with the Korean War, the horror of the Vietnam War, broadcast on the nightly news with its high casualties, contentious politics, and protracted duration, injected new urgency into the slogan "no man left behind."[51] In concrete terms, heightened repatriation efforts reflected improved logistical capacities to recover remains. While the helicopter gunship—what Viet Thanh Nguyen describes as "war machinery's pure sex . . . bristling with guns and rocket pods" that "personified America, both terrifying and seductive"—represented the United States' expanding reliance on air power to deliver violence, the ubiquitous Huey "slicks" inserted combat troops, and "dust off" medical evacuation helicopters extracted them, living and dead.[52] Evolving medical expertise and the positioning of triage facilities closer to the front lines, as well as improved forensic technology, meant that otherwise unrecognizable sets of remains, if found and repatriated, were more likely to be identified. It was, as Piehler notes, "one of the most elaborate efforts in the history of warfare to retrieve the bodies of those who died in combat and return them to their hometowns."[53]

The pledge to repatriate US war dead from Southeast Asia was also distinctly grounded in wartime and postwar politics, from the domestic turmoil of the late 1960s to the war's turning tides marked by the Tet Offensive in 1968 and eventually the peace negotiations in 1973. "Leave no man behind" cut to the core of a strained social contract. Unlike the world wars, in which the United States reluctantly entered the fray late, the conflict in Southeast Asia was a gradually escalated war of choice. The US government sent its men and women, historian Christian Appy explains, "one-third draftees, one-third draft-motivated volunteers, and one-third true volunteers," to fight in a distant land, and, following the emerging tradition of repatriation and individuated care, it was obliged to return them—and to name them.[54] Thus, when it met with the North Vietnamese in Paris in January 1973 to negotiate an end to the war, the Nixon administration insisted on including the act of accounting in the peace accords; Article 8(b) stipulated that "the parties shall help each other to get information about those military personnel and foreign civilians of the parties missing in action, to determine the location and take care of graves of the dead so as to facilitate the exhumation and repatriation of the remains, and to take any such other measures as may be required to get information about those still considered missing in action."[55] Underscoring its primacy, the United States specifically tied the POW/MIA issue and the North Vietnamese's cooperation in accounting for US missing service members to postwar aid for reconstruction, stipulated in Article 21.[56] The linkage had lasting effect. From Nixon to Clinton, the missing in action would become an opportune lever for US administrations seeking to eschew America's commitment to reparations and, by the 1990s, to pursue the formal normalization of diplomatic relations with the Socialist Republic of Vietnam.[57] "For the next-quarter century," historian Michael Allen notes, the Vietnamese would return in kind, insisting on "the reconstruction aid promised in Article 21 as the price for their cooperation in accounting for missing Americans."[58]

On the operational front, even as the peace negotiations were underway, the US military was formalizing a postwar accounting initiative. It established the Joint Casualty Resolution Center (JCRC) on January 23, 1973, activated first in Saigon and relocated to northern Thailand following the signing of the peace accords. Though its investigative and recovery efforts proved largely unsuccessful, accounting for a mere sixteen sets of remains by the time communist forces seized control of Saigon on April 30, 1975, JCRC became the first step in building the United States' contemporary MIA accounting mission.[59] And with that effort came a new phrase: "fullest possible accounting." In his televised address to the nation announcing the Paris Peace Accords, President Nixon pledged that "there will be fullest possible accounting for all those missing in action."[60]

IN THIS EVOLVING SET OF OBLIGATIONS to care for war dead and with the US military's increased capacity to recover and return remains, the decision to bury a Vietnam War Unknown Soldier at Arlington National Cemetery cut against the grain. If in the wake of World War I, the two poles of named individuals and monuments to unknowns facilitated both national and communal mourning in places like England and France, the gradually evolving enterprise of MIA accounting exposed their inherent tension in the American context.

The official interment of the Vietnam Unknown at Arlington National Cemetery took place on Memorial Day, May 28, 1984. For many Vietnam War veterans, the selection and burial were long overdue; while Congress passed legislation to inter a Vietnam War Unknown shortly after the peace accords were signed and the Vietnam crypt was added to the monument in 1975, the sarcophagus itself lay empty for the next decade.[61] For others in the POW/MIA movement, however, empty was better than filled. Many of the more politically mobilized families of the missing had fought against adding a Vietnam unknown to the tomb. To them it was another sign that the government was abandoning the search for POWs in favor of recovery efforts—giving up on the living to memorialize the dead.[62] Weighing it all, the Reagan administration saw the interment as a means to redefine the past conflict and revive the narrative of US exceptionalism, which the war in Southeast Asia had so forcefully called into question.[63] As had his predecessors Harding and Eisenhower, President Reagan presided over the burial rites as the symbolic father of the nation and titular "next of kin" for its unknown lost son.

In his address at Arlington that day before the "national funeral," the president walked the fine line between acknowledging still-unmet obligations to many of the MIA families and the need to memorialize the war. He asked the country to recognize the families' ongoing sacrifice:

> They live day and night with uncertainty, with an emptiness, with a void that we cannot fathom. . . . Vietnam is not over for them. They cannot rest until they know the fate of those they loved and watched march off to serve their country. Our dedication to their cause must be strengthened with these events today. We write no last chapters. We close no books. We put away no final memories. An end to America's involvement in Vietnam cannot come before we've achieved the fullest possible accounting of those missing in action.[64]

He then turned to the unknown, the symbol for "all our missing sons," and invited the American public to imagine him as someone who could have easily come from their own community, perhaps even their own family: "As a child, did he play on some street in a great American city? Did he work beside his father on a farm in America's heartland? Did he marry? Did he have children?"[65] By honoring a Vietnam unknown, Americans could, in his words, "transcend the tragedies of the past," as they learned to "trust each other again."[66] In this moment of public mourning, Reagan seized the opportunity to recast the Vietnam War as a "noble cause," whose memory could heal rather than divide the nation.[67]

Recall Benedict Anderson's words: "Sacrilege of a strange, contemporary kind!" What a violation it must have appeared when fourteen years later, on May 14, 1998, Department of Defense officials decided to open the Vietnam War crypt and remove the remains of the Unknown Soldier for forensic analysis. In his public remarks, a far cry from Reagan's interment speech with its attendant fanfare, Secretary of Defense William Cohen admitted the interruption was made with "profound reluctance."[68] And so, behind a screen of temporary walls and meshing to block the media, the disinterment of the remains began a six-week period of intense scrutiny and painstakingly careful analysis of forensic evidence. Much was at stake. In his *Washington Post* opinion editorial "Why We Must Know," poet and funeral director Thomas Lynch warned that "of course, reopened graves, like reopened wounds, seek a certain healing and run uncertain risks. Like the war that sent home this dead body and nearly 60,000 more, the right path is not well marked, the outcomes impossible to predict."[69]

By exhuming the remains of the Vietnam Unknown, on the one hand, the Department of Defense finally would have to address the whispers of political instrumentalism that had begun to swirl around the original selection of the war's officially designated unknown soldier. On the other hand, the disinterment offered a chance to write a new script about scientific innovation and integrity and demonstrate the state's willingness to mobilize the resources necessary to conform to a new standard of care. Rather than a story of bureaucratic negligence or breached trust, the exhumation spoke to an emergent ethos of exceptional care. The narrative turned on advances in forensic technology, DNA testing in particular.

An Uneasy Selection

To understand how in the span of fourteen years, the Vietnam Unknown went from being an intended symbol for national mourning and unity to an object of rumor and controversy, we need to start at the beginning—with his selection. The import of the story has as much to do with the behind-the-scenes *making* of the Unknown Soldier as it does with his unmaking.

The remains of 1st Lt. Michael J. Blassie, then unidentified, were one of four sets under consideration for the Tomb of the Unknowns in the late 1970s and early 1980s.[70] By 1982, nine years after Congress had passed legislation to add a Vietnam War crypt to the monument, the search for a suitable (unidentifiable) unknown intensified, and the task fell to the forensic scientists charged with accounting for the missing.[71] At that time, POW/MIA cases were processed by the DOD's JCRC and its associated forensic facility, the Central Identification Laboratory Hawaii (CILHI), located on Hickam Air Force Base.[72] With President Reagan bent on rede-fining the legacy of the Vietnam War, the DOD directive to produce an unknown for burial in the tomb came to the lab in unabashedly political terms. A special task force had been appointed to find the requisite "can-didate," and under the guidance of the lab's commander, Major Johnie Webb Jr., a Vietnam veteran himself, reluctant staff at CILHI were directed to review four potential sets of remains. That Webb headed the command was a telling sign of the times in and of itself; a military man assigned to the lab in Hawaii when it "stood up" in 1976 and then made its commander in 1982, Webb had no formal forensic scientific credentials.

The head of the task force, John O. (Jack) Marsh, told Webb in no uncertain terms, "We are going to place remains in the Tomb of the Un-knowns and we want you to sign a certification," a document stating that the remains were definitively unidentifiable.[73] Webb balked. He refused to sign the document and instead wrote a memorandum to the army in which he and his staff systematically argued against the premature and poten-tially negligent selection of an unknown from among the four sets. The memo tackled several troubling factors: the four sets of remains were rela-tively incomplete, with each consisting of only "minimal recovered por-tions"; there were far fewer "unknown" remains from the Vietnam War than from WWI, WWII, and the Korean War; and there was the possi-bility that additional remains might be recovered ("Perhaps there will be a breakthrough in our relations with SEA [Southeast Asian] governments"). The memo then addressed the sanctity of the tomb itself and what the very category of "unknown" should entail:

> 7. Any decision must be supportable and that decision must maintain the high dignity and place of honor that the Tomb now enjoys in the hearts and minds of Americans. If one of these re-mains is selected for interment in the Tomb a great amount of media interest can be expected. . . . The selection must not be flawed. The high honor attributed to previously selected Unknowns must not be compromised. A decision of non-selection may be more supportable than a decision of selection.
>
> 8. Consideration should be given to the distinction between 'Unidentified' and 'Unknown.' These remains are not completely unknown, the knowns are: (a) Race—All are caucasoid; (b) Sex—All are male; (c) The approximate height of each; (d) The approximate

age of each; (e) Two have name associations; (f) One has a good probability of being identified.[74]

The first point laid the grounds for the second. The objection raised in paragraph 7 of the memo stressed the symbolic weight of the monument, both the tomb and its already interred unknowns. At a time when the government, particularly the Pentagon, was under intense scrutiny for its handling of the POW/MIA issue, Webb and his staff knew that inquiries and close media coverage were inevitable. "The selection must not be flawed." The subtext was clear: the potential for error and, more damning, the taint of manipulation would be politically disastrous. Even worse, it could cast a pall over the entire monument, dishonoring not just the government that had forced a faulty selection, but the honored dead, the other three unknowns, as well.

The second point took aim at the troubling uncertainties (and in some ways, certainties) surrounding the four sets of remains—what was known, what could be known, and what might be known in the future. However faintly, Webb and his staff enlisted the idea of scientific progress to argue against not only sealing off evidence (the remains themselves) in the tomb, but also foreclosing the possibility of scientific advance. Someday, somehow, science might produce new tools and offer new insight to make the unknowable knowable.

The memo went on to dissect, case by case, the evidence in terms of the remains themselves and the context of their recovery. In response, a DOD emissary, an army general, traveled to CILHI to issue the ultimatum: they had six months to identify or hand over a set of remains for the Vietnam crypt. Under the time constraints, the lab staff scrambled to uncover clues previously undetected. They turned to categories of missing outside of the Department of the Army's conventional realms of responsibility. This included deserters, servicemen the army had written off as "discharged," not missing. Major Webb sent requests to each of the branches, asking them to forward the names of deserters. He also sought information on possible "black ops" MIA whose disappearance went undocumented because of the classified nature of the operations.

The inquiries led to the first breakthrough. With just two weeks remaining before the DOD deadline, the first of the four sets of remains, X-15, the one in best condition at 90 percent complete, including teeth, turned out to be those of a possible deserter. The information came to

CILHI serendipitously. That summer, a repatriation from Vietnam had taken place. Remains had been received through a unilateral turnover, and the US military had sent a delegation to escort them home. The aunt of a soldier who had never returned from the war saw the coverage and wrote her congressman asking whether the repatriated remains might be those of her nephew. After some investigation, it was discovered that the soldier had been declared a deserter (he had been absent without leave for thirty days) and so had been "discharged" rather than designated missing. Recalling Webb's earlier appeal, the army express-mailed their records on the young man, and using dental records, the lab quickly identified the first potential unknown.

The second candidate, X-32, entailed another slippage of responsibility and, more problematically, a wartime error in identification that subsequently went unaddressed. In August 1967, a helicopter and an F-101 Voodoo jet collided midair. While the pilot of the fighter managed to eject and survive, the helicopter crashed, killing all aboard. Of the five individuals on the helicopter, four bodies were positively identified, while the fifth, clothed in jungle fatigues, was assumed to be William McRae, a passenger listed on the flight manifest who was en route back to his unit, just released from the Long Binh jail, a military stockade, after having gone AWOL (absent without leave). Four months later, a reconnaissance team came across the same site and discovered a sixth set of remains. Compelling circumstantial evidence, including dog tags and an identity card, and forensic anthropological analysis pointed toward McRae. But the "first" McRae had already been sent home to his family in Boston, Massachusetts. Staff at the US Army mortuary on Tan Son Nhut Air Base, outside of Saigon, and later at CILHI, either did not recognize or ignored the discrepancy and so failed to inform the McRae family that they had buried someone other than their own relative. The remains of the sixth individual sat on the shelf until the directive arrived from the Pentagon to produce a Vietnam War unknown. Now designated the unknown set of remains X-32, the "second" William McRae, the sixth recovered body and the associated material evidence, underwent a more thorough examination. Major Webb wrote a memorandum to the army, indicating that he believed X-32 was "someone who has been misidentified." The lab pushed through the identification, and the first body, originally returned to the McRae family, was disinterred from the Boston cemetery and sent back to CILHI. Years later, it would emerge that the remains, dubbed "Boston Billy," were those of an unmanifested passenger, a civilian contractor who trained helicopter pilots and who had gone missing around the time and place of the loss incident.

With the first two sets of remains now dismissed, the lab turned to its third candidate. These remains, CILHI 0014-A-78, were too risky because of a particular doubt surrounding them. The remains had been received along with those of three other individuals as part of a unilateral turnover from Laos. Unilateral turnovers are remains acquired without American forensic personnel involved in their original excavation or procurement. In such cases, not only is the original provenience (the specific place where they came from) unknown, but the sequence of possession, from recovery to release—that is, who was responsible for and carried out the transfer of evidence—is also uncertain. Another, more niggling doubt arose from the context of the original accession: the remains had arrived commingled, and after examining and segregating them into four individuals, CILHI staff determined that two of the four individuals were of Asian, probably Southeast Asian, ancestry. In all likelihood, the remains were those of South Vietnamese Army of the Republic of Vietnam (ARVN) troops, or possibly members of the Montagnard populations who fought alongside ARVN and American forces in Laos.

The trouble lay with the limits of scientific knowledge, of knowability and unknowability: what could the forensic examiners at CILHI definitively determine about the remains and what kind of anxiety did their unknowable characteristics prompt? Typically, when generating an identification, forensic anthropologists seek to establish what is ascertainable, measurable, quantifiable, and comparable through a range of methods applied to a given set of individual remains. In selecting an unknown and thus designating that set of remains as unidentifiable, however, the concern stems from what cannot be known. In this third case, the lack of information about where the remains came from, who obtained them, and whose hands they passed through was further complicated by the other bones turned over to the US in the same group. Could the lab definitively rule out the possibility that the set of remains under consideration were not American? This was not to say that the remains were necessarily of Southeast Asian ancestry or that the lab was ignoring the fact that Asian Americans fought and died in Vietnam. Rather, without evidence otherwise, the lab was in a bind; the suggestion of unknowability that was introduced by the commingling effectively ruled out the third set of remains.[75] As Webb would argue in yet another memorandum to the army, the remains did not "satisfy the public law that [the unknown] would have to be an American fighting man who died in conflict during the war."[76] Although there was no way of proving that the third set of remains was not American, more compelling was what couldn't be proved. The scientists at CILHI could not say with absolute certainty that the remains were entirely and exclusively American.

From BTB (Believed to Be) to X (Unknown)

Having averted those three potential political disasters—burying a presumed deserter, a set of remains associated with a mistaken identification, or the chance, no matter how slight, of interring a "foreigner," perhaps even the enemy himself, in the nation's most hallowed of spaces—the forensic staff at CILHI turned to case X-26.

We know now definitively (and one could argue it was known then tentatively) that case X-26 was 1st Lt. Blassie. How he got there is as compelling a tale as that of his eventual disinterment and identification. To begin with, it is worth emphasizing that there was no doubt that Michael Blassie had died. As multiple accounts documented, on May 11, 1972, his plane was shot down by anti-aircraft artillery while he was carrying out a ground support mission, a "napalm delivery run," near An Loc City in southern Vietnam. The incident report bears the ominous words "no chute"—a fellow pilot witnessed Blassie's A-27 crashing into a canopy of trees in a ball of fire with no parachute sighted, a telltale sign that the pilot had not ejected.

The first gap in evidence appears early in the timeline. As Blassie's plane had been shot down over hostile territory, a search and recovery mission could not be mounted until the area was secure. In October that same year, an ARVN reconnaissance team located the crash site and recovered remains and personal effects, including Blassie's wallet, which in addition to "1,000$ RVN and $5.00 MPC" contained his MACV (Military Assistance Command, Vietnam) Form 5 and identification card. As crucial material evidence, those items, however, were not turned over when the remains were delivered to the mortuary facility near Saigon five days later. One of the reports hints that the mistake lay with a drunken South Vietnamese officer, head of the reconnaissance team, but the blame remained buried in the circumstances of a foreign war and an overstretched mortuary staff.

It was nevertheless an important omission. The missing MACV Form 5 and ID card, supposedly lost in transit, introduced a pivotal element of doubt, and staff at the Tan Son Nhut mortuary concluded that "there are not sufficient remains for a positive ID. All that was recovered was four ribs, one pelvis, one humerus, a small portion of Nomex flight suit, a raft, ammo pouch and part of a parachute."[77]

Rather than being sent home to his family in St. Louis, Blassie's remains were instead labeled BTB—"believed to be," and stored at the mortuary outside of Saigon, then transferred to northern Thailand, until they were eventually transported to the CILHI in 1976. The BTB designation in turn set in motion additional, more-problematic misreadings and misinterpretations. A forensic examination at the CILHI in 1978 yielded a trace hair on a fragment of the flight suit, the blood typing of which erroneously excluded Blassie. Well before the advent of DNA analysis, blood typing was an imperfect line of evidence at best, especially when chain-of-custody errors had already been introduced into the case. The CILHI staff also had to grapple with ambiguous findings about the remains themselves. Because they had so little to work with—just the right humerus and right pelvic bone could yield data about the individual's biological profile—the forensic examiners estimated the remains' stature and age at death to be outside those of the associated BTB (Blassie). They thought the remains belonged to a taller, older individual.

The final act that distanced Blassie's name from his remains happened when the DOD was trying to clear its docket of lingering unresolved cases. On April 24, 1980, Blassie's case, along with other unidentified remains, underwent a review by the Armed Services Graves Registration Office (ASGRO) to evaluate its status. By that point, the initial compelling circumstantial evidence connecting Blassie to his bones had been so eroded by mismanaged material evidence and misread forensic data that the ASGRO review board (made up of military officers, not forensic experts) opted to delete the name association; the tie to identity now cut, the remains were no longer "believed to be" those of 1st Lt. Michael J. Blassie. Rather, they had become an official unknown with an associated X-file.[78]

The review board's decision opened the door to Blassie's eventual selection for the tomb. Of the four sets of remains, in many ways, X-26 was the safest—untainted by the problematic associations of the other three candidates (desertion, misidentification, and possible non-American). Although hints of the former name association lingered, the lab had run out of options and arguments. With the three other candidates ruled out, the remains once known as BTB 1st Lt. Blassie in fact seemed an ideal fit to represent American military service and sacrifice. A graduate of the Air Force Academy and a decorated pilot, "Michael," as his cousin explained to me years later, "bled air-force blue."[79] And so, four years after the reclassification and despite serious misgivings about the potential someday to identify the unidentifiable, CILHI commander Johnie Webb acquiesced to the Reagan administration's demand to produce a Vietnam War Unknown Soldier, and X-26, candidate Number 4, was interred in Arlington.

Unmaking the Vietnam Unknown

It may be that forensic science has reached the point where there will be no other unknowns in any war.

—SECRETARY OF DEFENSE WILLIAM S. COHEN, *June 30, 1998*[80]

Flash forward to May 1998, when the crypt was opened and the Vietnam War Unknown removed. The notion of disinterring the remains stirred controversy from the start, and DOD officials came to the decision begrudgingly. Beginning in the mid-1990s, rumors surfaced about what some called "the worst kept secret in the Pentagon." Formal allegations of the known identity first emerged in an article published by Vietnam veteran and activist Ted Sampley:

In 1984, as a result of the US government's eagerness to lay to rest a Vietnam Unknown Soldier, it interred the remains of a missing American serviceman that today can be identified and accounted for through the U.S. government Central Identification Laboratory in Hawaii (CIL-HI). . . . The entombment of the Vietnam Unknown was at the very best premature and at the worst a politically expedient attempt to further close the books on the POW/MIA issue.[81]

In the same report, Sampley went on to detail the connection between 1st Lt. Blassie's case and that of the unknown, X-26, concluding that CILHI "should be able to right this wrong by determining through DNA if [Blassie's] remains" were in the tomb.[82] Here was the first hint that it might be scientifically possible to resolve the uncertainty that hung over the Vietnam crypt—to know definitively what had been deemed unknowable a decade before. Sampley's allegations were subsequently picked up by more mainstream journalists, including Vince Gonzales from CBS News, who, after an eight-month-long investigation into the matter, ran a report in January 1998 detailing the government's handling of the case.[83] The Blassie family soon fell into the public spotlight, forced to explain and, to some, defend their request to the Pentagon that the tomb be opened and the remains examined. Echoing Johnie Webb's memo to the US Army sixteen years before, the family's spokesperson, Michael's sister Pat Blassie spelled it out: "If it's Michael, he is not unknown. He might be unidentified, but he's not unidentifiable. And we want to bring him home."[84]

With pressure mounting, the DOD decided at last to disinter the remains for analysis. On May 14, 1998, the Tomb of the Unknowns was closed to the public, the sentinel charge of the Third US Infantry Regiment, the Old Guard, temporarily disrupted, and the marble slab atop the crypt removed. Beyond interrupting the national memorial, the disinterment marked a significant break from past scientific practice: this time, it would be board-certified forensic experts, not military personnel or mortuary staff, who would evaluate the evidence, and at their disposal they had the important new tool of DNA testing.[85]

The remains of the Vietnam Unknown swiftly shuttled from one realm of security and significance to another, going from being the object of national reverence to the subject of scientific inquiry. As with any rite of passage, ritual helped ease the transition from one to the next. Once removed from the crypt, the casket was draped with an American flag, and the following day, after Secretary of Defense William Cohen delivered brief remarks before the monument, a small procession of cars and honor guard departed Arlington National Cemetery for Walter Reed Army Medical Center and the Armed Forces Institute of Pathology. To ensure the remains' safe transit, the organizers took the added precaution of including two hearses in the convoy—one carrying the casket and a second present in case the first broke down while en route to Walter Reed.

Once there, the remains lay in state in the DOD laboratory. Where military ritual left off, scientific protocol picked up. Padlocks and laboratory regulations safeguarded the remains from a different threat of contamination—any intrusion, physical or procedural, into the evidentiary chain of custody that ensured legitimate findings. Having overseen the disinterment, CILHI anthropologist David Rankin performed the initial forensic anthropological review, cataloging and describing the skeletal elements present, while his colleague Bob Mann, another CILHI forensic anthropologist, and the director of AFDIL looked on to verify protocol. After his preliminary analysis, Rankin then prepared each bone in an evidence bag as a potential sample to be cut and analyzed by AFDIL. Working late into the night, staff from all three agencies and the Department of the Army shepherded the remains and associated material evidence through the channels of custody and analysis.

Internally, the answer came swiftly. Six samples had been cut from the remains, and "to insure blind testing," additional samples were submitted to AFDIL from an unrelated CILHI case.[86] It is important to note that Blassie was not the only individual potentially associated with the remains: CILHI scientists determined that nine other unaccounted-for American servicemen had been lost in the same approximate location (An Loc, South Vietnam) during the same one-month period (April 26–May 24, 1972). Because those individuals needed to be definitively excluded, AFDIL requested and received mitochondrial DNA samples—"family reference samples"—from maternal relatives of seven of the nine missing men.[87] The results were conclusive. DNA analysis matched the Unknown's sequence to the samples provided by Michael Blassie's mother and sister.

The scientists reviewing the case all agreed that the DNA evidence was the most crucial element of the identification. It was, as one external reviewer wrote in his report, "the key to the identification."[88] Moreover, the compelling DNA match with Blassie's mother and sister gave CILHI the evidence it needed to overcome the doubt introduced by the skeletal remains themselves with their outlier age and stature estimates, and lent further weight to the circumstantial evidence—the parachute and life support equipment—correlating the crash site with the recovered remains. The lines of evidence converged around Blassie's genetic signature.

The technology of DNA testing did more than just correct for past forensic errors or oversights. It allowed the government to refashion the narrative of the Vietnam Unknown's original selection and his identification into a story of the triumph of modern science (not the negligence or political pressures of the past). The DOD's news release extolled the advances of forensic genetics and the government's expertise that allowed Blassie's remains to be named: "After successful mitochondrial DNA comparison and forensic examination using state-of-the-art technology not available in 1984, the U.S. Army Central Identification Laboratory has determined that the remains interred in 1984 as the Vietnam Unknown are those of U.S. Air Force 1st Lt. Michael Joseph Blassie."[89] In this version of the story, DNA became the silver bullet, capable of establishing identity and reestablishing order.

The Blassie identification was in many ways a turning point for the US military's MIA accounting efforts. The promise of DNA raised expectations, and the Pentagon seized on that promise, emphasizing what it meant not only for missing war dead of past conflicts but also for contemporary and future US military members. When he announced the definitive news of 1st Lt. Blassie's identification, Secretary of Defense Cohen staked a new claim for future commemorations: DNA might well render unknowns a thing of the past. Here was a way for the state to sidestep past errors, to sweep under the carpet the political pressures that eventually caught up with a faulty MIA accounting mission, and instead look forward to the brighter future of war dead who can always be named.

The Vietnam Unknown's Legacy

In 2008, I met with Michael Blassie's sister Pat at her home in Crystal City, Virginia. Just a few days before our meeting, I had visited an exhibit at the National Museum of Health and Medicine titled *Resolved: Advances in Forensic Identification of US War Dead.* Among its other displays, the installation profiled the story of 1st Lt. Blassie's identification. In fact, the Vietnam War Unknown—then identified—airman served as a culminating moment of instruction. Wending its way through the various major conflicts of the past two centuries and the advances in forensic practice—the six "lines of evidence"—that comprised the US military's approach to postmortem identification, the exhibit's narrative eventually arrived at DNA testing and the example of 1st Lt. Blassie, whose fate it had resolved. "Due to advances in DNA technology, the Tomb of the Unknowns was opened and the remains of X-26 were removed for analysis on May 14, 1998. . . . On June 22, 1998, the Central Identification Laboratory identified 1Lt Michael J. Blassie using the results of anthropological and mtDNA [mitochondrial DNA] analyses to the exclusion of all other possibilities."[90] A glass display case housed objects recovered with his remains alongside photographs of Blassie in uniform and the white marble monument where he lay in rest for fourteen years.

When I visited his sister, she too had some of the material artifacts that had been recovered with her brother's remains and later interred with him at the Tomb of the Unknowns. She kept them stored in a suitcase. I remember being struck by the number and condition of the items—fragments and intact articles of life support and personal equipment. I ran my fingers over a piece of parachute, its orange silk seemingly untouched by the years of exposure, storage, even burial. After everything that had happened to her family, there was no trace of bitterness in her explanations of her brother's posthumous fate. He came home eventually, and that was as it should and had to be.

Pat Blassie had been asked many times to tell her brother's story to current military and veteran audiences, as well as to the general public. She had even prepared a PowerPoint presentation with slides to lay out the complicated details of his life, death, interment, and eventual identification, which she showed me that afternoon. It echoed much of what I had read and seen at the *Resolved* exhibit. In many ways, the act of storytelling is one of the Vietnam Unknown's/1st Lt. Blassie's most powerful legacies. His is the archetypal personalized narrative of the missing war dead whose return is made possible by the work of forensic science, the progenitor missing in action come home.

One can see this legacy on full display—literally—at the Tomb of the Unknowns in Arlington National Cemetery. Ride the official hop-on/hop-off tour up to the Memorial Amphitheater and listen to the guide instruct you about the cemetery, its decorated heroes, presidents, and statesmen buried there. When the trolley approaches the tomb, the story settles not on the anonymous unknowns from World War I, World War II, or the Korean War, whose mention is cursory, but on 1st Lt. Blassie, the details unfurled, as in Pat's slideshow, of his posthumous fate. The guide assumes the voice of the state: "With the advent of DNA testing we determined" the identity of the Vietnam Unknown, despite the scant remains interred. "We went to the family. 'Do you want to disinter?' They did." He runs through 1st Lt. Blassie's biography: where he was shot down in South Vietnam; his burial on Memorial Day in 1984 with President Reagan presiding; and his eventual disinterment and identification. "Michael J. Blassie is now 'known' and buried in Jefferson Barracks National Cemetery in his hometown of St. Louis."

"Modern forensics," the tour guide explains, has changed things. "With DNA, they can almost always identify remains."

Inside the Memorial Amphitheater, a recently renovated Memorial Display Room chronicles the history of the Tomb of the Unknowns, shining a similar spotlight on the Vietnam War saga. An entire wall of photographs and text tells Blassie's story. An image of his handsome face flashes for a few seconds on the monitor above the display case with the flag that once adorned his coffin and the Medal of Honor awarded to him as the symbolic "missing son." There is much more to say about an identified unknown than a set of anonymous remains, no matter how storied or symbolic the latter; there is much more for the visiting public to connect with and to remember. The account of 1st Lt. Michael J. Blassie's selection and identification is riveting, from the details of political intrigue to the scientific controversies and lessons learned. In some ways, it is perfect material for tour guide narratives and visitor center displays in the nation's capital. But the story of the making and unmaking of the Vietnam Unknown has done more than just draw in visitors to museums and national monuments. Returning to his family and to that quiet plot in Jefferson Barracks National Cemetery, 1st Lt. Michael J. Blassie ushered in an era of exceptional care that to this day underwrites, at times haunts, the US military's efforts to account for its missing war dead.

The Science of Accounting

In the Fall of 2017, a friend and I visited an exhibit at the Renwick Gallery in Washington, DC, that seemed to capture a certain popular cultural fascination with forensic science.[1] A few blocks from the White House, the Renwick doesn't attract the same crowds as the museums that line the National Mall—the Air and Space Museum, the National Gallery, or the recently opened National Museum of African American History and Culture, for example. The day was cold and rainy, the kind of weather that persuades people to stay put, and so I was surprised to find the first room of the exhibit packed with visitors. Peering over one another's shoulders and angling for better views of the individual displays, many using small flashlights to aid in their sleuthing, they were enthralled. They were investigating. They were playing forensic detective for the day.

The exhibit, *Murder Is Her Hobby: Frances Glessner Lee and The Nutshell Studies of Unexplained Death*, paid homage to Lee, known as the "mother of forensic science" and the country's first female police captain, by showcasing one of her most important contributions to the field: eighteen dollhouse-sized dioramas depicting various crime scenes that Lee used while serving as an instructor at the Department of Legal Medicine at Harvard University to train budding forensic investigators.[2] In the "kitchen," the figure of an apron-clad woman lies prostrate on the floor near the oven, a tiny Bundt cake resting on its open door. An old woman hangs from the rafters in the "attic," with papers strewn about and an upturned cane back chair at her feet. In the "three-room dwelling," a man lies face-down on a bedroom floor, his pajamas stained with blood, while his wife lies in the adjacent miniature bed, her head resting on a blood-soaked pillow.

Moving from one tiny "crime scene" to the next in the darkened exhibit hall, visitors speculated aloud—sometimes to themselves and with a striking level of assurance—about what clues they detected and what crimes of passion or negligence or avarice they thus deduced. Rather than focusing on the intricate handiwork, indeed artistry, of Lee's tableaus or the paradoxical rendering of such gruesome details through the classic medium of children's make-believe worlds, most people seemed to revel in the chance to discern the truth and solve the crimes. If only for a couple of hours on a rainy Sunday afternoon, they delved into the world of forensic science, albeit a fabricated and miniaturized one.

Writing about forensic fiction, particularly novels like those of Kathy Reichs, on which the television series *Bones* is based, anthropologist Zoë Crossland notes how "forensic work is commonly explained as a form of intellectual puzzle."[3] Assembling the facts and interpreting the signs, including those gleaned from the corpse itself, allow the scientist as puzzle solver to piece together the story, whether of violent death, guilt or innocence, or the identity of a nameless victim.

In some important ways, what the US military attempts through its MIA accounting resembles this crime-scene investigation puzzle-solving endeavor. They too seek to tell a story through the assemblage of forensic facts. They too bring to bear an array of investigatory tools to solve the puzzle. But unlike the protagonists of fictional TV series or forensic novels or even Frances Glessner Lee's trainees, the forensic scientists tasked with MIA accounting deal with vastly different sets of scales—of time, space, and, most significantly, numbers. Their scenes of investigation and recovery are sites of long-past wars. Their examinations focus less on the *how* or the *when* than on the *where* and, most pressingly, the *who*.

Then there are the numbers: some eighty-two thousand unaccounted-for US service members from the major conflicts of the past century (World War II, the Korean War, the Cold War, and the Vietnam War), at least half of which are cases requiring detailed archival investigation and scientific analysis—tens of thousands of "nutshell studies," enough to fill the Renwick Gallery exhibit halls at least two thousand times over, each dependent on multiple lines of evidence to discern the individual identity of a set or fragment of remains.

Finally, there is the simple fact that the forensic work of recovering and identifying remains is not just about investigation or resolution. It is about consecration. In restoring individual identity to a set of remains of an unaccounted-for service member, the process recognizes an individual life sacrificed to the nation. It is an act of setting apart the sacred.

I hadn't fully understood the scale or weight of that endeavor until I spent time in the forensic laboratory on Joint Base Pearl Harbor-Hickam. It was there that I learned of the scientific, archival, and operational facets of the accounting mission, both in the past and the present—how it started, how it changed over time, and what obstacles it continued to face. And it was there, through observing the fine grain of the forensic work of MIA accounting, that I came to appreciate how the efforts themselves to recover and identify remains form part of the rituals of remembrance and mourning attached to this country's missing war dead.

From Mortuary to Laboratory

The laboratory where I conducted my research in 2011 and 2012 and visited again in 2014 was not the same facility that currently serves as the hub for the forensic scientific work of the Defense POW/MIA Accounting Agency (DPAA).[4] That lab is now housed in a brand-new three-story building on the other side of the Joint Base Pearl Harbor-Hickam. It's an impressive structure, but in some ways its newness obscures the history behind the mission—namely its evolution from an endeavor defined primarily by mortuary practice to one dominated by forensic science. The evolution has had its growing pains, some of them with lasting effect.

It took time for me to learn this history, and in many ways, I first perceived it through the physical spaces of the laboratory, the Joint POW/MIA Accounting Command, the joint base, and the location itself—on the island of Oahu. The impression that history—and geography—matter came across right away through the setting of the two bases, Pearl Harbor Naval Station and Hickam Air Force Base, which were combined into the joint base in 2010. Driving through the art deco main gates of the Hickam entrance and along the winding roads fringed by palm trees and lush vegetation, past the roundabouts with fighter planes from various conflicts, past the buildings that still bear the scars of the December 7, 1941, aerial attack by the Imperial Japanese aircraft, I felt at times as if I were wending my way through a movie set. In fact, the two historic bases have lent their scenes to several Hollywood productions over the years—to films such as *Aloha* and *Battleship* and episodes of *Hawaii Five-O* (though, interestingly, not the 2001 blockbuster *Pearl Harbor*). Against that backdrop, the old lab was located in an unassuming, cream-colored, single-story building, its entrance announced by, unsurprisingly, the black-and-white POW/MIA flag. In the years since the 1976 transfer of the US Army's mortuary facility for the conflict in Southeast Asia from its temporary location in Thailand to Hawaii, a handful of brown trailers were gradually added as the original facility expanded from an initial staff of twenty-five to over four hundred personnel.[5]

The expansion reflected in part the geographic concentration of the previous century's absent war dead: of the more than eighty-two thousand unaccounted-for service members, 75 percent of the losses are located in the Asia-Pacific region.[6] Thus, Oahu, Hawaii, served as a convenient midpoint for remains retrieved from Southeast Asia, the South Pacific, and the Korean Peninsula. Furthermore, buried on the island in the National Memorial Cemetery of the Pacific, known as the Punchbowl, were also hundreds of Korean War unknowns and the unnamed dead from the Pearl Harbor bombings, whose remains would become critical to the expanded mandate and a congressional push for increased annual identifications beginning in 2010.[7]

Before setting foot in the CIL, I got a taste for the current organizational logic of the MIA accounting mission's scientific branch: standard operating procedure, or SOP. An SOP is a lab's playbook and regulations—it lays out the specific protocols for every element of the scientific work. For as much as they seem fixed in form, SOPs index changes—modifications, refinements, additions—that are integrated as knowledge evolves and practice improves. It's a "living document," one of the lab managers explained. "It constantly grows." To my uninitiated eye, the lab's SOPs were awash in detail. A few weeks before I flew out to Hawaii, a package arrived in the mail, a hard copy of certain sections of the various SOPs, which I was to review and be tested on before I could observe the laboratory. In addition to providing a DNA sample and my fingerprints as part of my induction into the world of the US military's forensic science, I also had to demonstrate my mastery of the fundamental rules for safeguarding evidence, accessing examination space, and keeping information secure.

Though an obvious artifact of any scientific laboratory, the SOPs of the Central Identification Laboratory had their own telling history. Like the Joint POW/MIA Accounting Command's (JPAC) evolving physical

space, they mapped the transition from mortuary practice to a more forensic, scientifically driven mission. Created in the mid-2000s, they also
flagged an initiative by the lab to maximize transparency and ensure the
scientific integrity of the identifications it produced.[8] The subtext here
was that more than just keeping apace with standardized practice in the
field, the SOPs sought to prevent problems of the past—past mistakes,
flawed approaches, and strained relations between civilian scientists and
military personnel that had characterized the early years of the Vietnam
War–era MIA accounting. Underwriting these aims of transparency and
integrity was the less tangible but equally vital issue of trust. People both
inside and outside the laboratory needed to have faith in the facts being
produced; they needed to see the basic processes of recovery and identification as trustworthy.[9]

Early into my research at the lab, I learned that there was a time when
the forensic work of MIA accounting had been publicly called into question. The details of the episode were recounted to me by five leading figures
in forensic anthropology and odontology (dentistry), who as academics
and/or practitioners had served as external consultants, that is, peer reviewers for the CIL. Two of them had been working with the lab since the
1980s; three had provided the external reviews for the identification of
1st Lt. Michael J. Blassie, the former Unknown Soldier of the Vietnam War.
My first month of research at JPAC coincided with their annual visit to the
laboratory, and I was able to meet with them as a group. As we sat in the
lab's library, surrounded by hundreds of identification packets (closed
cases), their plastic-comb-bound volumes lining the shelves, the overwhelming majority of which these men had personally peer reviewed, they
chronicled the changes they had witnessed over the past two decades. They
started with what brought the lab to their attention and to that of their colleagues in the wider academic and professional community: mistakes. At
that time, the mid-1980s, the scientific director—in fact, the lone "scientist" at the lab—was Tadao Furue, who held a bachelor's degree in science
from the University of Tokyo but no advanced degree in a relevant field of
forensic science.[10] He had, nevertheless, worked for the US Army in Japan
from 1951 to 1977 processing Korean War remains (those unidentified
during the policy of concurrent return) and later remains from the war in
Southeast Asia. In 1977, he joined the laboratory in Hawaii.[11] To be fair,
there was little appetite within the Department of Defense in those early
years to throw resources at developing forensic expertise, let alone hiring
personnel with proper scientific qualifications. Again, it was still a mission

largely governed by military mortuary practice—recovering remains and trying to make identifications based on archival, circumstantial, dental, and limited forensic anthropological evidence.

By the early 1980s, rumors of unsupportable identifications had begun to surface—around the same time that the remains of the Vietnam War Unknown Soldier were selected for interment at the Tomb of the Unknowns at Arlington National Cemetery—culminating in a lawsuit filed by Anne Hart, wife of an MIA. Hart rejected the US military's identification of her husband's remains and demanded that they be examined by an external scientist.[12] Michael Charney, who was the director of the Center for Human Identification at Colorado State University, undertook the review of the remains, a mere seven fragments, none more than six inches in length, and denounced the military's identification as "incompetence of the worst sort." He explained that "the fragments were so minute, there was no way they could be identified as Lt. Col. Hart. The things Furue claimed to detect from the bones—age, sex, race—were just not possible."[13]

By that point, the external consultants explained to me, Congress was paying attention. In December 1985, three independent forensic scientists, leading figures in their respective fields—William Maples, Ellis Kerley, and Lowell Levine, two anthropologists and one odontologist—were sent to evaluate the lab. (Levine, the odontologist, was one of the five consultants filling me in on the lab's early history.) Tasked with "conduct[ing] an in-depth review and analysis of identification procedures and associated documentation used in the [lab]," the independent reviewers found a pattern of errors with data collection and analysis.[14] They reported their findings to Congress and made twenty-three recommendations, including that "positive identifications" be made by direct fingerprints or X-ray comparisons; "unidentified commingled, fragmented remains should be presented as such and recommended for mass burial"; a "nationally or internationally known anthropologist" become lab director; the Armed Services Graves Registration Office's review board include two forensic anthropologists, two odontologists, a lawyer, and forensic pathologists; and the lab's scientists be encouraged and financially supported to attend scientific meetings on the mainland.[15] The recommendations underscored the need to address the scientific integrity of the MIA accounting process by ensuring good science carried out by qualified scientists—from the top down, personnel not only trained in the relevant fields but knowledgeable about evolving practice. In short, they needed to reestablish trust in the government's capacity to care for its fallen service members. The US Army accepted all twenty-three recommendations, and the evaluation proved a watershed moment. By 1987, Ellis Kerley—one of the anthropologists— became the lab's scientific director, whose "standing in the field helped the lab gain needed credibility in the scientific community," members of which he brought out to Hawaii as visiting scientists and external consultants.[16]

A Civilian-Military Gap

Kerley's directorship also heralded an important shift in how the scientific component of the MIA accounting mission was conceived and structured. Gradually, the CIL became more of a civilian rather than military-led operation. As Lowell Levine, a veteran himself, explained in less diplomatic language, "You had to divorce the science from the tree suits, the mean green machine [the army]," to ensure the integrity of the forensic efforts—that is, CILHI needed to demonstrate that the science wasn't beholden to extrinsic interests. Though change was slow and resources lacking (despite the 1985 recommendations, the lab still had only one computer in 1990, available to staff for thirty-minute slots), the consultants noticed a subtle transformation in the language of the reports—from the formerly definitive statements that nevertheless lacked supporting evidence to more cautious scientific analysis that acknowledged the limits of the available data.

But getting good scientists, especially well-trained forensic anthropologists, not only to move to Hawaii, so distant from the mainland, but also to work for the military, wasn't an easy task. In the wake of the Vietnam War, anthropologists, including forensic anthropologists, were skeptical of the US government, and especially the military. As Tom Holland explained, "the relationship between universities and the military was so tainted by the Vietnam War. Coming out of WWII is the exact opposite. The scientists were seen as the saviors. The scientists were the ones that gave us the atom bomb that ended the war. But that was a whole different world."[17] Four years after assuming the position of the lab's scientific director, Ellis Kerley, then president of the American Academy of Forensic Sciences, was fired by Lieutenant Colonel Johnie Webb, deputy to the commander at CILHI. Kerley's successor, Kimberly Schneider, lasted even less time. Holland recalled arriving at the island and his post as one of three newly hired forensic anthropologists only to find its management in turmoil. "About a month after I was here, she [Schneider] had a blow up with the Command concerning what she felt were intrusions into scientific integrity brought about by the Joint Task Force-Full Accounting, JTF-FA. At that point, JTF-FA was run by a two-star general by the name of Thomas Needham, whose nickname was Nuke 'em Needham. He was a real piece of work and didn't have much regard for scientists. So I think Kim probably had a very legitimate concern."[18] Holland took over the permanent position of scientific director in 1994. Despite Kerley's efforts to reform the laboratory, the military emphasis on expediency still extended to field operations. Hired the same year as Holland, anthropologist Bob Mann spent much of his first few years deployed to Southeast Asia, where, under General Needham, the military's "gauge of success was the number of investigations that were done, the number of sites that were excavated and closed. Emphasis on closed." The civilian anthropologists were only advisors on excavation sites, and the attitude was "get in there and get it done."[19]

To protect the integrity of both the archaeological work of recovery and anthropological work of identification, Holland sought an external guarantor for quality assurance and transparency. He achieved this by getting the lab accredited. Accreditation is used to verify a laboratory's quality management system and assure that it can perform certain test methods properly.[20] "Given what they do, with life and liberty at stake," he explained, "forensic laboratories probably more than any other laboratory need maximum transparency." In December 2000, the lab's management began their campaign to make the CIL the first forensic anthropology laboratory to be accredited by the American Society of Crime Laboratory Directors/Laboratory Accreditation Board (ASCLD/LAB). They petitioned for the accreditation not on the basis of human identification, but rather on trace evidence.[21] Holland used the analogy of a car crash to convince the ASCLD/LAB reviewers of the parallel. Reassembling and analyzing the shards of a broken headlight from a car crash was like reassembling and analyzing a human skeleton that had been recovered at an air crash site, he argued. It worked. In 2003, they secured the accreditation, and in 2008, CIL succeeded in becoming the second federal laboratory to pass the ASCLD/LAB-International program (based on the International Organization for Standardization's general requirements for the competence of testing and calibration laboratories, or ISO 17025).

To a layperson, the lab's accreditation might seem like a lot of extra bureaucracy—from quality assurance to peer reviews and SOP revisions. But it did critical work. The achievement raised the lab's profile both nationally and internationally—CIL, its facilities and scientists, soon led rather than trailed the field in postmortem identification, especially in the context of mass fatalities—and, equally significant, the move effectively placed a buffer between the scientific wing and the military operations within the Command (Levine's "mean green machine") and the larger accounting mission. In that sense, the forensic efforts of MIA identification had a new master to serve—namely, the standardized protocols demanded by an external scientific accreditation agency, not military leaders. In sum, accreditation raised the bar: it required the consistent execution of exacting science, an element integral to the ethos of exceptional care.

Although accreditation increased transparency and ensured scientific integrity, at times it compounded tensions between civilian scientific and military expertise within the Command.[22] Lab staff often squared off with military leadership over questions of authority—who knew better, whose purview it was, who was the expert in the room. Part of the problem was that résumés didn't translate. The military personnel in the Command had their achievements and experience fixed to their chests: bars, pins, and medals. Intelligible to one another, such records of service made sense in what one of the lab's archaeologists described as the "last true rank society," where individuals are ranked—that is, have more social status or prestige—according to their genealogical distance from the chief. But the scientists at the lab could only gesture to degrees. "Scientific smarts don't count," remarked one anthropologist. "The military folks can't evaluate how well you know your science." Whether a scientist had earned her PhD at a nationally top-ranked forensic anthropology program or was considered a leading figure in the field didn't register because—like the bars and pins—it only fit within its own value regime, recognized by other anthropologists and archaeologists. Further compounding that disconnect was the fact that the military staff typically rotated every two to three years through the official process known as permanent change of station. Such constant hitting of the reset button undermined respect for corporate knowledge, including the specialized knowledge of scientists—anthropologists and archaeologists—deployed on recovery missions.

While there were scientists at JPAC who had previously served in the military or came from military families, they were still seen as personnel from the civilian-dominated laboratory. Archaeologist Bill Belcher's father served his entire career in the US Army. He fought at the tail end of World War II, throughout the Korean War, and completed four year-long tours in the Vietnam War. "I grew up with the sensation of knowing—and my mom would talk about—[how] he might not come back. He might get killed." He remembered "her fear of a car coming into the driveway and a specific kind of car—a government car—that was black, a black sedan, because she said that she knew at that time, her husband, my father, would be either dead or missing in action." He brought that sensibility and respect for the military to the mission. But sometimes it didn't feel reciprocated. "It boils down to they want us to respect them and their position and experience, which I think is great. And I think we should. But they don't want to do it back. They don't want to respect our education and our experiences outside of here. . . . It takes a lot of work to get a PhD."[23]

Echoing this impression, but from the other side, a former JPAC military staff member explained what he saw among his colleagues, many of whom had deployed to Iraq or Afghanistan (himself included):

> They get that mentality of working up to being a first class or a first sergeant or whatever. They don't want to take orders from civilians because, I think, you know, coming into the military out of high school, you get all this praise for being in the military or working hard. . . . I remember from basic training that civilians—it was drilled into our heads—that civilians, I don't want to say, [were] a piece of shit, but it was basically that they didn't do anything when they got out of high school. They're just at home worthless doing nothing. You're going to go back and they're still going to be doing the same thing but look what you've done. You've sacrificed yourself, your family, and time.[24]

For many members of the military at the Command, a JPAC deployment was a way-stop along a career dedicated to either training for war or going to war, and while they wholeheartedly supported the goals of MIA accounting, working alongside civilians who did not fall within their same chain of command could be challenging, especially during recovery missions. No matter how exacting, no SOP could manage expectations about clashing authority when the metrics of expertise were so divergent.

The Archaeology and Anthropology of MIA Accounting

When Lance Corporal Merlin Raye Allen returned to his hometown of Bayfield, Wisconsin, few if any of those who lined the streets to welcome him home might have imagined what little of his physical body remained—a single tooth. Nor could many have guessed the painstaking efforts to lo-cate the proper site to excavate—where to dig for his remains—and once recovered, how to identify them as definitively belonging to him. Yet those underlying, undetected aspects were among the most important insights I gained from my time at the lab: that the processes of recovery and identi-fication are complex and each case is unique, with its own set of compli-cations and contingencies, and that definitive, scientifically sound identi-fications depend on the convergence of *multiple* lines of evidence, which may take years to compile. In short, there's a lot more to the forensic sci-ence of accounting than meets the eye.

I would also add that the remains of war dead from long-past conflicts aren't what you might picture. In 2011 and 2012, the bones laid out on the examination tables at CIL were rarely complete—a far cry from the articulated skeleton that hangs in an anatomy classroom or as a prop on the set of a forensic detective show. Much more often fragmented and partial, they defied assumptions about what lies within the flag-draped coffins photographed coming home to Dover Air Force Base or interred at Arlington National Cemetery. Instead, these heterogeneous collections of skeletal remains were all that was left, or all that could be recovered, of young lives cut short, of once vital bodies, of human beings sent off to fight for their country. In looking out at those tables, you see war's destruction and a limited, if rigorous, attempt to answer its violence.

The science of identifying human remains starts with accession, the process by which remains are formally received at the laboratory and en-tered into its system of analysis. But to be accessioned, remains have to come from some place. They must first be recovered, which means their original loss must first be researched. In most instances, years of archival analysis, intelligence gathering, and field investigations drive recovery missions. "Historical investigation," DPAA historian Michael Dolski explains, "is more of an art than a science," and yet "historical analysis provides the starting point for the scientific staff."[25] Coupled with "human intelligence"—for example, statements by local villagers con-cerning a loss incident or the burial of remains, collected by DOD ana-lysts working in Southeast Asia—historical investigations help determine where to seek remains (which site to excavate) or assist in evaluating the context that has resulted in remains arriving to the laboratory.

The cases laid out on the tables in CIL's inner sanctum of the forensic anthropology examination room come from a finite number of sources. In the past, the majority of the remains accessioned to the lab resulted from a recovery effort, for example an excavation of an air crash site or a burial site in Southeast Asia, such as that which unearthed Merl Allen's tooth. They may also come from a unilateral turnover, where a third party has handed over remains to the US military. While unilateral turnovers have been the source for multiple Vietnam War identifications, the most significant example to date relates to the Korean War, when in the early 1990s, the North Korean government handed over 208 boxes of "individual" remains. The 208 cases in fact turned out to represent approximately six hundred individuals whose bones were commingled and which the lab's scientists are still working to segregate and identify.[26] Finally, since 2015, the DOD has aggressively pursued a program to disinter unknowns— service members buried as unknowns in national military cemeteries, principally in Hawaii at the National Memorial Cemetery of the Pacific— the Punchbowl—from the Korean War and World War II.[27] In the case of unilateral turnovers and disinterred unknowns, provenience may be uncertain—that is, the precise location of where the remains were originally recovered might be unknown, or at least less certain. Just as an art historian might seek to authenticate or verify the origin of a painting, so too the analysts at the lab try to ascertain the original associated loss site through archival and historical research. Even when it is known, such as a crash site in Vietnam or Laos or Cambodia, the link between the remains and the site is still best understood as putative until all evidence is aggregated and analyzed. In that instance, the archaeological investigation of the location, its physical features and its material remnants, provides the first depths to plumb for evidence of identity.

The field recoveries that the US military undertakes as a part of the MIA accounting mission aren't the fine brush-and-trowel digs of classical archaeological sites. Because of limited time and resources—in Laos, for example, US recovery teams were for years allowed in country for a maximum of only thirty days—they operate at a breakneck speed. That said, they still adhere to the fundamental tenets of archaeological theory, including that an excavation is an inherently destructive process; the site is destroyed in pursuit of remains and any correlating material evidence— artifacts such as dog tags or blood chits, personal effects, aircraft data plates, military-issue equipment, and so on. All the more reason to document it carefully, to draft "soil profiles" tracing out the color, consistency, and compactness of the earth to define the boundaries of an impact crater or a burial site. As Greg Fox, a veteran archaeologist and former manager at the lab explained to me, archaeological evidence often reveals distinctions between war and peace, between expediency and ritual; wartime burials are usually "not actual interments but rather field sanitation," where graves are hastily dug and bodies haphazardly placed.[28] He likened recovery and identification efforts to processing metal. The excavations, he explained, were never guaranteed success. The recovery team mined veins to yield raw material. But it was the laboratory, in its process of "smelting the ore," that was expected to produce the "zero-defect" product within a system of inevitable defects, no matter how slight.

While I learned the principles of field archaeology in the abstract during that first period of research at the lab, I came to appreciate the work of forensic anthropology through up-close observation and occasional hands-on experience. When the opportunity arose, I joined forensic anthropologists at the CIL as they analyzed and reviewed assigned cases, either producing their own report or peer reviewing that of another scientist. In shadowing them, I began to recognize interconnections across the scientific component of the mission, including how knowledge gained from one conflict's unaccounted for advanced efforts to identify the missing from others. Observing casework also helped underscore differences in conditions of recovered remains among those conflicts, especially between those excavated from crash sites versus the disinterred unknowns from the national military cemeteries. For example, one of the few times I encountered a complete (or nearly complete) skeleton was when I joined two interns at the lab in assisting an anthropologist as he prepared the remains of a Korean War unknown for analysis. The case was one of two disinterments on the same day. Unearthed from the nearby Punchbowl, the coffins were hammered open and their contents revealed and recorded. They were then transferred to the lab's autopsy room, where, led by the forensic anthropologist, the interns and I set to work "cleaning" the remains. We gently removed the cotton batting and cloth still wrapped around or stuck to the skeleton. We felt around the wool blanket that had ensconced the remains, patting and smoothing down its folds in search of smaller bones or teeth that might be hiding in the clumps of a chalky substance, a formaldehyde-based embalming powder. With the remains freed from the fabric, we began to wash them. Slowly, bone by bone, dipping tooth brushes and occasionally hands into the flowing water, we gently bathed and coaxed the powder off the skeleton. Its varied colors emerged, the effect of long-term contact with different elements, such as metal or soil: a darkened femur, coal black on one side, shades of brown on the other; rust-colored tones, light and dark, for most of the other bones. After several minutes of careful labor, the layers of powdery dust that had protected this individual's remains for the last sixty years dissipated. Now clean, the bones were arranged in anatomical order on an examination table, ready for the next step in unearthing the unknown service member's identity.

In examining remains, forensic anthropologists sort and classify; they measure, assess, and interpret the physical evidence of a skeletal element, or set of elements—that is, a bone, a bone fragment, or a collection of bones/fragments. They read the skeletal elements for clues to identity. This phase happens in the "blind"; the anthropologist is not provided with any information about the case or who it is suspected of being. The veiling is done to ensure that the analyst is not subconsciously biased to draw a conclusion or to see a feature that may not exist. To begin with, they must determine how many individuals are represented by the remains arrayed on the table—a calculus of the principle of "minimum number of individuals," the basic idea of which is to "avoid counting the same individual twice."[29] Once remains are segregated into discrete assemblages or a single set of remains (and human remains at that), the forensic anthropologists seek to build a "biological profile" based on four features: age, sex, stature, and ancestry.[30] Presented with a fully articulated, complete set of remains (again, think of the anatomy classroom skeleton), an anthropologist can come up with an almost definitive assessment of sex; a very close calculation of age and height; and a relatively strong estimation of ancestry (for example, whether the individual's ancestral background is European, Asian, or African).[31] Certain bones are instrumental in indicating particular aspects of this profile. Unsurprisingly, the pelvic bones help differentiate sex, and the surface of one area, the pubic symphysis, provides an indication of age, as do signs of growth with long bones, such as the femur and humerus, as well as clavicles and teeth. Long bones are also used to calculate height, and metric and morphological analysis of the skull, including the teeth, are typically the basis for estimations of ancestry.

I once asked one of the anthropologists if after so many years of generating biological profiles, he started to look at people, living people, differently, imagining their skeletal structure, like Ismail Kadare's protagonist in *The General of the Dead Army:* "'What a damned business this is we've got on our hands,' the general said. 'I can't even pass anyone on the street or see anyone in a café now without automatically checking to see what type his skull is.'"[32] He assured me he didn't. Prior to joining the CIL, he had gained extensive experience studying and identifying human remains, including remains that had to be macerated (the flesh removed) in order to analyze the skeleton. If he didn't assess the skulls of strangers passing him on the street, did he do the reverse? Did he imagine features traced out from the skeleton before him? No. "I take skin off, but I don't put skin on." His task was analyzing bones, not imagining flesh.

In addition to the four features of a biological profile, the anthropologist looks for traces of events and conditions during life, what Laqueur calls "the marks of the life that once clothed them": an injury such as a healed-over broken bone; illness, diet, and nutrition; repetitive physical activity; and, key for the CIL investigation, trauma, both peri- and postmortem (at the time of and after death).[33] Taphonomy, the study of the various factors affecting the preservation, condition, and recovery of skeletal remains, also provides telltale signs of the posthumous life of the remains—were they exposed to the elements, stored above ground, buried in acidic soil?

But what biological profile can emerge from a handful of bone fragments? Recall Michael Charney's scathing critique of the US military's identification of Anne Hart's husband: "There was no way they could be identified as Lt. Col. Hart. The things Furue claimed to detect from the bones—age, sex, race—were just not possible." Thus, only when the available evidence supports it, forensic anthropologists at the lab present their estimations of age, sex, stature, and ancestry, acknowledging in each instance where that assessment falls along a continuum of probability. Indeed, the notion of probability—that is, probable versus absolute terms—is critical to how remains are analyzed in forensic anthropology. As one anthropologist explained, though the "moment of death freezes the skeleton in a particular instant of development," there is nevertheless a certain "slushiness," a gray area between the definitive and probable, that the scientists invariably encounter. Their work therefore employs calculable error rates that can be translated into a probability of certitude. Those conclusions undergo scrutiny by peer reviewers and case managers before they are accepted as fact. "There is no room for error," stressed another anthropologist.

Old Versus New Proof: Dental Versus DNA

Like archaeological findings and material artifacts, forensic anthropology constitutes only one line of evidence. There are other vital means of determining individual identity. In the field of forensic science applied in incidents of mass fatality—whether missing persons, victims of state-sponsored violence such as in Argentina or Bosnia and Herzegovina, the September 11, 2001, World Trade Center attacks, or victims of natural disasters—much has been made of the probative strength of DNA analysis.[34] Forensic genetics does indeed present a very powerful tool. But in the case of the US military's MIA accounting efforts, dental analysis often proves equally effective. This has to do with recordkeeping. The military recognized at the start of the 1900s that dental records offered an expedient way to identify its service members. Military dental records were kept with an expectation that they could be used for that purpose—not unlike how DNA samples are now collected from all service members upon entering the military.[35] Even when X-rays were not taken, there were graphic "odontograms" made with great care and detail.[36] Thus, if teeth are among the recovered remains, forensic odontologists review the case and compare the X-rays of the recovered teeth against dental records. This dental comparison typically operates on the principle of concurrence—that is, on evidence that concurs, as opposed to definitively identifies or excludes. Take, for example, a case in which three teeth have been recovered, two of which are unrestored and one restored. The two unrestored teeth could merely concur with dental records (as the examining dentist would not have marked anything on the chart for teeth that were normal); the restored tooth, on the other hand, could be used as evidence for identification or exclusion, because the dentist would have noted the specific type of restoration and material used.

In Vietnam War cases, teeth can present a twenty-first-century dilemma of scientific promise. Encased in enamel, the crown is the most durable element of the human skeleton—the remains that best defy the decaying properties of the acidic soil found in Southeast Asia—and they endure in ways that bones don't. Given the military's archive of radiographic and dental chart records, dental analysis is therefore not only a comparatively inexpensive tool, but also a highly effective one.[37] In the popular imagination, however, dental analysis has taken a back seat to DNA testing. MIA families often want the "certitude" of genetic evidence, even when the odontological analysis, coupled with the archaeological record and material evidence, provides sufficient proof for a definitive identification. I saw this dynamic firsthand at a regional family update, when a relative insisted on speaking with the scientific director, Tom Holland, because she wanted an explanation as to why the lab hadn't ordered DNA testing on the recovered remains. Holland was summoned, and over the next several minutes, they reviewed the case, step by step, from the excavation to the recovered remains. Among the tiny fragments recovered was a single tooth that had been conclusively shown to match the missing man's dental radiographs. It was the only element large enough to undergo DNA testing, but the sampling and extraction process would take additional time and would use up some portion of the sample (i.e., the dentin, the boney tissue that makes up the bulk of the tooth).[38] Doing so to obtain unnecessary DNA confirmation of a conclusive identification, Holland gently explained, could mean that the family would have less to bury.

With epithets like "gold standard," "truth machine," or "God's signature"—not to mention the touchstone event of 1st Lt. Michael J. Blassie's identification—it is understandable how DNA testing has raised MIA families' expectations regarding what evidence should constitute the principal proof of their missing relative's identity.[39] Indeed, DNA in some instances is the only tool that can segregate commingled bones or identify highly fragmented remains, and the technology has improved significantly from the days of 1st Lt. Blassie's identification. For example, whereas in the past, forensic geneticists at the Armed Forces DNA Identification Laboratory (AFDIL) needed a minimum of 2.5 grams of bone to produce a DNA profile, since 2006, they are able to do so with .25 gram.[40] Still, much depends on the conditions of the remains: "The majority of remains submitted to AFDIL for testing have been subjected to harsh environmental elements for at least 30 years. Some individuals were involved in aircraft incidents, which contributed to the highly fragmented nature of the remains. Some remains have been subjected to years of burial in highly acidic or basic soils or trapped in pockets of jet fuel or saltwater."[41] Either cut from bones or as fragments themselves, bone samples are sent from the CIL in Hawaii to AFDIL, located on Dover Air Force Base in Delaware.[42] There, they undergo mitochondrial DNA (mtDNA, transmitted along the maternal line) testing at first, with additional nuclear DNA—either Y-chromosome (Y-STR, from the paternal line) or autosomal (auSTR, both lines)—as necessary and if the relevant references exist. Nuclear DNA is found in the nucleus of a cell, while mtDNA comes from the mitochondria, the "power generator" organelles found in the cytoplasm of most cells.

For DNA testing to succeed in identifying a missing person, there needs to be something to compare it with—that is, the genetic profile from a bone sample must be compared against DNA sequences collected from surviving relatives or, if possible, from "self-references" such as old envelopes (e.g., where the flap or stamp was licked), baby teeth, a hair brush, or some object that might yield a viable DNA sample of the missing person.[43] Since the early 1990s, AFDIL has sought "family reference samples" from relevant donors among MIA families.[44] Historically, they have emphasized donors from the maternal line, given that mtDNA is more prolific (most human cells have only a single copy of nuclear DNA but an average of two hundred copies of mtDNA per cell) and more durable, meaning less susceptible to degradation from the environment and over time. But the preference for mtDNA also had to do with another set of related factors: first, the limitations of extraction and testing methodologies; and second, the demographics of the missing.[45] To begin with, the overwhelming majority of the missing war dead are young men who did not have children. To use nuclear autosomal DNA, family reference samples are required from one or both parents, siblings, or children of the missing service member.[46] Given the amount of time passed since death (several decades), finding the required nuclear DNA donors can be difficult. But with mtDNA or Y-chromosomal DNA, AFDIL needs only one viable sample from the maternal or paternal line.

AFDIL's early emphasis on mtDNA also reflected the times. Short tandem repeat (STR) technology, which analyzes repeating sequences of DNA that are highly variable from individual to individual, was in its infancy in the 1990s, and due to the limitations in the extraction process, which failed to digest all bone material, not enough nuclear DNA was recovered to allow STR systems to work. It wasn't until 2003 that Y-STR kits were available. In 2006, AFDIL devised a method to overcome the problem of chemically treated bones—called the demineralization protocol—which allowed for all bone material to be digested (the same method that reduced the required sample size from 2.5 grams to .25 gram). The advance freed up all nuclear DNA and mtDNA for purification, and thus, with additional modifications, enabled AFDIL to test for nuclear DNA.[47]

As the genetic technology improved, so too did AFDIL's outreach program. Its Family Reference Collection Form maps the vast potential network of donors, expanding outward from the "missing individual" to relatives as distant as great grandnieces and fourth cousins. The numbers of references collected reflect family mobilization and awareness across the various conflicts. As of 2018, an mtDNA, autosomal, or Y-chromosome sample, provided by a relevant donor, was on file for 85 percent of the missing personnel from the Vietnam War, 92 percent from the Korean War,

Familial Relationship

Please Circle Your Relationship To The Missing Individual

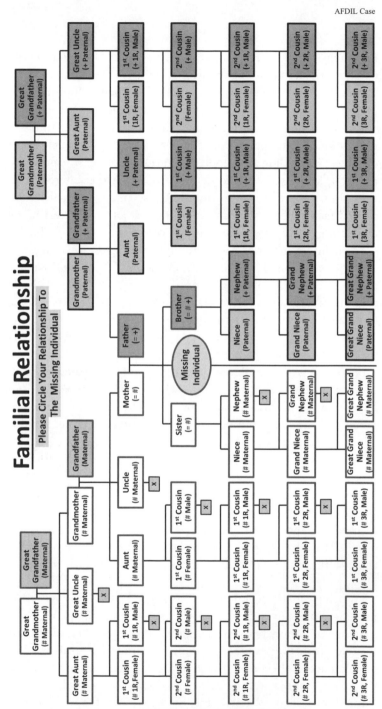

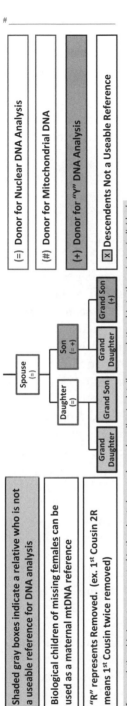

_

Shaded gray boxes indicate a relative who is not a useable reference for DNA analysis

Biological children of missing females can be used as a maternal mtDNA reference

"R" represents Removed. (ex. 1st Cousin 2R means 1st Cousin twice removed)

If your relationship is not represented in the chart above, please describe, in detail, your relationship to the missing individual:

(=) **Donor for Nuclear DNA Analysis**

(#) **Donor for Mitochondrial DNA**

(+) **Donor for "Y" DNA Analysis**

X **Descendents Not a Useable Reference**

Family Reference Sample chart.

85 percent from the Cold War, and 6 percent from those missing from World War II.[48] Notably, despite their role in driving the US military's MIA accounting mission and their decades-long engagement, the Vietnam War families in fact have a comparatively low participation rate, at least relative to the historically less organized and less politically active Korean War families.

Two Cases Compared

While I also saw cases from World War II and the Korean War, it was the examples from Southeast Asia, in particular excavations of air crash sites in Vietnam and Laos, that drove home the complex, contingent course of investigation, recovery, and forensic analysis that leads to an identification. In those cases, recovery missions typically yield highly fragmented and partial remains, bits of bone and teeth that may barely fill your palm. Their examples also made clear how identifications necessarily derive from *converging* lines of evidence—the various forms of proof, from archaeological and material evidence to anthropological, dental, and DNA analyses, that come together to point definitively to an individual service member. There is no single evidentiary silver bullet, though DNA and dental analysis often provide the data that tip the scales of probability and exclusion.

Seen side by side, two cases I reviewed in my first year at the lab—REFNO (reference number) 1895 and REFNO 0738—stand out as particularly good illustrations of these points. Their specific histories map the arc of accounting over decades and across investigations that unfolded in fits and starts, shutting down and circling back. In them we can see the ethos of exceptional care gradually taking shape and coming to fruition as it insisted finally on pinpointing sites of loss whose surfaces then had to be scoured to retrieve the scant traces of the almost entirely disappeared. In them we also glimpse the labor required to "smelt the ore" of recovery to produce an identification and return remains to surviving kin.

REFNO 1895:[49] On July 10, 1972, Commander Frank C. Green Jr., pilot of an A-4F Skyhawk, failed to recover from an attack dive and crashed into a high karst mountaintop in North Vietnam.[50] Because of the crash site's location in hostile territory, friendly forces were unable to return, and Cdr. Green was designated killed in action/body not recovered. After initial confusion regarding the exact location of the crash, several investigations and field surveys were conducted at the presumed site, with United States and Vietnamese (Socialist Republic of Vietnam or SRV) joint teams traveling there four times between 1994 and 1997 to interview potential witnesses, survey the site, and assess conditions for recovery. In 1997, the site was deemed too hazardous for a recovery mission, and for good reason: the potential recovery locations entailed an area of rock fall at the base of a karst outcropping and an area near its summit. In 2005, however, a US/SRV joint team returned to resurvey the location, and in 2007, they returned to resurvey again. By 2008, excavations began. The first mission (October–November 2008) tackled the base of the karst outcropping; the second covered the much more dangerous terrain of the summit itself. The archaeological report spells out the challenging physical conditions: "The primary excavation area during JFA 10-1VM, Section II, is located near the summit of the karst outcropping that is approximately 133 [meters above mean sea level]. Section II is accessible via an approximate 100 m near-vertical to vertical ascent from Section I requiring the use of fixed ropes and ladders. The recovery scene is located on a 30° to 45° north-facing slope with numerous small to large limestone boulders."[51] The report includes photographs of team members clipped into rappelling harnesses and attempting to move large boulders.

Despite the formidable terrain, the two missions were successful. In addition to locating correlating wreckage and pilot-related equipment, both teams recovered human remains: in aggregate, there were two tooth fragments and "numerous fragmentary elements in fair to poor condition," including portions of the skull and fragments of long bones, vertebrae, and other elements, as well as "numerous non-diagnostic bone fragments" and "a small quantity of minute bone particles mixed with sediment."[52] Although it may sound like a lot of remains, in fact, as the identification memorandum explains, their size and condition "preclude[d] the determination of any individualizing biological characteristics." In other words, nothing definitive could be gleaned from an anthropological examination of the recovered bits of bone that could associate them with Cdr. Green. The same was also true of the two tooth fragments; not even the tooth type of either could be determined. DNA, on the other hand, proved the key line of evidence. Though only two samples cut from the skeletal remains yielded mtDNA profiles, they matched family reference samples provided by two maternal-line relatives (cousins) of Cdr. Green. Thus, in the end, the archaeological and material evidence of the crash site, coupled with the DNA analysis, "allow[ed] for the remains to be attributed to CDR Frank C. GREEN, Jr., to the exclusion of all other reasonable possibilities."

REFNO 0738:[53] On June 21, 1967, Captain Darrell J. Spinler, pilot of an A-1E Skyraider, crashed along the banks of the Xe Kong River in Xekong Province, Laos. Though a second pilot remained in the area for two hours searching for any signs that Capt. Spinler had survived, he was eventually given the status of killed in action (body not recovered). In October 1993, a joint US/Lao People's Democratic Republic (LPDR) team investigated the purported crash site and interviewed two witnesses who claimed to have seen the pilot's body on the nearby river bank; they "speculated that the remains likely had been washed away during the ensuing rainy season(s)." During that same investigation, the team surveyed the site and located wreckage consistent with an A-1E Skyraider. A year and a half later, the US government evaluated the case for its recovery potential, and the case was officially designated "no further pursuit," effectively suspending future investigations or site surveys. But as happens periodically with Vietnam War–era cases, eventually the government's decision was revisited, and another team was sent to investigate the site in 1999. Four years later, the no further pursuit designation was reaffirmed. For six more years, the case lay dormant, until a joint US/LPDR team working in the same province returned to the site once more and located additional A-1E Skyraider wreckage. After sixteen years of tacking between pursuit/no pursuit, these latest findings pushed the site up the priority list for excavations. From October 31, 2010, to November 11, 2010—just under two short weeks—another joint US/LPDR team excavated the site and recovered "human remains, personal effects, and pilot-related equipment from amid the sparse wreckage field."

Remains in this case consisted of small fragments of three "disarticulated" teeth (meaning disarticulated from the mandible, i.e., the jaw bone): #10, #18, and #28 in the Universal Numbering System used in dentistry. Their condition precluded the use of DNA testing, "given the current state of that technology," the identification memorandum explained. But dental comparison, the historical mainstay of the US military's forensic accounting, carried the day. One of the three teeth (#18) had a restoration—a "mesial-occlusal amalgam filling." Though Capt. Spinler's dental records had no radiographs, they did include an odontogram that documented that same type of restoration on tooth #18. Notably, with this particular case, the lab also had to exclude the possibility that the dental remains might belong to another A-1E pilot—that is, that the site might be corre-lated with another Skyraider loss in the area. In fact, there were two other such pilots unaccounted for within fifty kilometers, but both of those sites had been located, and the recovered tooth fragment—that of tooth #18—did not match the dental records for either of the other two pilots. Here, the aggregated evidence, as partial as it was, had to exclude other poten-tial unaccounted-for service members in order to attest definitely to Capt. Spinler's identity. The material evidence recovered at the site played an equally weighty role—specifically, the recovered wreckage including blue canopy glass that correlated exclusively to an A-1E Skyraider. Thus, the dental analysis, coupled with the associated "non-biological material" recovered at the site, allowed "the remains to be attributed to Capt Dar-rell J. SPINLER to the exclusion of all other reasonable possibilities." Iden-tified on January 5, 2011, Captain Spinler would return to his family on Father's Day weekend of that same year.

Encounters and Expectations

There are families who, for a variety of reasons, have not followed the MIA accounting issue, the science, or even their individual relative's case over the intervening years. For them, news of identification—be it driven by DNA, forensic anthropology, odontology, material artifacts, or some com-bination of those lines of evidence—may come seemingly out of the blue. In 2011 and again in 2012, I saw this reaction repeatedly during family visits to the lab, when relatives of a recently identified service member trav-eled from the mainland to Hawaii in order to take custody of the remains and escort them home.[54] World War II, Korean War, and Vietnam War families arrived at the lab with different levels of knowledge about their individual cases—about the recovery efforts and the identification itself. Some had obviously pored over the identification packet, the bound col-lection of documents that include the official memorandum of identifica-tion and supporting scientific and historical reports, and knew its details intimately. When asked whether he had read through his father's packet, the son of a Vietnam MIA nodded his head earnestly: "Absolutely every word."

Met at the front desk by a photographer, families were first shown to a wooden plaque bearing the names of each individual identified since 1976 and given the opportunity to have their picture taken beside their relative's newly inscribed brass plate. Then they headed down the hall to a conference room to meet with members of the External Relations Office within the Command. With boxes of tissue and coffee service in fine china at the ready, they viewed the JPAC informational video, which, set to sweeping orchestral music, extolled the personnel, technology, and lengths taken to recover and identify the remains of the unaccounted for. They had a chance to ask questions, often of Johnie Webb, who long since had left the position of deputy commander of CILHI to head JPAC's External Relations Office and had perfected the art of offering soothing, if somewhat stock, condolences. "You take your loved one home and give him the proper burial that he as a hero deserves," he would say, and as his face lit up, "This is the moment we live for."

From there, visiting family members proceeded to the lab, where they were given a brief informational tour by one of the forensic anthropologists—JPAC science on display. It began just outside the forensic anthropology examination room, where glass walls offered a clear view onto the work of analyzing remains. The anthropologist gave an overview of the forensic science of recovery and identification, referring periodically to various props laid out on a nearby table—plastic bones and model skulls, laminated photographs of excavation sites, dental X-rays, even a diagram of a cell with the mitochondria, cytoplasm, and nucleus marked. Most visitors readily admitted they knew little about the science, and their questions often related to information they had come across in their identification packet.

The welcome photograph, the video, the tour, all set the scene for the main event, when families were invited to step into the family visitation room to see the remains of their missing—now recovered and identified—service member. The first time I accompanied a family into the room, I was reminded of Bosnia and that singular moment when the coffins of the identified victims of the Srebrenica genocide are unloaded one after the other and placed in symmetrical rows stretching the length of a stark gray warehouse, ready for burial the next day. Women aren't allowed to assist with carrying the coffins, and so instead, they look on, some trying to spot their loved one's name on the identification placard at the foot of the slender pine box draped in green cloth. Some walk along the rows stooped over, checking each coffin until they find their son, husband, father, or brother. I heard a mother once remark as she watched two men swiftly, without strain, hoist a coffin above their heads, "they are *so* light." There was so little left of the person, just a handful of bones, that there was barely any weight to shoulder. These memories came back when I watched the niece of a Korean War MIA encounter her uncle in the quiet space of the family visitation room. She was three years old when he left for the war; her siblings never knew him. There on the table was a clear plastic bag—an evidence bag—laid neatly atop a green wool army blanket. Its sight brought tears to her eyes; the rest of us—her husband, JPAC staff, the military escort, and I—stepped back into the shadows of the dimly lit room.

She reached out to touch the bag, her fingers tracing the bones within. After a moment, she wiped away tears and remarked wistfully at how it was just "one person in such a small bag." She asked about teeth, as she knew her uncle had had special bridge work done when he was seventeen years old, but the teeth were tucked beneath the rest of the skeletal elements in a separate bag and out of sight. Did she want to touch the remains, to have them brought out of the bag? She shook her head. Did she want time alone with the remains? Again, she declined. But something had caught her eye instead: a handwritten number on the white slip of paper attached at the bag's seal was unclear—was it 2007 or 2001 (the year of accession)? The evidence coordinator left the room to prepare a more carefully printed version. When he returned, he gingerly sliced open one end of the bag and replaced the slip, extracting a smaller plastic pouch from inside, the one containing the teeth. The niece held the tiny packet in her hands for a moment.

Finally, she was ready to take her leave. The evidence coordinator began the final step of the lab's care for the remains, one of the most symbolically striking acts of the entire recovery and identification process. Sometimes assisted by families or a military escort, sometimes on his own, the evidence coordinator, a young man named Ben, would fold the blanket around the remains, already secured in the evidence bag, and then fasten the edges of the thick wool fabric together with six large golden safety pins. This was no slapdash effort. There is a strict protocol to the position of each pin: all facing the same direction, four along the long edge and one on each end. Ben learned firsthand that there was no room for error. He had once allowed someone else to attach the pins but hadn't double-checked the work. The person had made a mistake, and not long afterward, the Army Mortuary Affairs Office on island got a call from Arlington National Cemetery, reprimanding them for the slip.

The ritual swaddling of the remains signaled the end of the scientific inquiry into individual identity and the beginning of the military rites of homecoming. It also enfolded the remains into the longer history of the United States military's care for war dead. The same woolen blankets have been used to wrap the dead since World War I. In a laboratory where remains from all three major conflicts—World War II, the Korean War, and the Vietnam War—might be laid out on the tables in the forensic anthropology examination room at any given moment, the blankets and their uniform ritual leveled—if only temporarily—distinctions in conflict, branch of service, rank, and martial valor. Named and known once again, all were dressed in the plain cloth. All were headed home, some to the astonishment of surviving kin.

"You know, we didn't expect any of this." Having watched her uncle's remains fastened atop a funeral home stretcher, and wheeled outside the building to the waiting hearse, the Korean War MIA niece turned to the anthropologist who had given the tour to say her thanks. It was a response I would witness repeatedly during such family visits—expressions of gratitude for events wholly unexpected. *"We didn't expect any of this,"* echoed the daughter of an identified Vietnam War pilot a week later. She had come with her husband to take custody of her father's remains and bring them home. "We got the call out of the blue, the day after Presidents' Day." Her husband had been the first to hear the voicemail message from the service casualty officer and told her to listen to it.[55] "I thought at first it was a hoax. And then I said, 'I think this is about my dad.'" *"We never expected this day to come,"* yet another daughter of a Vietnam War MIA explained. She was six years old when her father was shot down, and her brother just four. "We had resigned ourselves to the fact that it would be left to our imagination."

Encountering the physical remains of their missing relatives after such prolonged absence, families thus grappled with this curious amalgam of memory and imagination, often expressed in terms of what they did and did not expect. As we will see in the following chapter, it is such expectations, with all their emotional and political force, that both drive and frustrate the US military's scientific processes of "fullest possible accounting."

· 3 ·

Trust, Expectations,
and the Ethics of Certainty

"We've become like the pilgrims in the Middle Ages. We keep on and on
while the rest of them"—he pointed away toward where he reckoned the
men's families should be—"imagine we just press a button and the bones
come popping out of the ground. They just have no idea what it's like."
—ISMAIL KADARE, *The General of the Dead Army*[1]

IN THE FALL OF 2017, after news broke of a failed special forces campaign
in Africa, the US military faced questions regarding its care for service
members missing in action and killed in action. Rather than stories of
unfulfilled obligations to Vietnam War MIAs or unaccounted for from
other past wars, the topic in this instance was "current conflict" fallen.
The controversy centered on US Army Sergeant La David Johnson, a
member of a special forces team that came under attack in southwest Niger
on October 4, 2017.[2] Johnson was one of four US soldiers and five Nige-
rien troops killed in an ambush by Islamic State militants, but it was his
case that garnered the most media attention. Grabbing headlines was the
political dustup surrounding President Donald Trump's interactions with
the Johnson family.[3] The coverage also seized on the story of the soldier's
remains—the delayed recovery of them (Sgt. Johnson's remains were retrieved two days after his fellow US soldiers' bodies), as well as their
condition.[4]

On October 21, 2017, two days after her husband's funeral, Myeshia
Johnson, the wife of Sgt. La David Johnson, voiced her concerns in a

televised interview with George Stephanopoulos of ABC's *Good Morning America*:

MJ: The questions that I have that I need answered is I want to know why it took them forty-eight hours to find my husband; why couldn't I see my husband? Every time I asked to see my husband, they wouldn't let me.

GS: What did they tell you?

MJ: They told me that he's in a severe, a severe wrap like I won't be able to see him. I need to see him so I will know that that is my husband. I don't know nothing. . . . They won't show me a finger, a hand. I know my husband's body from head to toe. And they won't let me see anything. I don't know what's in that box, it could be empty for all I know. But I need, I need to see my husband. I haven't seen him since he came home.

GS: And what have they told you about what happened in Africa?

MJ: I really don't know the answers to that one neither because when they came to my house, they just told me that, um, it was a massive gunfire and my husband as of October 4th was missing, they didn't [know] his whereabouts. They didn't know where he was or where to find him, and a couple days later is when they told me that he went from missing to killed in action. I don't know how he got killed, where he got killed or anything. I don't know. That part they never told me and that's what I've been trying to find out since day one, since October 4th.[5]

Her account prickled with anxiety about what was known and not yet known, but Myeshia Johnson addressed the lingering uncertainties head on. Why was her husband's body not recovered immediately, with the three other American soldiers? Why was she not allowed to see his remains for herself? How did his status go from being missing in action to killed in action? Her questions turned on expectations of care gradually forged from the conflicts of the past century. Yet they were also quintessentially the products of the Vietnam War POW/MIA movement. If he died on foreign soil fighting on behalf of the nation, Myeshia Johnson expected the immediate recovery and repatriation of her husband's remains and a full accounting of his last moments of life and death. Faith in the US military's capacity to retrieve and identify bodies (and body parts) had clearly taken root, as had Defense Secretary Cohen's DNA-inspired wager of "no other unknowns in any war." And yet however understandable Johnson's reaction might be in the contemporary context, its timeframe—the expectation of immediate recovery—fell far outside the experience of most Vietnam War MIA families, for whom delayed recovery had long been calculated in decades not hours.

Expectations are more than hopes. Whether well founded or not, they posit something, they forecast something, they are tethered to some premise that anticipates a future course in light of a past one. Over the past century, expectations of care for war dead have evolved, with the Vietnam War the driving force in setting benchmarks for the forensic scientific work of recovery, repatriation, and identification—that is, in giving rise to a mission that pledges "fullest possible accounting" and includes the unaccounted for from the major conflicts of the twentieth century. Expectations also turn on trust. It's what allows the next of kin to accept that a petri dish full of bone shards or a single tooth *is* in fact their relative—not some stranger's, but the remains of their husband or father or brother—and is *all* that might ever be returned of that person. MIA families must trust in the scientific integrity of the recovery and identification process and in the qualifications and competence of the scientists carrying out that process. Such trust once built, however, is never guaranteed; rather, in the world of MIA accounting, it sits on a precarious perch, within easy range of the jabs and swipes of outsized expectations of exceptional care and its concomitant memory politics. When trust does exist, the forensic scientific process transforms the meaning of a set (or shards or just one piece) of human remains, connecting them once again to a human life, as to memories of that life. When trust is missing, truth claims of even the most exacting of scientific methods are called into question.

"WHY COULDN'T I SEE MY HUSBAND? Every time I asked to see my husband they wouldn't let me." Thwarted expectations and breached trust can also produce a powerful cocktail of disaffection and frustration. In recent years, the US military's MIA accounting efforts have faced a series of attacks. Much of the criticism has centered on questions of leadership, efficiency, and results. But underlying these controversies, we can discern a more fundamental disjuncture between heightened expectations of care and the limitations of knowledge and practice. Science played a central role in the saga. On the one hand, it offered an obvious metric for assessing efficiency for a mission that costs US taxpayers upwards of $130 million per year; on the other hand, it invited speculation about what was possible and therefore required by twenty-first-century techno-scientific innovation.[6] When

the two clashed, forensic science became an easy foil for critiques of the MIA accounting mission and its agencies, with the memory politics of the Vietnam War that defined the endeavor in the 1970s and 1980s resurfacing in powerful and public ways. The war's myriad disillusionments, ones that the promise of exceptional care had sought to address in the individually parsed-out measure of returned remains, echoed in accusations of "risk-averse" and "outmoded" science. Once again, it seemed as if the state was failing the missing and betraying their families' trust.

And yet these renewed debates about how best to care for the missing and the unidentified—to account for their absence—also belonged to a wider set of cultural concerns. They tapped into existent preoccupations about the reach—and the limits—of scientific expertise and military power.[7] Frustrations with less-than "fullest possible accounting" rose to the fore when ideals of high-tech, precision warfare collided with the lingering, unruly tolls of unidentified remains. In this regard, the debates swirling around the forensic work of accounting weren't limited to the Vietnam War per se, nor to the general issue of missing war dead, but on some deeper level played into public skepticism—and layperson assumptions—about what science could and should do.

Since the controversies concerned national politics more than local experience, the debates tended to privilege views from "inside the Beltway," playing out on the pages and through airways of national media outlets. The point here isn't that national and local realms of discourse are inherently distinct. On the contrary, because they continually feed into one another, they can never be entirely disentangled. But the heightened public scrutiny of the mission's process and results illustrated how often the voices of the political elite within the MIA accounting community tend to influence popular understanding of the nuanced, idiosyncratic experience of this particular phenomenon of absence, loss, and memory.[8] In this instance, the people most publicly engaged with the topic—legislators, policy makers, journalists, paid consultants, and MIA advocates—drove the narrative about disappointed expectations. Not everyone affected by the missing in action shared those disappointments, but understanding how they came to be is an integral part of our story—that is, how such a robust scientific enterprise, fortified by accreditation, standardized protocol, and transparency, came under such withering attack and what changes followed.

An Expanding Mandate

"*I DON'T KNOW WHAT'S IN THAT BOX, IT COULD BE EMPTY FOR ALL I KNOW.*" Just as Myeshia Johnson's expectations regarding her husband's remains and their swift recovery had context, so too did the niggling uncertainty she expressed. To Ann Mills-Griffiths, POW/MIA activist and sister of navy pilot James Mills, declared MIA in 1966, uncertainty was and is "a great motivator." The uncertainty that hovered over the missing in action—not knowing the fate of those service members, whether living or dead—she explains, was what mobilized the Vietnam War POW/MIA families, her own included, both during the war and in the immediate postwar years, and what has kept them engaged for the past four decades:

> All of us who had people who were POW/MIA can remember waiting for the phone call right after the agreements [the Paris Peace Accords] were signed. And it was a terrible thing. You're—that's what you're hoping for. Something concrete. You're hoping they're on the list and coming home. But if not that, then it means remains recovery and did they know for sure he died. Did they know anything? Well, if you don't know anything, uncertainty is a great motivator. Whether it's about your social relationships, your children, your health—uncertainty motivates getting answers. And it's just across the board. If you're uncertain, you're gonna push. [That's] what's kept this issue going all these years.[9]

As the National League of POW/MIA Families' executive director from 1978 to 2011 and current chief executive officer (in addition to chairman of the board), Mills-Griffiths is by far the most influential non-governmental actor shaping the US government's MIA accounting process—"*the* civilian player," as one reporter styled her.[10] Holding top-secret clearance for several years, she has had unprecedented access to policy makers, Pentagon officials, even the White House. "Every official meeting between U.S. and Vietnamese officials that occurs throughout the Reagan administration involves Mills-Griffiths directly, and this is an extraordinary thing."[11]

To this day, an imperious Mills-Griffiths presides over the organization's annual meeting in Washington, DC, held in conjunction with the US government's annual briefing for the Vietnam War families. For these last thirty years, from the dais of the Crystal City Hilton banquet hall, she has issued orders and demanded answers of the government officials attending the three-day meeting, especially at its final session, the notorious Saturday morning Q and A. The meetings operate according to this tacit dynamic of antagonism, whereby league members push the DOD bureaucrats for accountability, and the various agencies in return seek to perform their competence, champion their achievements, and elicit the families' support.

It was at these meetings, and again in the smaller regional family updates in places like Syracuse, New York, and Durham, North Carolina, where I first observed the charged relationship between the governmental agencies and these most mobilized members of the MIA community and how trust between them was frequently tested. I rarely witnessed hostility; many of the families and government officials had gotten to know one another well over the years, and some forged close ties, sitting down to meals and drinks in the hours between panels and events. But personal goodwill was no substitute for results and no salve for the corrosive effects of unabated uncertainty. Questions posed by MIA relatives often invoked the urgency of time—firsthand witnesses in Southeast Asia were dying, acidic soil was eating away at remains, tracts of land were under threat of development, and, most of all, relatives feared they might not live long enough to learn the fate of their missing or welcome home their remains.

In the face of such threats, scientific advance offered some measure of reassurance. More than any other tool in the MIA accounting tool box, the forensic science of recovery and identification operated according to the tenets of empiricism and the promise of innovation. PowerPoint slides at the briefings I attended beginning in 2008 highlighted cutting-edge approaches—DNA testing, isotopic analysis, an innovative technique of radiographic comparison, even feats of underwater archaeology. The Armed Forces DNA Identification Laboratory staffed a table outside the banquet hall with personnel ready to collect a "family reference sample," a swab from the inside of the cheek to gather DNA for extraction and analysis.

To congressional eyes, science also presented an important yardstick of accountability and efficiency within the now four-decade-old mission of "fullest possible accounting." By 2010, the cold hard facts of forensic science had become the mission's privileged currency—that is, the means to produce measurable results and a path to achieving certainty, or as close to it as possible, for a mission that, though deemed sacred to the nation, nevertheless cost significant taxpayer dollars. The change came about because of a particular piece of legislation: the National Defense Authorization Act for Fiscal Year 2010. In it, Congress set out a specific number for expected annual identifications, what they termed an "accounting for goal": "the Secretary of Defense . . . shall provide such funds, personnel, and resources as the Secretary considers appropriate to increase significantly the capability and capacity of the Department of Defense, the Armed Forces, and commanders of the combatant commands to account for missing persons so that, beginning with fiscal year 2015, the POW/MIA accounting community has sufficient resources to ensure that *at least 200 missing persons are accounted for under the program annually* [italics added]."[12]

In the same legislation, Congress made another important change to the statutory requirements for the DOD's MIA accounting mission. It added World War II and Persian Gulf losses to the list of conflicts included in its mandate, raising the number of unaccounted-for service members from approximately ten thousand to eighty-two thousand.[13] "Fullest possible accounting" now encompassed World War II, the Korean War, the Vietnam War, the Cold War, and the Persian Gulf War. Given that "between 2002 and 2012, DOD accounted for an average of 72 persons each year," the two hundred figure more than doubled the annual identification rate.[14]

But perhaps the most surprising and significant change came in the legislation's definition of "accounting," which singled out language already written into Section 1513 of Title 10 of the United States Code, the Missing Persons Act. Until that point, there had been only three possible means to "account" for a missing person:

(A) the person is returned to United States control alive;
(B) the remains of the person are recovered and, if not identifiable through visual means as those of the missing person, are identified as those of the missing person by a practitioner of an appropriate forensic science; or
(C) credible evidence exists to support another determination of the person's status.[15]

The first two methods were pretty straightforward: either the person returns alive or remains are recovered and identified through scientific means. The third method required credible evidence as to why one of the first two couldn't be achieved. But it was never used. Tom Holland explained:

We would go excavate a site, for instance an aircraft crash site. We know we can exclusively associate that site to an individual. The ejection seat is present, life support [equipment] is present, we know he was onboard the aircraft the time it impacted, and no remains were recovered. . . . So you could make a case that based on the crash dynamics, he was in the plane, he died, but soil acidity, fire, etc., [means] there are no remains to recover. So we could probably make a case for accounting for that individual. That was never perceived to be palatable politically.[16]

The 2010 Defense Authorization Act cut to the chase, setting aside the first and third methods, and stipulated that accounting could only result from forensic scientific findings: "The term 'accounted for' has the meaning given such term in section 1513(3)(B) of title 10, United States Code."[17] Coupled with the goal of two hundred IDs per year and the addition of the WWII losses, this narrowed definition meant that a new set of expectations was being placed on the forensic scientific component of the MIA accounting community—on the forensic archaeologists, anthropologists, odontologists, and geneticists at the Joint POW/MIA Accounting Command's Central Identification Laboratory and the Armed Forces DNA Identification Laboratory (AFDIL).[18]

Lab director John Byrd recalled his surprise at the time, both at the number of identifications that the scientists were expected to make and how Congress had narrowed the definition of accounting to scientific means only: "We were alerted to it in late August or early September by somebody outside the government. Just called and told me about it. I went and pulled it up on the computer and I read it. I was like, 'Oh my God.' I went and showed it to the [JPAC] commander [Admiral Crisp]. She had never heard of it. Our legislative affairs person had never heard of it."[19] He quickly learned that the two hundred number had originated with the House Armed Services Committee, some of whose staff were concerned that the mission wasn't being pursued as "aggressively and efficiently" as it should be. "That's why they put a two hundred marker on the wall as a goal." For Byrd, the phrase "by practitioner of the appropriate forensic science" was especially revealing. "And that's very clear that they don't want some kind of trumped-up nonsense, where people that aren't qualified are trying to identify remains using substandard methods and try to sell that to the families. They clearly don't want that. They said it has to be solid— professional forensic identifications is what they want. And that's the only way. You have to do two hundred individuals a year through this means." As both Holland and Byrd anticipated, the decision had a profound impact on the mission. My research in Hawaii began as the ripples of the

2010 act were being felt across the agencies and especially within the Central Identification Laboratory on Oahu, Hawaii. By 2013, the entire MIA accounting process was under the microscope, as Congress pressed to see the results of the redefined and expanded mission.

Accountability

What can you tell me about plans to change this ridiculous organizational structure that is supposed to be working on a very focused problem? It is not like this problem is disparate. . . . We are talking about locating the missing remains, which involves, obviously, science, it involves personnel, it involves cooperation of the various branches, but if we do not get this fixed, they are going to be back here in twenty years yelling at you guys.

—SENATOR CLAIRE MCCASKILL, *August 1, 2013*

If you look at the MIA accounting community's track record writ large, Senator McCaskill had a point.[20] In the wake of the 1986 and 1987 congressional hearings into rumored misidentifications, the Government Accountability Office (GAO) was tasked with evaluating the Central Identification Laboratory Hawaii (CILHI) operations and management. Its 1992 report detailed reforms introduced by the newly installed scientific director Ellis Kerley to "minimize" misidentifications and addressed the problems that still persisted.[21] Two decades and several congressional hearings later, the GAO once again was called on to take stock of the US military's MIA accounting mission and once again issued a report documenting recurring obstacles to its effective pursuit of "fullest possible accounting."[22] But in 2013, Congress wasn't worried about the wrong bones being sent to the wrong family; it was worried about efficiency. McCaskill noted that although Congress had appropriated an additional $50 million toward the effort, the money hadn't "yet yielded any significant increase in identifications. We cannot put a price tag on this mission, but we can and must ensure that hundreds of millions of dollars that taxpayers have earned are being spent as efficiently and effectively as possible."[23] With the World War II losses added to the MIA accounting mandate, swelling overnight the number of unaccounted for almost eightfold, and the 2015 deadline fast approaching, Congress was growing frustrated and the DOD agencies nervous. Where would the blame fall?

To be sure, there was plenty of blame to go around, and congressional members like McCaskill saw the POW/MIA accounting troubles in the light of other recent military-related scandals, including the examples of mismanagement and negligence at both Arlington National Cemetery and the Department of Veterans Affairs.[24] Criticism of interagency "squabbling," redundant mandates, and overall waste had merit; personal politics and rivalry over authority, especially between the Joint POW/MIA Accounting Command located in Hawaii and the Defense Prisoner of War/Missing Personnel Office outside of Washington, DC, stymied interagency collaboration.[25] Addressing the heads of the Defense Prisoner of War/Missing Personnel Office, the Joint POW/MIA Accounting Command, and the Life Sciences Equipment Laboratory (LSEL), Senator Kelly Ayotte remarked, "But what bothered me most was reading about the petty squabbling between the three agencies which each of you has been charged with leadership."[26] The very fact that LSEL, with a staff of five non-scientists and holding no accreditation, was given a direct voice at the hearing over that of management from the Central Identification Laboratory (CIL) or AFDIL revealed the fundamentally flawed channel of communication between the Department of Defense and members of Congress regarding the science of the accounting mission.

Moreover, the public handwringing over efficiency overlooked the role Congress itself had played in ratcheting up expectations for the mission that it had substantively redefined through the National Defense Authorization Act of 2010. Part of the problem lay with the act's overly aspirational benchmarks—outgrowths themselves of an ethos of exceptional care sharpened in response to the Vietnam War and underwritten by pledges already long-embedded in the war's language of remembrance, from the POW/MIA flag's "You Are Not Forgotten" to Hollywood's "The War's Not Over Until the Last Man Comes Home" and the Joint POW/MIA Accounting Command's own motto, "Until They Are Home."[27] Even if the American public understood that about half of the estimated eighty-two thousand unaccounted for were deemed non-recoverable—lost at sea—the various congressional hearings and ensuing media coverage rarely touched on the complexities of locating and identifying remains (recall the two case studies from the previous chapter, REFNOs 1895 and 0738).[28] Senator McCaskill insisted, "It's not like this problem is disparate." Yet how else to describe the monumental task of recovering and identifying some forty thousand individual sets of remains, missing service members from three major conflicts spanning more than eight decades, scattered across four continents (Asia, Europe, Africa, and North America, with its unknowns buried in national cemeteries) in vastly diverse sites, whose conditions varied significantly, including highly fragmented, partial, and/or commingled bones? Furthermore, the entire enterprise, with the exception of national military cemeteries, presupposed the American right to enter another sovereign state's territory and, with teams of military personnel, to labor on its soil in search of American missing (and thus sometimes enemy) war dead—a request that was no small matter for countries such as Vietnam or Laos, which are still grappling with the legacy of chemical agents and unexploded ordnance, or for North Korea, which has rejected it for over a decade.[29] But since the 2010 National Defense Authorization Act, "fullest possible accounting" for over forty thousand missing war dead, achieved by a "by a practitioner of an appropriate forensic science" has become a quantifiable sacred obligation.

"Failed Science"

On March 31, 2014, Secretary of Defense Chuck Hagel announced that the US military's MIA accounting mission would be restructured, combining the three entities—the Defense Prisoner of War/Missing Personnel Office, the Joint POW/MIA Accounting Command, and the Life Sciences Equipment Laboratory—into one agency, formally established on January 15, 2015, as the Defense POW/MIA Accounting Agency (DPAA). "These steps will help improve the accounting mission, increase the number of identifications of our missing, provide greater transparency for their families and expand our case file system to include all missing personnel."[30] The DOD created the Personnel Accounting Consolidation Task Force (PACT) to oversee the reorganization, whose informal—and mildly discomfiting— motto was "we're fixing this plane while we fly it"—and for a cool $6.7 million hired a DC-based consulting firm, aptly named the Clearing, to advise the task force.[31] Some families roiled at the expense. "Just think how much research we could have accomplished for that kind of money," said John Zimmerlee, executive director of the Korean War POW/MIA Network.[32]

The task force and the consulting firm were intended to bring a dispassionate, outside perspective to bear on reforming the accounting mission, a decision that placed significant authority over the reorganization process in the hands of temporary personnel. In the case of AFDIL, not a single person from the Clearing ever came to the laboratory to learn its processes; in the case of the CIL, not a single person on the PACT team reviewing the forensic scientific work was an actual scientist. Instead, lab management found itself fielding questions such as, "What is the acceptable margin of error for an identification?," a query that signaled not only an ignorance of the MIA accounting mission's history, but a fundamental misunderstanding of the mission's pledge of exceptional care. Such questions also flagged the task force's focus on output and efficiency. With a former Guantanamo Bay detainee policy director, Alisa Stack—who later would leave the DOD to join the cannabis industry—largely spearheading the effort, the reorganization followed a decidedly business-model approach in which MIA families were redefined as the "customer."[33] As Michael Lumpkin, the acting undersecretary of defense for policy, explained in yet another congressional hearing on July 15, 2014, "The most important piece that we came to conclusion, and this is kind of a business perspective, is that who is the customer here? . . . We need to focus on the families as the customer because the missing service member can't speak for their case."[34] The market logic of costs and benefits, efficiency and accountability, customers and services, had infiltrated one of the military's most sacrosanct spheres—the care of its fallen. Its rhetoric inched the public debate closer and closer toward an implicit calculus of dollars per identification, thus recalling the body-count metrics of the very war that gave rise to the "fullest possible accounting" mission.

With this "business perspective" restructuring, the science of MIA accounting was again in the crosshairs. A military medical examiner, subject to pressures that a civilian forensic anthropologist was not, would assume the role as scientific director, and, as Lumpkin explained, the new agency would also seek to partner with private organizations to "fully embrace progressive science"—the implication being that the forensic science of MIA accounting had fallen behind the times.[35] Indeed, his language echoed criticisms already raised in mainstream media of "outdated" science and "risk-averse" scientists whose attention to exactness—archival, mathematical, and methodological—seemed to be getting in the way of speedy resolutions.

The rhetoric upended what many in the broader scientific community knew of CIL and AFDIL. In 1998, AFDIL was the first forensic laboratory to be accredited for mitochondrial DNA testing and remains one of only ten such laboratories in the country.[36] Moreover, it has been on the forefront of human remains DNA testing technology since its establishment. For example, its 2006 pioneering demineralization protocol revolutionized human remains DNA extraction by reducing the amount of sample needed for extraction and opening up testing to any bone present in the human body.[37] CIL, as the largest facility of its kind in the world, had been the first forensic anthropology laboratory to be accredited by the American Society of Crime Laboratory Directors/Laboratory Accreditation Board. Its management sat on boards for international and national forensic scientific institutions, such as the International Committee of the Red Cross and the International Commission on Missing Persons, and with the Federal Bureau of Investigation had established the Scientific Working Group for Forensic Anthropology to "determine best practices and to develop consensus standards" for the field.[38] And its scientists were routinely recognized for academic achievements at the American Academy of Forensic Sciences annual meeting. By all measures, both labs and their personnel were in excellent standing within their respective scientific communities.

But academic accolades and peer esteem offered a poor defense against snowballing negative press. From Associated Press stories and military publications to mainstream news outlets, the 2013 GAO report and subsequent congressional hearings attracted attention, especially around predictions that the two hundred IDs per year goal for 2015 would not be met.[39] Reports alleged dysfunction, poor leadership, and questionable scientific practice—from NBC and CBS to the *New York Times, Washington Post,* and finally an extensive joint investigative piece by ProPublica and National Public Radio (NPR).[40] With its headline telegraphing the criticism to come—"Grave Science: America's effort to bring home its war dead is slow, inefficient and stymied by outdated methods"—the NPR/ProPublica piece focused on the science of MIA accounting and its so-called risk-averse scientists:

Kelly McEvers on *All Things Considered*: One reason we found it to be so slow, JPAC uses an outdated scientific method, not the DNA-led method used by most missing persons' labs worldwide. Add to that a crippling bureaucracy that slows cases down, plus scientists who are so risk averse they'd rather leave people in the ground than make a false ID.[41]

ProPublica: The Pentagon spends about $100 million a year to find men like [an individual unaccounted for profiled in the story], following the ethos of "leave no man behind." Yet it solves surprisingly

few cases, hobbled by overlapping bureaucracy and a stubborn refusal to seize the full potential of modern forensic science.[42]

NPR, "Grave Science": A joint investigation by NPR and Pro-
Publica found JPAC's process of identifying remains is hindered by
several layers of bureaucracy, an aversion to risk and a reluctance
to lead with DNA testing.[43]

The portrait drawn by NPR and ProPublica of CIL and AFDIL was
damning in its hyperbole—labs stuck in the proverbial dark ages, em-
ploying outmoded science and resisting advances in the field, especially in
forensic genetics. Most of the claims about outdated science centered on
DNA. Why wasn't CIL prioritizing DNA as a line of evidence over archaeological, anthropological, or other methods? According to their sources,
not only had the military's science failed to keep up with the times, the
entire process should be led by DNA.[44] "Forensic scientists elsewhere use
this approach, first developed in post-conflict Bosnia."[45] The individual
quoted in the NPR/ProPublic reports comparing Bosnia and Herzegovina
and its DNA-led model was Ed Huffine, former geneticist at AFDIL and
one of the scientists who helped identify First Lieutenant Michael J. Blassie.
Following his tenure at AFDIL, Huffine worked in Bosnia and Herzegovina
with the International Commission on Missing Persons from 1999 to 2002.
In 2004, he joined a private forensic genetics laboratory, Bode Technology,
where he served as vice president for international development. Among
its other ventures, Bode sought and secured contracts from the US Congress to work with Latin American countries identifying missing persons.[46]
In 2014, the biotech firm was touting its successful identification of a World
War II MIA on the basis of a "nuclear based 'DNA-Led' approach."[47]
Neither NPR nor ProPublica mentioned Huffine's conflict of interest.

The reports' overarching line of questioning and drawn conclusions
ignored several facts. First, CIL used DNA testing whenever possible and
considered it the most powerful line of evidence when sufficient profiles
could be extracted from bone samples. Second, remains had to be recovered in the first place (a bone found, for example, often through archaeological excavations) and then examined and prepared for DNA sampling
by a forensic anthropologist before a DNA test could be run. And third,
beyond the blatant conflict of interest, Huffine's comparison of the US military's MIA accounting efforts to postwar Bosnia and Herzegovina with
its mass graves filled with the commingled bones of hundreds of victims,
many of them relatives, was, in effect, comparing apples to oranges.[48]

Bosnia's missing persons, like other examples of post-conflict "disappeared," are all considered modern-day losses, where appropriate nuclear references are often available and nuclear DNA is prevalent in the samples. Bits of bone recovered from a high-impact air crash or an unknown disinterred from a national cemetery like the Punchbowl, whose skeletonized remains had been treated with a harsh, DNA-degrading chemical compound, required different approaches. In some instances, DNA might in fact be the most effective line of evidence; in others it could prove ineffectual.

But the negative reporting didn't stop at the labs' supposed underutilization of DNA testing. The criticism got more specific. Why didn't AFDIL rely more heavily on autosomal, particularly nuclear DNA testing, rather than mitochondrial DNA (mtDNA)? The question overlooked the scientific and social realities of MIA accounting for conflicts five, six, even eight decades past. The "ancient," meaning here fifty-year-old (plus) skeletal elements, that constitute the remains recovered from the three major conflicts, including the often partial, fragmented, and degraded remains from the Vietnam War, typically yield mtDNA profiles more consistently than autosomal.[49] This fact becomes even more salient given AFDIL protocol that requires the lab to perform two independent DNA analyses from the same skeletal specimens tested to ensure against contamination.[50] Moreover, finding relevant donors for nuclear DNA testing is much harder when parents are deceased (as is overwhelmingly the case for WWII, Korean War, and Vietnam War families), and surviving kin are now two and three generations removed (nuclear DNA comes from both parents, and thus becomes increasingly diluted over generations). The shared maternal lineage thus makes mtDNA particularly effective when viable nuclear DNA references are unavailable. "For example, a maternal fourth cousin will still have the same mtDNA profile as a sibling, making this type of testing invaluable as the cases extend further back in time."[51] The reports also overlooked innovations in the wider field of forensic genetics, namely around next generation sequencing (NGS), a high-throughput sequencing technology that enables an entire human genome to be sequenced rapidly and at lower costs.[52] At that point in time, AFDIL had already invested in NGS instruments to develop a mtDNA control method to be used with highly degraded samples. By 2016, AFDIL became the first—and is still the only—forensic laboratory in the United States to utilize an NGS method for mtDNA sequencing, which for the first time enabled obtaining mtDNA results from chemically modified samples. But such nuanced explanations didn't make it into the NPR/ProPublica exposés; rather, their reports cast the civilian scientific personnel as progress-thwarting bureaucrats who, in their risk aversion, were more worried about making a mistake than providing families with answers.

In their reporting, both NPR and ProPublica tacitly subscribed to the ethos of exceptional care without considering the attendant ethics of certainty. The fundamental premise of exceptional care is that there is no margin for error—the motto is not "Until the Last Man Comes Home, and These Are Probably His Remains." There was no going back to expeditious but erroneous identifications, because too much was at stake. "It defines us as a nation," explained JPAC commander Major General Kelly McKeague in the NPR piece.[53] For his own part, Tom Holland stressed that rushed or flawed science risked the trust of surviving kin, from World War II, the Korean War, the Vietnam War, all the way to relatives of current-conflict war dead and current members of the US military serving in conflict zones. "Our credibility is only as good as our last misidentification. It doesn't matter that I've identified five hundred people correctly. If I misidentify one, that's what's going to be the focus. That's what's going to be on the news. That's what is going to erode the credibility. So that's what I go home with every night."[54] As he knew well from the lab's early years, misidentifications destabilize the entire accounting mission, casting doubt on every identification made prior to the mistaken identification. But the gravity of such a breach of trust failed to translate. Spliced from its context and from the larger history of Vietnam War MIA accounting—the Hart case, the flawed science of the 1970s and 80s, the selection of 1st Lt. Michael J. Blassie as the Vietnam War Unknown Soldier—the NPR/Pro-Publica pieces conveyed neither the scientific staff's ethical commitment to the unaccounted for and their families nor the institutional viability that precluded a margin of error greater than zero.

At the time, the negative media pieces were puzzling. Why was their criticism so convincingly and successfully trained on the scientific component of the MIA mission? As the GAO report and congressional hearings pointed out, there were other serious problems to be addressed across the agencies (e.g., lack of leadership, duplication of personnel and tasks, etc.). One answer lay in the silence coming from the Pentagon itself. As the media coverage about "outmoded science" and "risk-averse" scientists escalated, the DOD issued a gag order to all civilian and military members of the MIA accounting mission; they were not to engage, not to speak with the media, unless otherwise authorized. So there were few opportunities to refute the misinformation circulating about the science or the individuals practicing it. Members from the larger scientific community who came to the lab's defense—former employees, current and former external consultants, and leading figures in the fields of forensic anthropology and odontology—were pointedly missing from the analyses, despite their efforts to correct the record publicly.[55] Those within JPAC who were allowed to speak with journalists faced the frustrating task of dispelling preconceptions. Lab director John Byrd recalled having two polar-opposite interviews in one day about the same subject—innovation at the lab. One journalist demanded to know why JPAC wasn't pushing innovations more; the other pressed him on why they didn't stop playing around with innovations and get to work. Byrd also spoke with Kelly McEvers of NPR for a two-hour follow-up interview to address the erroneous information presented in the NPR/ProPublica reports. But NPR chose not to publish any portion of it.

In the end, the failed science narrative gained traction and fed into decisions guiding the reorganization of the MIA accounting agencies within the Department of Defense. By 2015, Tom Holland, the civilian scientist, lost his job as scientific director, replaced by a medical examiner from within the military, a move that brought current and past conflict accounting under one roof.[56] His replacement, Captain Edward Reedy, a forensic pathologist who specialized in DNA, was to become the "single identification authority" and oversee the Central Identification Laboratory (eventually renamed the DPAA Laboratory, and later the Scientific Analysis Directorate), as well as a satellite laboratory established in 2013 in Omaha, Nebraska, and the Life Sciences Equipment Laboratory located in Dayton, Ohio.[57] Reedy himself would retire within two years, and notably, Michael Linnington, appointed in 2015 as the director of the newly formed DPAA, would last even less time, tendering his resignation in June 2016, despite having publicly pledged to remain in the position for ten years.

On one level, the failed-science narrative made sense. It rejuvenated a long-held skepticism regarding the federal government's commitment to fulfill its obligation to missing war dead, a sentiment cultural historian H. Bruce Franklin explored in his analysis of the politics of POW/MIA "myth-making" from the 1970s to the early 1990s.[58] Following that strand of skepticism, the faulty forensic efforts thus represented the most recent iteration of the government's failure to care for MIAs. But this time—in this version's apportioning of blame—it was negligent scientists, not cowardly members of Congress or duplicitous administrations, who willfully abrogated their duty to care for the fallen. Removed from its historical context and denied its complexities, the adherence of the two labs, especially CIL, to standard operating procedures, multiple lines of evidence, and external reviews smacked of bureaucratic foot-dragging to some, or worse, a willful subversion of the mission so sacrosanct to the military and to the nation. In the words of NPR's Kelly McEvers, they're "so risk averse they'd rather leave people in the ground than make a false ID." Like the POW/MIA films of the 1980s (*Uncommon Valor, Missing in Action*, the *Rambo* series) that "exposed" government cowardice perpetuated by bureaucrats and politicians, this caricature of pluckless, careerist scientists represented the betrayal not just of the MIAs themselves, but also their families, still grieving decades on.[59] It is important to note that however provocative it was, such a portrait did not accurately reflect the sentiments of the majority of MIA families—not simply the mobilized core such as members of the National League of POW/MIA Families, but also families who had remains of their missing service member recovered because of advances in the forensic scientific knowledge and practice at the labs. As JPAC commander Major General Kelly McKeague (who would eventually replace Michael Linnington as DPAA director) testified at the 2013 congressional hearing, quoting a sister of an army helicopter pilot missing in Vietnam who told him, "The vast majority of the families who are involved have tremendous trust in your mission and in those who work our cases."[60]

The portrait of "outdated" science and "risk-averse" scientists also made sense in terms of popular culture. Feeding into contemporary public understandings of forensic science, the narrative clashed with *CSI/Bones*-fueled imaginaries in which crime labs produce lightning-fast and definitive results and where DNA reigns supreme as the gold-standard line of evidence in postmortem identification.[61] However erroneous or misrepresentative their facts, exposés such as the NPR/ProPublica report could rely on popular cultural biases forged from fictionalized forensic work. And yet given this appetite for cutting-edge science, there was little if any mention in the media coverage (including the NPR piece) of the innovation pioneered by CIL forensic anthropologist Carl Stephan. An Australian national who served with JPAC on a fellowship from 2008 to 2013, Stephan devised a radiograph analysis comparison technique that overcame the challenges of the Korean War unknown cases for which DNA couldn't be extracted. He utilized chest X-rays that had been taken at recruiting stations to screen for tuberculosis for comparison with postmortem radiographic images of clavicles and cervical vertebrae.[62] "They were photographing five hundred to seven hundred people a day," Stephan explained in an interview with Australia's ABC News. "And so the Department of Defense had all those records. My task [during the fellowship] was to develop some sort of method to use those radiographs to identify those individuals." He described both the mission and his American colleagues' work ethic: "In the US, the government makes that unofficial promise to everybody that you will be returned home. It's an admirable ideal. They have three hundred employees around the clock, full time, each year, working on this. It's a massive operation."[63] Validated through peer review and awarded for excellence at the American Academy of Forensic Sciences annual meeting in 2013, Stephan's technique jumpstarted the disinterment program for the Korean War unknowns. But it fell outside the dominant storyline of CIL and ADFIL's "outmoded" methods of MIA accounting, at least in US media coverage.[64]

Why was this the case? What assumptions were driving these partial and often misguided conclusions about what the forensic science of MIA accounting should look like and achieve? The example of Renwick Gallery and Frances Glessner Lee's Nutshell Studies comes to mind. It's quite likely that not a single person in the gallery that rainy afternoon, not even those who inspected the tiny dioramas with their flashlights in search of clues, had ever worked a real crime scene or seen a body visited by malice. And yet the majority had an opinion on how to interpret the evidence before them and a high level of confidence in that interpretation. As Ian Burney and Neil Pemberton write in *Murder and the Making of English CSI*, "Though they may have never physically encountered one themselves," most people "will have an idea about what a crime scene looks like, what takes place within it, and why." It's a familiarity, they argue, born from "a seemingly inexhaustible fascination with the forensic investigation of crime," brought to us on "our television screens and in our newspapers."[65] That appetite has bred more than interest; it's fostered a sense of layperson expertise. Ironically, the friend who accompanied me that day, himself a trained forensic scientist who has worked murder scenes and dealt with the realities of violent deaths, wasn't drawn there for the opportunity of vicarious sleuthing. Rather, he marveled at the attention to detail in the miniature tableaus and the craftsmanship of Lee's models. As I look back on that day and on the public rhetoric surrounding the science of MIA accounting in 2013 and 2014, the contrast between the museum goers and my forensic scientist friend comes into focus. In the late 1980s, when the lab in Hawaii came under scrutiny—justifiable scrutiny—it was the professional scientific community that led the investigation. Forensic science, in many ways, was still a relatively young field and a mystery in and of itself to the general population at that time. With the exception of the popular television show *Quincy, M.E.,* which ran from 1976–83, or perhaps late-night reruns of the Sherlock Holmes movies of the 1940s, the general public had very little exposure to the science of forensics.[66] As a field, it was something intangible, performed by people with expert knowledge and training, and few within the general population fancied it an area within their own wheelhouse.

But by the 1990s and into the 2000s, things had changed. With a spate of forensically themed television shows and a lucrative market for forensic-based novels, the realm of forensic science had been demystified and popularized.[67] And so, when the lab again came under scrutiny in 2014, it was no longer the professional forensic scientific community that led the way, soberly evaluating the quality of the science against an external standard. Now the criticisms were voiced most loudly, and like the visitors to the Renwick that afternoon, most confidently, by those who had little understanding of what they were seeing.

Science and Its Discontents

Nevertheless, at the time, the unspooling negative media reports took me by surprise. Coming on the heels of my fieldwork at CIL and on the recovery mission in Vietnam, the depictions in the various mainstream media pieces of flawed science and risk-averse scientists didn't compute. They didn't match what I had learned from my time in Bosnia and Herzegovina and from colleagues in the broader field of missing person identification efforts, they didn't fit with what I knew of the academic world of forensic anthropology or forensic genetics, and most of all, they didn't reflect the work I observed in the labs. They did, however, intersect with two broader trends in contemporary American society—public reckoning with scientific knowledge and the complicated expectations tied to the US military.

On the first point, the failed science narrative was itself a product of our own particular moment in time. For just as much as the negative press and ensuing reorganizational turmoil fit within the US military's freighted record of accounting for the missing (especially Vietnam War missing), it also belonged to a larger context, to a longer history of "discontent with public facts" in American society.[68] Questioning the expertise of the experts was not new and certainly not exclusive to the forensic science of

MIA accounting. Rather, as sociologist Steven Epstein points out, "Growing distrust of established experts is magnified by our culture's ambivalent attitude toward institutions of science and their technological products."[69] Scientific authority in the late twentieth and early twenty-first centuries thus had already become less fixed, and debates about expertise unfolding in mainstream media—from the "science wars" of the 1990s to "post-truth"-era anti-vaccination campaigns and climate-change denialism—already made manifest how much science as the generator of "public facts" couldn't be divorced from its political climate: "Questions of what and how we should know go hand in hand with questions of how we should govern."[70] Seen in this light, the negative coverage of the MIA science also offered a comment on governance, namely how our nation governs war dead and their living kin. Rather than insulating the MIA accounting mission from criticism *because* of its expertise, the science, in all its imagined/expected certitude, provided a ready vocabulary and a sharp tool for lay critics. "It's not rocket science" scoffed the WWII family member profiled in the ProPublica report.[71]

The emphasis on the scientific rather than merely the bureaucratic or operational side of the accounting mission wasn't accidental. It signaled how much value had accrued around the forensic efforts of caring for the missing. The scientific component could materialize the state's commitment to MIA accounting in ways other realms of the mission couldn't. Through investments in the scientific labor, resources lavished on the care of remains became an index of social regard, the mark of a country in its singular pursuit to repatriate, identify, and return its missing to their kin. The science translated both ethos and effort. For if, as Jay Winter tells us, "language frames memory," mediating how we know and understand war and its effects, the lexicon of forensic science, especially DNA, had come to color how the American public conceived of its unaccounted-for war dead and set its expectations regarding their proper, indeed exceptional, care.[72] Such heightened expectations had ready and concrete metrics—quantifiable ways to gauge whether the state was in fact fulfilling its obligation of "fullest possible accounting"—through the medium and language of science. In a more recent example of the military's forensic expertise under fire, in May 2017, the *New York Times* profiled seven families of WWII unknowns who had banded together to sue the government—specifically, the Defense POW/MIA Accounting Agency—to force the disinterment of remains they believed to be those of their relatives buried in the national military cemetery in the Philippines. Among the legal arguments presented, the plaintiffs claimed that the government was "not using readily available DNA testing to identify the remains."[73]

While criticism leveled at the forensic scientific component of MIA accounting may have resonated with broader public skepticism of scientific expertise, it also drew on twenty-first-century American ideals about the nation's military, part of what historian Andrew Bacevich defines as the "new American militarism." In this gradually configured relationship between American society and its military, he argues, there is "a tendency to see military power as the truest measure of national greatness, and outsized expectations regarding the efficacy of force."[74] "Henceforth, swiftness, stealth, agility, and precision," in the new era of high-tech warfare, "would characterize the operations of modern armies," while "uncertainty, risk, waste, and error" would be lessened if not eliminated.[75]

The ideals apply to war's tolls as well. From surgical strikes by unmanned aerial vehicles to ground-based robots and biometrics to track human bodies, what Rosa Brooks calls "individualized killing technologies," the efficacy of destructive force thus requires its equal in an efficacy of postmortem care—cutting-edge, not "outmoded" science—to recover and identify the remains of its fallen service members. Anything less is a breach of trust with the nation's military and their families.[76] In the logic of such militarism extended to the exceptional care of its missing war dead, it's no wonder, then, that the media's failed-science narrative centered on DNA. The twenty-first-century molecular dog tag, if only harnessed properly, seemed the best bet to achieve the new benchmarks of increased output, the elusive two hundred IDs per year goal. Chest X-rays and dental charts paled in comparison; this was the stuff of the past, not the promising science of the future. Overlooking the fact that "smart" weapons nevertheless have devastating effects, a militarism championing precision and efficacy left little room for the messy realities of war's destruction—commingled skeletons, fragments of bone too small or degraded to yield DNA profiles, or, worse still, remains that could not even be located. Therein lay the presumed betrayal: the forensic scientific component of MIA accounting was denying the entire process's sacrosanct end—the white gloves, the neatly folded flag, the three-volley rifle salute, and a fallen hero finally returned home. The mission's science, having generated the "new sacred thing" of an ethos of exceptional care, in an ironic twist of fate had outstripped itself, now seen to be the very thing profaning that which it helped to define. For within this "new American militarism," it should be high-tech, cutting-edge forensic science, properly executed, that set the United States apart from other nations in fulfilling its sacred obligation to the missing, their families, and their brothers and sisters in arms.

In the end, whether one looked at the media coverage and the reorganization through the narrower scope of MIA accounting history and politics or the bigger picture of science and the military in contemporary American society, there were ample signs of an *ideal* of a scientific endeavor that had failed to deliver. And that failure demanded explanation. The science of MIA accounting bore the brunt of the criticism because its particular language of remembrance held out the most readily available metrics. As Senator McCaskill argued, though the mission's value was incalculable, the resources dedicated to it must nevertheless be managed well and wisely. How better to measure efficiency and effectiveness than through the number of identifications per year? And so the principal explanation for the failure to achieve the 2015 goal became "failed science"—laboratories whose bureaucrats refused to embrace high-tech tools, refused to put their shoulders to the wheel, and thus refused to fulfill the nation's promise to its war dead. It was a seductive, but deeply problematic, narrative, and yet one that laid bare the powerful reach forensic science had in shaping how the wars of the past century, especially the Vietnam War, are remembered and their costs quantified, at least at the national level.

But beyond the scope of these national debates, the experience of caring for those missing in action from the war in Southeast Asia took shape in markedly different ways, both with and without the benefits of forensic science and its advances. It is to these more particular histories of loss and remembrance that we now turn.

⟡ 1967 ⟡

"Memorial Days"
May 1967, I wrote a poem.
I said, No, you *are* not dead. You are *not!*
You are too young. I am too young. Death is not real.
I didn't really know that I would never see you again,
that you would never come home to this place.
I thought, "No body equals no death," so maybe you'll
come back.
I said, "Now & forever, you are"—but you weren't—here.
I said, "I can't be sad"—but I was.
Now I'm 42. I am younger and wiser now.
My wiser soul knows that you are really gone,
that you won't come home again.
And sometimes now I cry.
But inside my younger heart, and in my memories,
and in my dreams,
you are as alive & real as when you were my
young and living friend.
My heart knows that your spirit did come home.
Sometimes, especially in the spring, I feel the
presence of your spirit, and I know that you know
you were not forgotten.
—MARY E. DEFOE (April 1990)

In July 2017, I met with Mary Defoe to talk about the Vietnam War
and about the two young men from her high school class who fought
and died in it. We sat tucked in the shade of the local Veterans of Foreign Wars (VFW) post, angling the wrought iron patio chairs toward
one another. Cars and trucks periodically whizzed by on Highway 13,
part of the steady flow of summer traffic headed toward the Red Cliff

Band Reservation casino or lakeshore property further up the Bayfield Peninsula. Though early afternoon, the post had already begun to fill up with members, and it seemed the best spot to avoid both the sun's glare and the rising din of the conversations inside.

Mary and I hadn't formally met before this day. In fact, I had only encountered her—on April 30, 2017—at the fiftieth remembrance ceremony held at the post for Duwayne "Wotsy" Soulier, still MIA/KIA. As his classmate and friend, Mary was among those who stood up and shared aloud memories of his life and his death, or in her case, the news of his death. At the time, I was struck by the clarity and poignancy of her remarks. She had come prepared that day, reading a poem she had written years before entitled "Memorial Days" and half-apologizing to the assembly for not being able to find the original verse she had penned when she first learned the terrible news.

So when I returned to Red Cliff three months later in July, I sought out Mary, hoping she might share the poem and tell me more about what her friend's absence had meant to her over the years. Once again she came prepared. Balanced on her lap was a Bayfield High School Trollers 1965 yearbook, its pages filled with jottings and well-wishes from her classmates, among them Merl Allen and "Wotsy" Soulier. Wotsy teased her for having turned him down for a date—she had been too afraid her mother would find out ("mama's girl") if she said yes—and thought her destined to be a successful lawyer. One of thirteen children, Mary had grown up mostly in Bayfield and moved to Red Cliff later in life with her husband, Ken. Despite Wotsy's predictions for a career in law, she started her college education in English and eventually turned to medicine, working as a registered nurse for over four decades.

The Vietnam War had indelibly marked her life—not simply for the classmates who served and those from her community who died, but also because of her husband's own struggles with posttraumatic stress disorder (PTSD). As Mary put it in a letter she wrote to the Department of Veterans Affairs in 2015, two years after his death, she saw him "suffering more from his PTSD than his lung cancer."[1] In that same letter, she described their "good relationship" fueled by his steadfast, daily commitment to remain sober, alongside her love for "the person underlying the PTSD symptoms and the hope that this special man would be able to emerge, stay with me, and not go back to Vietnam." This sense of metaphorical travel returns in the final lines of the letter, as Mary noted that even though her husband was "'only'" in Vietnam from May 1967 to July 1969, "he spent more of his life there than anywhere else."[2]

As we sat in the shade on that summer afternoon, Mary helped me appreciate the complicated notion of homecoming, as well as the wider circle of loss in which her community's experiences of missing in action/killed in action/body not recovered were nested. She also helped paint a picture of Merl and Wotsy and their high school lives before they left for the war. We leafed through the yearbook's pages, Mary pointing out Merl and Wotsy in various photographs, from sports teams and extracurriculars to their formal class pictures and senior quotations: "Ruff and tuff and all that stuff" (Merl) and "I have never let my schooling interfere with my education" (Wotsy). I asked her how people in Bayfield and Red Cliff had thought about the war at that time, what the prospect of serving in Vietnam meant to the boys in her class. "We were the baby boomers, it was all U-Rah-Rah. We won wars and saved the world. Like the movies. But it came out good. And of course with President Kennedy, 'Ask not what . . .' They thought they were doing the right thing to go into the service. And it turned out different."[3] Later, I would ask the same question of Butch, the VFW post commander. "I joined in '66 because I wasn't gettin' nowhere in Bayfield," he explained. "There was nothing here, so me and another friend of mine, we just joined up. . . . I wasn't really scared of being drafted, I never thought about it that much."[4]

I paused on the yearbook's "Athletics" page. Superimposed on a photograph of the iconic Iwo Jima Memorial in Arlington, Virginia, was a quotation by Adlai E. Stevenson: "If we win men's hearts throughout the world it will not be because we are a big country but because we are a great country. Bigness is imposing. But greatness is enduring."[5] A friend had written classmates' names over the six figures struggling to hoist the flag. In 1965, in the Bayfield High School yearbook, these were the words and images shaping their view of service, honor, and sacrifice—abstractions to the youthful and invincible.

Stock tributes like these are nothing new. So much of contemporary media coverage of a successful instance of MIA accounting champions ideals of national sacrifice, of the "fallen hero" come home to flag-waving crowds. And there is truth in those scenes; as Bayfield itself demonstrated with Lance Corporal Merlin Raye Allen's homecoming, the return of remains holds an extraordinary power to gather people in mourning and remembrance. In tending toward the celebratory, however, such stories of national sacrifice often eschew the unruly, complicated, and, most of all, local histories of loss. They offer happier endings instead, wrapped up in gauzy claims of "closure." The impulse to silence or smooth over the raw experiences of war—Mary's bitter, disbelieving rejection of Wotsy's death, "You *are* not dead, You are *not*!"—may well be a twenty-first-century mode of effacing sorrow. But if nothing else, it is a partial one. What does it mean, to "give" one's life for the nation, if that life was wrested from one's family, friends, and fellow service members? How can one return home if home no longer exists? What if his remains will never be recovered?

When I first visited the VFW in Red Cliff, and Randy, the post's quartermaster, told me of the three men who died in Vietnam—"one came home right away, one came home forty-six years later, one will never come home"—I was intrigued by the span of the community's wartime and postwar experience, that such a small place had encountered the range of loss that it did.[6] In some ways, I romanticized its capacity to reveal the Vietnam War MIA phenomenon. I know now that a community can only ever explain its own particular history of the war. But it is enough—and yet never enough—to try to make sense of that history for what it might teach us: that homecomings are never a single, bounded event, just as the individuals coming home are never merely emblems of a nation or a society, and that accounting for loss requires considering the effects of absence in the immediate and the long-term.

HOMECOMINGS INTIMATE AN END, but they necessarily have beginnings—stories that underwrite how and why young men went off to fight and die on behalf of something larger than their families, their communities, and their hometowns. The more I dug into the particular history of Merl Allen's and Wotsy Soulier's hometowns, the more I recognized a common theme that framed familial and communal experiences of wartime loss and that to this day colors how those losses are recalled and reconciled—*dispossession*.

To dispossess means to deprive of the possession of a thing; it's usually used when talking about land or real estate. A person can lose possession of land or property and still have a sense of belonging to that place. But that kind of dispossession can come with a steep emotional price. In the case of Bayfield and Red Cliff, the Vietnam War MIA experience is imbricated with instances of dispossession, both on an individual level and a broader historical plane of tribal rights and federal decrees. Furthermore, dispossession is not limited to land or property alone.[7] To have a child sent off to war is also a type of dispossession. To have that child (or brother or father or uncle) die and yet receive no remains or have no coffin to bury represents a deprivation of a categorically different nature. Layer those dispossessions, one atop the other, and you have a central thread in the particular history of service and sacrifice in Vietnam War–era Bayfield and Red Cliff.

As hometowns go, these two places are linked in obvious and more subtle ways. Just three miles from one another, the village of Bayfield and the community of Red Cliff share a highway and a lakeshore. They bask in the natural beauty of Lake Superior and the backdrop of the northern woods. But they stand apart in certain essentials. Differences in wealth and demographics are easy to spot. While Red Cliff, as the seat of the Native American reservation on the peninsula, has largely missed out on the tourist boom of the past four decades, Bayfield developed in leaps and bounds with the establishment of the Apostle Islands National Lakeshore in 1970.[8] Anointed by the *Chicago Tribune* as the Best Little Town in the Midwest in 1997 and by the *Smithsonian Magazine* as one of America's Best Small Towns in 2015, Bayfield has become a favored getaway for tourists from the Twin Cities and throughout the Midwest.[9] "How far away is Bayfield?" asks its Chamber of Commerce. "Far enough to let you escape from strip malls. And drive-thru meals. And 3pm budget meetings."[10]

But the Bayfield of 1997 or 2017 is quite different from the close-knit community rocked by the news in the spring and early summer of 1967, of Wotsy Soulier and then Merl Allen—one on the heels of the other—as missing in action/killed in action. Far removed from the anti-war protests erupting on college campuses "down south" in Madison that same year, the town and its residents, along with members of the Red Cliff Band, were engaged in their own battle with the federal government.[11] At stake—at least in the eyes of people like Merl Allen's and Wotsy Soulier's families—was the question of land rights. Of ownership and inheritance. Of home.

"I, Merl Allen, will my beach at Sand Bay to the future senior class for their swingers next summer." In 1965, for his senior year-book "Class Wills" section, Merl wrote about the place he loved, the strip of lakeshore where he and his siblings and their friends spent long summer days soaking up the sun, frolicking on the beach, and enjoying the water. Two years later while stationed in Vietnam, he penned a letter to the United States Congress, beseeching his elected officials not to take this land away from his family. He was writing to oppose the creation of the Apostle Islands National Lakeshore, which would force the Allen family to sell its property, York Island and lakeshore acreage along Sand Bay, to the federal government.

First imagined by landscape architect Harlan Kelsey in 1930 as a way to redress the scars of the timber and mining industries, the idea for adding the twenty-two islands and the lakeshore to the national park system was the brainchild of Wisconsin governor Gaylord Nelson (the founder of Earth Day) beginning in 1960.[12] President John F. Kennedy lent support to the project after visiting the region in 1963 as part of a national conservation tour, flying over the islands in a presidential helicopter.[13] By 1967, the first lakeshore bill was introduced before the Congress and a series of contentious hearings ensued.[14] And so, from halfway around the globe, Merl Allen wrote to register his protest.

His sister Marilyn Neff read his words into the record during the Senate subcommittee hearing on S. 778, "A Bill to Provide for the Establishment of the Apostle Islands National Lakeshore in the State of Wisconsin, and for Other Purposes":

I am a Marine in the 3d Reconnaissance Battalion. I understand that you will shortly hold hearings on a proposed bill to create an Apostle Islands National Lakeshore Recreation Area. I wish to go on record as being unalterably opposed to this bill. I am presently engaged in fighting a war not of my seeking because the leaders of my country tell me it is necessary that we combat Communism whenever and wherever it threatens a free people. Is the taking of private lands for uses other than those necessary for common safety or necessity very much different than the seizure of private lands by the state in a foreign land of a different ideology?

My parents made many sacrifices that they might acquire a part of our great country. As children I and my brothers and sisters had to forgo many things dear to a child's heart in order that mortgage payments and tax payments might be met. Since I was a child my vacations were spent on our property on Lake Superior in Bayfield County. Later my parents built a home on this property and the family moved there, although for several years my father continued to work down state, spending only weekends with the family. Now he has managed to build up a small business and live in the area [he] has loved so many years.

It is ironic and unfair that we should now be forced to give up that which we all worked so hard to acquire. My personal plans had always been predicated on my living on our property on Lake Superior. Am I to be denied this right to further a vote getting plan of ambitious politicians? Why is it that people trying to push this bill have no property in the area? . . . Is this the reward for serving my country to be deprived of my inheritance and that of my brothers and sisters?

Yours very truly,
Merlin R. Allen[15]

Marilyn finished and walked back to her seat to a standing ovation, after adding her own stinging line about the government being better off concentrating on winning the war in Vietnam rather than worrying about "playgrounds for the idle people."[16]

A savvy letter for such a young man, Merl Allen's argument drew on dovetailed notions of sacrifice and home, with his service in

Vietnam—"fighting a war not of my seeking"—bookending his message. Just as his family sacrificed for their land—to acquire York Island and the beach he so loved at Sand Bay—so too, by enlisting in the marines, he sacrificed for—and only weeks later would be sacrificed to—the nation. "Is this the reward?" he asked with tragic prescience. Is the federal government, seeking to take ownership of business, residential, and, notably, tribal lands, so very different from North Vietnam (presumably what he meant by the "state in a foreign land of a different ideology" that seizes private lands)? It was a bold question to pose at the time. Two years into Rolling Thunder, the aerial bombardment campaign, by the spring of 1967, US troop levels in Vietnam were inching toward half a million. Increasingly, those numbers were drawn from working-class communities spread out across urban, suburban, small-town, and rural America, from places like Bayfield and Red Cliff.[17] In the mid- to late 1960s, Bayfield High School, which included students from the Red Cliff Reservation and the nearby township of Russell, saw four or five young men, out of graduating classes of twenty-five to thirty students (half of them girls), shipped off to the war in Southeast Asia.

The hearings before the Subcommittee on Parks and Recreation of the Committee on Interior and Insular Affairs, held on May 9 and June 1 and 2, 1967, touched on the war, but only tangentially. When it was invoked, alternately by both sides of the debate (as Marilyn, Merl's sister, did), at issue were costs—either the park would divert federal funds from the war efforts, or, for the bill's proponents, bring much needed public funds to an economically depressed region. A representative of the Wisconsin Farmers Union explained, "We do not deny that great spending on the forces of destruction is necessary in our present predicament, but let us not lose sight of the compelling needs to expend some of our great wealth on the forces of construction that are imperiled by delay."[18]

Though their subject was the creation of a national park, the hearings focused largely on local lives and local benefits versus impacts. More than just lamenting the potential loss of land as an acquired or inherited good, many who gave testimony opposing the bill spoke of the lakeshore, the islands, and the lake itself, as a place of belonging.[19]

Among those convened—from elected officials, developers, and business owners to residents, conservationists, and outdoor enthusiasts—it was members of the local Native American population, including the Red Cliff Band and Bad River Band of the Lake Superior Chippewa, who viewed the plan to take over land and set up the national park within a broader sweep of time and a larger history of racial inequity. In that same 1967 subcommittee hearing, mother of ten children ("not one of them old enough to be on their own") Jeanette Gordon cut to the chase:

> I may be dead within the next twenty-five years. What will happen to my children? Will you turn them loose into the woods with wild game or will you use them for Indian totem poles in this so-called national park? I know one word in the Indian language, Gau-Wie, which means "No . . . I am not for the park."
>
> Let the Great White Father settle with the Indians first the treaty they made with great Grandfather, and let the Great White Father put more cream on the cake before I will say "Ave-Sau," which means "Yes."[20]

Another mother from the Red Cliff Band spoke that same day. Just as the Allen family (Merl's sister Marilyn and their father, Alden Allen) traveled to Washington, DC, to voice their protest, so too did Duwayne "Wotsy" Soulier's mother. Her statement was short; she did not dwell on her pain. But her son's death—or, as she phrased it, his "loss"—stood at the heart of her stated opposition:

> I am Caroline Newago of the Red Cliff Band, also a member of the council. I oppose this proposal as to selling my allotted land. . . . One son I have in Vietnam who I lost. This allotted land was willed to my children and myself. I think a vote should be taken [to assess] the [true] feelings of the Indian people.[21]

If Caroline Newago's testimony was an exercise in understated grief, her sister-in-law, Mrs. Walter Newago, made no bones about her deep skepticism of the bill's intended beneficiaries. Speaking right before Caroline and echoing Jeanette Gordon, she took aim at what she perceived to be yet another instance in a centuries-long pattern of betrayal:

> I am Mrs. Walter Newago, a Chippewa Indian from the Red Cliff Reservation. From what I understand, we Indians are supposed to be your main concern, but it seems to me that all you people are giving us is a bunch of promises again, just as you did one hundred years ago. Why should we believe the promises you are making now will be kept, when the ones made one hundred years ago were never kept?
>
> You want our last remaining land we have. Then what will we have? Nothing but a lot of people we have no understanding for. . . .
>
> I see no good for my people if this park did go through. The people who live here have no education that would qualify them for a job that would be available at the park, except maybe to pick up paper and such things, after the white people left. We can do that now without the park.[22]

The treaty "with great Grandfather" and the unfulfilled promises of a hundred years ago refer to an important chapter in the region's history of dispossession—namely, the 1854 Treaty of La Pointe. The treaty arose in response to an 1850 removal order issued by President Zachary Taylor, which, in breach of 1837 and 1842 treaties guaranteeing hunting, fishing, and gathering rights, the US government threatened to remove—literally to displace and push west—the Lake Superior Chippewa villages to Sandy Lake, Minnesota.[23] To understand the magnitude of that threat requires understanding the symbolic and cultural value of the lake and its islands to the Chippewa people. The Red Cliff Band is one of 154 Bands of the Anishinaabe, a larger nation whose people extend across the Great Lakes region of North America, both in the United States and Canada—or, more precisely, as the Red Cliff Band official "origins and history" notes, "as far east as the Atlantic Ocean, as far south as Iowa, as far west as Montana, and as far north as Hudson Bay."[24] Known as the "Hub of the Ojibwe," Red Cliff sits at the geographic heart of the Anishinaabe nation, located just across from Madeline Island in Lake Superior: "The Anishinabe [sic] people know Madeline Island as the final stopping place of their migration from the Eastern sea. Moningwanikoning, Madeline Island, is the name that was given to this island by the people who saw this place as a spiritual center."[25] As Red Cliff Band member Andy Gokee explains, the Chippewa, led by Chief Buffalo, a "gifted diplomat and highly regarded orator" in his nineties, resisted Taylor's order and, through the 1854 treaty, successfully negotiated for land to be set aside for himself and his band, including what would later become the Red Cliff Reservation.[26]

Over a century later, members of the Red Cliff Band, some of them direct descendants of the storied chief, faced another push by the federal government to cede their land. The lakeshore bill intersected with a complex history of tribal lands granted and ceded, leased and alienated, of treaty rights negotiated but often challenged and rescinded.[27] Thus, many tribal members resisted it, seeing the initiative through the lens of the historic deprivation of Native American land and treaty rights. After two years of hearings and vigorous debate within their respective tribal councils, in 1969, the Red Cliff and Bad River Bands of the Lake Superior Chippewa decided to oppose the national park bill, Duwayne "Wotsy" Soulier's mother included. She had lost one son on behalf of the United States—the nation that only forty-three years before had granted Native Americans citizenship—and was unwilling to give up the land allotted to her and her surviving children.[28]

The Allen family was left with no choice. As part of the National Park Service's plan to acquire property from private landowners, the federal government exercised its power of eminent domain.[29] In exchange for just compensation (what the government deemed a "fair price"), they were compelled to give up their island and lakeshore property, which included the family's house and its two businesses, a bar and machine shop. But the takeover didn't happen easily. As president of the South Shore Property Owners Association, Alden "Skip" Allen fought hard to hold on to his property—in Merl's words, "what we all worked so hard to acquire." Eventually, however, the government prevailed. It condemned the mainland property in order to seize it and establish park headquarters there. In the winter of 1978, a US Marshal appeared at the family home with a notice that they had ninety days plus a six-month extension to vacate the property. Mr. Allen was so incensed by the government's forced takeover of his lakeshore property that he relocated the bar and shop, and having purchased his family's house back from the government, he moved the entire structure, every last brick and board, to another plot within the nearby township of Russell.

Several years earlier, with his son missing in action in Vietnam, sacrificed to the nation but his remains unrecovered and unreturned, Skip Allen had already undertaken a symbolic act to defy the dispossession of his home and land and to honor his son's question, "Is this the reward for serving my country?": in 1970, before the federal government could assume full possession of the island property in 1974, he deeded a sliver of land on the southern-most tip of York Island to the township of Russell—with the guarantee that he and his wife, and possibly his son who fought and died in Vietnam, would someday be buried there. Little did he know the extraordinary journey his son's remains would make to come home to the shores of Lake Superior and the beautiful beach Merl once willed to his high school friends.

· 4 ·

A Recovery Mission

I met Merl Allen on the airstrip at Khe Sanh.[1] I was gathering up my gear when this tall skinny kid with a big grin says "You here for recon? Name's Allen, from Bayfield, WI. How long you been in country? Oh . . . FNG [fucking new guy] huh? Recon's this way." That was the start of a short but everlasting friendship.

FNGs were the new guys. They were frowned upon because they usually screwed something up right away. Also, you just never made friends quickly because it was too hard seeing them hauled off in body bags right away. Hard to explain, but that's the way it was. A friendship was earned and just sort of established itself over time.

Merl was my mentor, he took me under his wing and he taught me about Recon, and he taught me about Vietnam. He was my friend when I needed one. That's how Merl was.

We had a lot in common—both from the Midwest, both took ships to Vietnam, both radio operators, both big dreamers. We were both extremely proud to be in Recon. We talked, constantly, about "the world"—home, girls, cars, hunting, fishing, Bayfield, what we'd do later, after Nam. We laughed, and talked, and dreamed. Just like the two teenage kids that we really were. The war hadn't hardened us yet.[2]

ON JUNE 30, 1967, Jeff Savelkoul survived the enemy fire and helicopter crash in Thừa Thiên–Huế Province in central Vietnam. On its final approach to insert a reconnaissance team, the helicopter came under attack, and despite the pilot's efforts to maneuver the aircraft, it crash landed into the tree line.[3] The attack and ensuing explosions killed his best friend, Merl Allen, and four others: the pilot, Captain John House II, and three members of Team Striker from the US Marine Corps' Third Reconnaissance Battalion, Alpha Company—Michael Judd, John Killen III, and Glyn Runnels Jr. A sixth man from Third Recon, Dennis Perry, died two days later from the wounds he sustained in the fiery crash, and a seventh, Eugene Castaneda, would return to battle and be killed on another patrol mission two months later.

Savelkoul himself was severely wounded that day, with broken bones and over 65 percent of his skin burned. He and Perry were evacuated to a military hospital in Japan for treatment. He woke up on a gurney, a few feet away from Perry. "He looked me straight in the eye, and just died."[4]

For years, Savelkoul thought he had been the sole survivor—as did Mariano "Junior" Guy. In the aftermath of their chaotic extraction, each knew nothing of the other's fate. It wasn't until twenty-three years later that they reconnected and pieced together the story of that day. Savelkoul wrote out a detailed description, which he uses when speaking to various audiences about his wartime and postwar experiences. He shared it with me after we met, after he learned that I had taken part in the excavation of the crash site that recovered the remains of his best friend Merl. In it, time slows down as he recounts the chaotic scenes of the downed helicopter, loaded with men and explosives. His are visceral recollections of death and survival:

> As we descended into the LZ [landing zone], the tailgate was down and we were all in our positions for departure. Just above the ground we started to take SA [surface-to-air] & AA [anti-aircraft] fire. The pilot pulled up and we were hit with a rocket. It blew a huge hole in the side of the chopper, severed the fuel line, sprayed jet fuel all over the chopper, and us—and ignited. This inferno, the rocket blast, and all the rounds we were taking killed most of the team at that time.
>
> The inside of the chopper was like an 8-foot culvert with a pile of burning tires in it—that thick, black, orange, oily, smoke-like acetylene without oxygen. You couldn't see and you couldn't breathe. *Everything* was on fire! I needed air. I stuck my head out a broken window and came back in with burning plexiglass stuck to my face—but I got some air!
>
> I could see streaks of light coming in where bullets were coming through, but I couldn't see anyone else. How I didn't get hit was a

miracle! My clothes were burned off and my pack was on fire. I remember thinking of the ammo and 12 frag grenades I had in my pack. And that Merl would have his radio. So I threw off my pack. Our M-16's were already melted at that point. . . .

Capt. House, our pilot, tried to fly us over a ridge to safety, despite being already shot through [the] arm. (This was the same pilot that hovered with one wheel on a stump, taking heavy fire while his crewman ran out and rescued all of Team Hawk in April '67.) We were losing altitude fast and he couldn't make the ridge. About three-quarters of the way up the steep hill we hit the trees, sheared off the rotors, and free-fell 90 feet to the jungle floor. When we hit the ground, the chopper split open, the air rushed in, and it exploded.

Those of us who were alive had worked our way up to the gunners' opening on the right side of the chopper. Somewhere between the treetops and the ground, we were blown out that small window. I remember flopping back down through the branches of a big tree . . . and landing in the dirt below. Junior was stumbling around holding his head. Perry was laying in a heap. There was a leg laying outside the chopper. Cass [Eugene Castaneda] was pounding on the windshield in frustration trying to get the pilot out, who was trapped and burning to death. All the other Reconners were dead.

At this point in the narrative, Jeff turns to the panicked moments that ensued as he and the survivors fled to the mountain ridge, a site I had come to know well by the time I read his account. It was there, four decades later, that we—the US military recovery mission—would labor for days, sifting through dirt and debris to locate remnants of the helicopter and remains of the pilot and the fallen members of Team Striker:

We had no radio. We had no weapons. We had one hand grenade, six pencil flares, a half a canteen of water, the co-pilot's .38 cal revolver, and Junior's machete. The NVA were everywhere, you couldn't see them, but you could hear them coming!

Cass and Junior gathered up Perry and me and started us up the hill. We stumbled, fell, clawed our way to the top of the hill. I had to grab onto branches to keep us going, there was no skin left on my hands. We got up the hill and I collapsed leaning against a tree with Perry in my lap. Junior came up to me and put our one

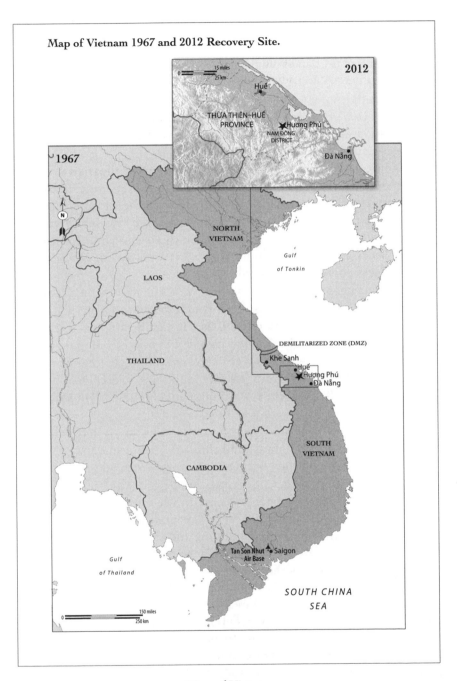

Map of Vietnam.

grenade in my raw hand, wrapped my fingers around it, and pulled the pin.

He stuffed my hand between me and Perry and told me not to let go unless the NVA got to me. We wouldn't be POW's!!!

I kept passing out from the pain. I would lurch awake and tell myself, "Don't close your eyes. You'll never wake up." I'll bet I said that a thousand times. My hand hurt so damn bad, but I held on to that grenade.

We were all gathered up on top of the hill, under the trees when a chopper came in and hovered over the wreck below us. We had no comm [communications], so Cass fired four of the six flares. They didn't see the flares and went back and reported "no survivors." About two and a half hours later we heard choppers again. One flew right over us and Cass fired the 5th flare. It was a dud! My heart sank, I was going to die here.

Another chopper was getting closer so Cass fired the last flare. All we knew was that it went up through the leaves. Years later I finally found the pilot who rescued us. He said he dropped a reactionary force in the valley behind us and was hover-taxiing up the ridge to look at the wreck and go back, [when] he glanced out his side window to check his rotor clearance and saw a flare. I told him it was our last flare. There was a long pause, he said, "Honest, it was just a glance."

He came over to where it came from and his crew chief yelled "There's guys on the ground, and I think they're Americans."

They couldn't get a sling down to us through the jungle, so Junior climbed up a tree—under fire—and chopped off the branches to clear the way. The chopper hovered there, under fire, as they winched each of us up the 100 feet. Cass and Junior stayed to be the last two. Each put a foot in the sling and came up together, neither wanting to leave the other. They selflessly risked their own lives, putting the rest of their team first.[5]

In his account, Jeff Savelkoul is quick to highlight the selfless acts of the pilot, Capt. House, of Junior Guy and Eugene Castaneda, even Merl Allen, whom he credits with shielding him from the explosion that tore apart the back end of the helicopter and thus saving his life. He is not a person who covets the spotlight; rather, over the past four decades, he has sought to hold the men from Team Striker who died on June 30, 1967—and the two who died a few short days and weeks later—in the bright light of memory. He explains in his public talks, "I don't expect that you'll remember their names, but I hope you will remember their story, and pass it on to others, so that they are never forgotten."[6]

This notion of a memory shared, a story that in its circulation animates and thus prolongs the essence of lives lived and lost, fits within a larger history of caring for war dead, what historian Jay Winter has called the "work of remembrance."[7] In the wake of the Great War, he argues, individuals and groups came together to create a space in which "the story of their war, in its local, particular, parochial, familial forms, [could] be told and retold"; this memory work was neither wholly individual nor exclusively national (i.e., part of the "national theater of collective memory choreographed by social and political leaders").[8] Rather, Winter saw it as a generative force that operated in the in-between spaces of grief, "at a point between the isolated individual and the anonymous state."[9] It forged bonds of "fictive kinship," extending the work of remembrance beyond the strict parameters of family to other members of a community. Though emerging from a very different war and in a very different era, Jeff Savelkoul's attempts to share the details of June 30, 1967, as we will see, have brought about their own forms of fictive kinship.

I met Jeff in Superior, Wisconsin, in September 2016, already three years after I had started researching the story of Lance Corporal Merlin Allen and had traveled on a few occasions to the Bayfield Peninsula. Like many conversations that have informed this book, our first real talk took place at a diner, over coffee and between slices of French toast and bacon. For all the files I reviewed at the Central Identification Laboratory in Hawaii in preparation for the 2012 recovery mission, I still knew little about the reconnaissance patrol, or even the events that led to the crash itself; I had no idea of what happened to the men who survived the incident. Speaking with Jeff was a chance not only to fill in the gaps, but also to think about MIA accounting from an entirely different perspective and within a larger chronology.

It helped that he brought photos.

We spoke for about three hours that day. Over the course of our meal and the meandering discussion, the restaurant gradually emptied out and filled up again with a second wave of customers; we sat absorbed in the past, pushing along topics of the war, the helicopter crash, and his recovery. As conversationalists go, Jeff is subdued—not standoffish or reserved, but not someone who runs at the mouth—and so it was I who asked the questions, gauging as best I could what might be wading too far into troubled pools of recollection.

The photographs, stored in an old checkbook box, came out after we had set aside our plates of diner fare and the coffee had grown cold. Internally, I fussed at the thought of sticky smudges of syrup marring their surface, and I wiped my hands again on the now crumpled napkin at the edge of the table.

"Here's Merl and me."

"That's Khe Sanh."

"We're on patrol there."

Scenes of bare-chested young men smiling into the camera, cocky, goofy, relaxed. I searched for war's sharper edge, but it wasn't there among the faces, or at least not yet. Later, Jeff's words would return: "We laughed, and talked, and dreamed. Just like the two teenage kids that we really were. The war hadn't hardened us yet."

He left the photos for me to look through while he went to the restroom. I gingerly pulled them out, one by one, and scanned their faded scenes. In his absence, they felt different in my hands. There were so many of them, and yet they each deserved time. I began to move more quickly as the scenes sorted themselves into categories. They conjured up landscapes, bonds of camaraderie, and the labor of war on someone else's soil.

One image stuck out for its inescapable suggestion of violence. With tattered white rags as blindfolds, two Vietnamese men crouched on their heels, hands bound behind their backs. I think I remember there being other figures, legs that hinted at a circle of onlookers, but I can't be sure.

As the ice melted and a water ring spread beneath my plastic cup, I wondered how to ask Jeff what happened to those men.

Often in studying war, scholars adopt a narrow scope, privileging one experience over another, drawn to one side or the other. Here was an abrupt reminder of my own tunnel vision, what Viet Thanh Nguyen might call the blinders of "remembering one's own." In his book *Nothing Ever Dies: Vietnam and the Memory of War,* he writes about the connection between remembering and forgetting, explaining that it is a relationship "more fundamentally about remembering our humanity and forgetting our inhumanity, while conversely remembering the inhumanity of others and forgetting their humanity."[10] While Nguyen admits that "total memory is neither possible nor practical," he resists easy lines cordoning off war's events and actors, because doing so fails to capture its enduring effects.[11]

"Haunted and haunting, human and inhuman, war remains with us and within us, impossible to forget but difficult to remember."[12]

When Jeff returned to the table, I asked him about the picture of the Vietnamese prisoners. He didn't know what had happened to the men. Weighed down by the guilt of his own survival, he was doing his best to remember those who hadn't gotten off the mountain slope alive. The prisoners' memory was not his to safeguard. In a similar vein, just as Jeff cannot tell the story of the North Vietnamese troops who shot down his helicopter and killed his best friend, so too the account that follows cannot capture Vietnamese experiences—neither of the war itself, nor what it meant to the Vietnamese who witnessed and, in some cases, labored alongside the US military recovery team. Such are the limits of lived experience, of fragmented and unstable memory, and of our endeavor to make sense of both in the present. Perhaps it is best then to acknowledge that the attempt to locate and repatriate the remains of US service members is, like an archaeological dig, an act of partial reckoning. It seeks to account for lives lost on *one* side of a war that lingers, haunts, and defies easy recollection. That is to say, MIA accounting for the missing is a singularly American enterprise, an extension of an American tradition, undertaken for American surviving kin, veterans, current military, and public. And yet it's carried out on Vietnamese soil, by permission of the Vietnamese state and with the indispensable aid of Vietnamese laborers.

That acknowledgment should give pause. It should invite us to imagine, alongside the events described below, what exceptional acts of care might be required to recover and sustain the memory of Vietnam's missing—the three hundred thousand lives lost on the *other* side of what the Vietnamese call the "American War."

THE EXCAVATION "UNIT," the four-by-four-meter patch of rust-colored earth, had taken all day to hollow out and in the process had left each dig team—the pair of Americans who rotated in and out of the shallow trench for an hour apiece—drenched in sweat and physically spent. We only had to cut into the jungle floor about fifteen centimeters to reach the bottom— where signs of helicopter wreckage disappeared—but the unit's loamy earth and maddening network of roots and rocks required extra strength behind each swing of the pickax or shovel. With the temperature well over ninety-five degrees and humidity well above 90 percent, the jungle seemed to be steaming. Even the young Vietnamese men who manned the bucket line, the human chain that ferried soil and debris up the mountainside, tried to press themselves into the shade, with the unluckiest among them suffering under the blazing sun.

Bác Thuận, one of the Vietnamese laborers, whom members of the American team had nicknamed "Old Man Shovel" for his finesse with the tool, was also bathed in sweat. From the beginning of the dig, he had strategically positioned himself at the bottom of the bucket line. As US military protocol allowed only American personnel to dig within the unit itself, he took up one of the most arduous tasks at its edge—filling the buckets with what had just been unearthed. He worked there each day, nonstop for hours on end. Though he rarely spoke and, in the early days of the dig, rarely smiled, he quickly won the American team's respect as his labors set a pace of steady but intense exertion that everyone working beside him followed, American and Vietnamese alike. That he too felt—and showed—the strain of the dig that particular day signaled just how challenging the unit had been. After the last rotation, looking down over its hard-won, though still partial, "floor" and neatly trimmed "walls" (terms of archaeological excavation whereby destruction gives way to superimposed order), I took stock of the sight, this section of land in the middle of the jungle in central Vietnam, and the day's accomplishment. Those few hours, perhaps more than any other during the month-long mission, impressed upon me the extraordinary physical effort of MIA recovery: tearing into and scouring the land—the soil of a foreign land—to find whatever bits and scraps of human remains and material evidence that had endured from the CH-46 helicopter crash some forty-five years before.

The clearing sat on a draw at the intersection of two steep slopes, with inclines ranging from thirty-five to seventy degrees. Heavy rains and the natural force of erosion of the past four decades had pushed the wreckage downward, along a central and two smaller washes that empty into a creek below. While gravity had played a hand over time in dispersing the wreckage farther and farther away from the initial site, not all the disturbance stemmed from the laws of motion. Much more had occurred at the hands of people—local villagers and itinerant scavengers—who cut up and carted off the metal of the downed chopper.[13] They themselves relied on gravity for help, using the slippery incline of the draw to haul vast sections down off the mountain. Following the logic of war and its deprivations, they took what they could and put it to use in their houses and gardens, fields and farms.[14] More valuable scrap metal could be sold on local and international markets.

Helicopter wreckage was not the only object of interest on the slope. Reports containing the names of the five missing in action eventually surfaced from nearby Huế and Hồ Chí Minh City, as well as from farther-flung refugee camps in Thailand where thousands of South Vietnamese had fled after the war ended in 1975.[15] As Deputy Assistant Secretary of Defense James W. Wold explained in a letter updating Mrs. Amy House, wife of the pilot Captain John House II, of their ongoing efforts to investigate her husband's case, "Over the years, we have received refugee reports with identification media information on each of the five servicemen."[16] These dog-tag rubbings, identification media, and secondhand stories of remains recovered in the jungle inland of Huế pointed toward a different kind of scavenging: in the limited but active field of "remains trading," bones associated with American MIAs became articles of exchange in the region's wartime and postwar market.[17]

Between 1993 and 2011, Reference Number (REFNO) 0746 (the case number assigned to the June 30, 1967, CH-46 helicopter crash) was investigated eleven times, including as part of several joint field activity (JFA) missions conducted with the host state—that is, alongside Vietnamese officials from the central government (e.g., its Ministry of Foreign Affairs, Ministry of National Defense, Ministry of Interior) and at the provincial level. During this period, investigative and recovery efforts centered on two sites in Thừa Thiên–Huế Province: first, the record loss location near Hương Phú commune, Nam Đông District, with site surveys conducted on the 23rd JFA in May 1993, the 27th JFA in January 1994, and the 55th JFA in May 1999; and second, at another helicopter crash site where personal artifacts—a wristwatch, a card from a deck of playing cards ("2" black ace), a rosary necklace, and a piece of an ink pen—and "several pieces of aircrew/troop related items" were purportedly recovered, in Phú Lộc District.[18] Survivors of the crash had recognized some of the articles said to have been found at the second site—Jeff Savelkoul, in particular, his own rosary. But preliminary investigations during the 60th JFA in May 2000 and excavations carried out at the site during the 68th JFA in January 2002 and again on the 70th JFA in June 2002 proved futile. No remains were recovered and the location could not be definitively correlated with REFNO 0746. Finally, as part of the 83rd JFA, in November 2005, the Joint POW/MIA Accounting Command returned to the site near the original record loss location in the mountains near Hương Phú commune, Nam Đông District; they resurveyed the site and documented "numerous fragments of metal, composites, and fiberglass consistent with possible aircraft wreckage." Before departing the site, the recovery leader (a position filled by either an anthropologist or an archaeologist) set a "datum"—a "poured concrete slab on the ground with a bundle of nails immersed at its center"—at specific grid coordinates determined by a GPS receiver.[19] Found, then sidelined, then found again, the original loss site was now pinpointed geographically. Seven years later, the United States military returned once more to search for the five service members missing in action from REFNO 0746.

OUR THIRTEEN-PERSON RECOVERY TEAM from the Joint POW/MIA Accounting Command (JPAC) arrived in May 2012 and set to work on the mountain, with its dense canopy and unforgiving underbrush. My fieldnotes detail my initial discomposure:

> May 22, 2012: Ospina leads a small group of us up into the draw, into the chaotic mess of vines and branches, slippery rocks and wet leaves. Gone is my fear of leeches, thrust to the back of my mind out of sheer necessity—I'm grabbing on to whatever tree trunk or root gives me leverage to ascend yet another few feet on this treacherous, dense slope. Where on earth have I come to and how, how, are we going to find human remains in the middle of this damn jungle?

The first days were disorienting: the jungle vegetation was thick, and initial surveys proved futile in locating the datum, the key marker left in November 2005. Laurel, the civilian forensic anthropologist leading the excavation, worked with the EOD (explosive ordnance disposal) technician, Jimmy, a twenty-three-year-old who had already cut his teeth locating and disarming UXO (unexploded ordnance) in Afghanistan. Canvassing the swaths of land that local workers cleared with deft strokes of their machetes, he swept his Excalibur II metal detector across the jungle floor. When its hum intensified, he pulled out the more exacting tool, a hand-held detector that beeped and whined with its own insistent pitch at the presence of larger pieces of metal, most of which turned out to be "bomb frag," portions of exploded bomb casings unrelated to the helicopter crash. Central Vietnam remains the country's most affected region of UXO contamination, a punishing legacy of US bombing campaigns.[20] By the Vietnamese government's tally, there are still some eight hundred thousand tons of ordnance present, including bombs, mines, missiles, artillery shells, mortar shells, and other UXO.[21]

On the second day of the recovery mission, before the US team moved into the base camp, we got a taste of that legacy. Not two minutes into the walk on the logging road that led to the dig site, one of the team members signaled for everyone to head back to the main road. Jimmy had spotted a munition. There, in the middle of the dirt track, lay a 100 mm artillery round. Someone had carried it in and purposefully placed it along the route. As we filed back toward the main road to await the bomb disposal, nearby construction workers chuckled knowingly, perhaps having seen who left the round earlier that morning. The munition hinted at a subtext left mostly unexamined by the American team: the resentment felt by some Vietnamese about recovery efforts for US missing (with little regard for Vietnamese missing), and the destruction wrought by US bombing.[22] If the source was unclear, the action demanded was obvious. The dangerous vestige of war required care too, as much as, if not more than, the remains of American war dead.

Jimmy would earn his keep that mission, disposing of three other munitions back on the slope, including three M381s—40 mm high-explosive fragmentation grenades, one fired and two unfired. It was his first assignment as a JPAC "augmentee," sent by the US Army's Sixty-Fifth Ordnance Company to support the mission, and so he had done his research in the run up—consulted manuals, read up on Vietnam-era munitions, punched data into a blast frag calculator to anticipate how far he'd need to push people back from one round or another. Protocol on the dig was different from what he was used to, and he would have to adapt. Rather than detonate a munition in place, as he would have with an IED (improvised explosive device) in Afghanistan, in these circumstances he needed to protect both personnel and the dig site itself by moving the round to the UXO pit he had built on the ridge above the base camp.

On the mountainside, Jimmy's task was not only about identifying and mitigating munition risks. He was there to help Laurel, the anthropologist, map the crash site. Working in tandem, they stuck brightly colored pin flags in the soil for each of the "big hits" from the metal detector, and gradually a pattern of debris began to emerge. It was an intimidatingly large field of subterranean traces; the wreckage was so dispersed, there was no clear sign of where to begin digging.

A breakthrough eventually came when a local man, a bee gatherer from a nearby town, encountered one of the laborers and in passing mentioned that he knew something of the original crash site. Shortly thereafter he made his way up the mountain slope to speak with the Vietnamese officials, personnel from the Vietnamese Office for Seeking Missing Persons (VNOSMP or VNO for short), tasked with providing logistical support for the recovery mission and day-to-day management of the Vietnamese laborers at the site. While there were local and provincial representatives assigned to the VNO team, the majority of them were from Hanoi and thus had limited connection to the district and limited knowledge of the crash site itself. The local "witness," however, was confident that he knew the spot.

The man dropped to his heels, squatting on the slope as he surveyed the thick vegetation to his right and left. There, he indicated, was where he had seen the helicopter wreckage back in 1995, what remained of it at least—a charred section with two seats, possibly from the rear of the chopper. Other segments had been hauled off the mountain slope, with a crane and big trucks brought in for the task, and he himself had scavenged what he could from the remnants.[23]

The conversation between the Americans and Vietnamese proceeded haltingly. The anthropologist posed questions to gauge the witness's intentions as much as the accuracy of his recollections. The man nodded his head nonchalantly as the interpreter relayed the wary, compact questions.

"What did he see? Ask him to describe exactly what he saw painted on the tree trunk."

"A skull and crossbones, spray-painted in pink, with an English word. It started with P and ended with E."

Laurel shook her head. "We wouldn't have left that kind of mark." JPAC field investigation protocol precluded the possibility of such signage, and thus the proof offered raised more questions than it answered. Not long afterward, the man, nonplussed, rose to his feet and collected his machete. Nodding at the Vietnamese officials standing nearby but brushing past the US personnel, he took his leave, heading down the rocky wash that led back to the base camp and, beyond that, the main road. While the man lent support to the general location of the crash site, he also openly acknowledged the ongoing practice of scavenging that stripped the area of evidence definitively correlating the loss incident with the site.

IN A MATTER OF DAYS, the excavation site was transformed, with brush cleared and units plotted. Given the complex terrain, with the central draw and the rocky, steep, and uneven topography, the key, Laurel explained, was to set the grid in a manner that conformed to, or at least worked with, the natural features of the landscape. Moving outward from her transit lines centered at N500/E500, she plotted several units with string and wooden stakes; first, four meters north, then another four meters east. In the course of an afternoon, we established the parameters for eight units, four on each side of the wash. An exercise of laying down order onto a landscape of natural chaos, old and new technologies, complementary tools of measuring, reading, and taming—the transit and its precise electronics, the hand-held GPS instrument, the Excalibur II wand, alongside machetes, stakes, pin flags, and string—soon rendered the site legible to the eyes of the anthropologist who would in turn determine the course of the excavation.

By the time the main body of the recovery team arrived on site, the land that served as the base camp had also been cleared by the villagers and thus, apart from large trees, was emptied of the same thick vegetation that covered the crash site. The villagers had been hard at work, clearing and building not only the base camp structures, but also seventy-five yards worth of steps up to the landing zone, itself utterly denuded of trees and ground cover. Much of the equipment and supplies were flown in by helicopter and carried down the hill to the camp, about a fifteen-minute hike from the excavation site. We set up our individual tents, the three women on our own separate platform, the ten men on theirs, and a kitchen "hootch" where at the beginning and end of the day, we ate rudimentary meals of oatmeal, tuna, and dehydrated noodles.

For my own part, as the social anthropologist—not the forensic anthropologist directing the dig—I ordered my space on the women's platform with an eye toward how best to write up fieldnotes. Behind my tent I created a makeshift desk with my footlocker, which stored thirty-five days of non-perishable food, and a lawn chair. For the next twenty-some days, after dinner ended and the kitchen hootch emptied out, I would retire to that space. To the hum of the generator and the unfamiliar sounds of the jungle at night, I would type up the day's observations and reflections.

Before that, however, I had to figure out how to open up an army-issue cot. Mark, the team's medic (whom everyone on the team would call "Doc"), knew ineptitude when he saw it, and came over to assist.

All of this building and ordering had its literal price. Generally speaking, the process of clearing the land is especially big business when it comes to US-Vietnamese negotiations around MIA accounting, and it takes shape in two forms of monetary compensation that the US teams provide Vietnamese officials, either directly or negotiated on behalf of local landowners: "land comp" (compensation for land clearing and use) and restoration (money provided to restore the land to its pre-excavation conditions). In addition to land compensation, recovery missions involve the intricate task of planning for and utilizing local labor. Ours was a typical mission in terms of such labor, starting with a core group of about thirty Vietnamese workers and expanding to upwards of sixty when the excavation began in full force and villagers manned bucket lines and helped screen the dirt removed from the crash site. Hired directly through the VNO, the Vietnamese local workers are supposed to receive approximately thirty dollars per day (in a region where the per capita GDP at that time was $1,003), but in actuality pocket far less after the government takes its cut.[24] Indirect channels of redistribution exist but are opaque—at least to the US teams—following complex networks that exist at local, regional, and federal levels. Thus, although the explicit policy is that the US government does not pay for remains, it pays steeply to *access* those remains.[25] With an operation and maintenance budget for the Defense POW/MIA Accounting Agency (DPAA) of approximately $130 million per year, nearly 70 percent is allocated to the agency's operations in Southeast Asia.[26]

The postwar politics of the arrangement are unmistakable: the victors let the vanquished back in to collect their losses, but they control each move, set the tone, and dictate the terms, monetary terms included—the land comp prices, the workers' wages, the helicopter flight ("blade") hours, and so on. In carrying out its investigative and recovery missions, the US government seeks to drive its own hard bargains in purchasing local goods and services. For the recovery missions during May–June 2012, when first entering and later exiting the country, US personnel stayed at a newly built resort hotel in Đà Nẵng, down the road from the wartime air base with its concrete B-57 hangars tucked just beyond view from the posh grounds of the beachside resorts. With the promise of at least four missions annually of sixty to seventy members apiece, the US government receives a steep discount for the deluxe accommodations, one-third the regular charge for a night's stay.

If the interactions among the official parties hewed closely to prescribed roles during negotiations about the excavation's logistics and operations, more spontaneous, personal exchanges took place between members of the US recovery team and the local workers at the excavation itself, often out of sight of the VNO officials. After the first week of the dig, lunch break became an icebreaker.

> June 12: One of the nice developments has been lunch with the workers. It began with Le relaying their invitation to eat with them, and slowly a small contingent of us have taken to bringing food for the group—like a potluck—in addition to their myriad dishes of rice, bamboo shoots, curried fish, pork, soup, pumpkin stalks, and morning glory. It's a veritable feast that we embellish with our tins of soup and Chef Boyardee and packets of tuna and snack-packs of peaches and cookies. Originally, we joined the group over on their side, where it's cooler and shadier, but today they placed two screens (upside-down) in the shade between our two "areas" and we all gathered around. They had brought roasted duck among other dishes, and we ate until we were all full. We rely on Le and Baker to translate, but we also do pretty well in understanding one another in the basic enjoyment of company and generosity of spirit.

The meals encouraged conversation, and the US interpreters helped navigate the early tentative exchanges. Is she married? Does he have children? How old are they? A few of the older workers spoke of the past and of the war, and Bác Hùng ("Uncle" Hùng), a former Army of the Republic of Vietnam (ARVN) medic, sought out Doc, our recovery team's medic, to talk about their common work. The wiry old man, always first to the site in the morning and first to shoulder the heaviest loads up the mountainside, still remembered a few of the English phrases he learned during the war and would try them out each day with Doc. He too enjoyed the collective meals, telling the Vietnamese American linguist, "It could be the same food but the people I sit with make the difference of how much I can eat."

For Doc, the highest-ranking member of the team as a senior chief petty officer in the navy, the lunches offered an important opportunity for cultural exchange. "I've been around the world. I can name a list of all the places that I've been, more than I've been in the States. That's one of the things I've learned is I'd rather get away from the mainstream and hang out with the people and learn the culture and learn the people, because it gives me a better respect for them and them a better respect for me."[27] He took note of how each day, the workers asked us to eat with them, and how, after each lunch, one of the men would invite him to go have a smoke. It bothered him that some among the American team rejected the workers' hospitality by rejecting their food. Their refusal missed the point. "We didn't come all this way to eat pizza."

THE EXCAVATION SOON GAINED its own rhythms and routines—the sound of shovels biting into the earth, buckets being filled and rocks against mesh screen. Like clockwork, by late afternoon, the skies would open and it would rain hard, if only for a few minutes. The workers anticipated this each time and left the site before they got caught in the downpour.

Most days, after the last bucket had been screened, a few of us remained to watch Laurel and the life support equipment expert examine the day's finds at a smaller screening station to the side. The two of them picked through the articles slowly, sorting out wreckage to be disposed of at the end of the dig and the more important material evidence, including fragments of life support equipment, that would eventually return with us to the laboratory in Hawaii. The consequential recoveries they sealed in evidence bags, recording the contents of each. The act hinted at the chain of evidence gradually emerging from this harsh landscape to establish definitively the area we were digging as the location of the crash site and to document the precise provenience of any human remains that might turn up in our screens. The sifting and sorting also gave Laurel a chance to see what the day's unit had yielded. The amount and kind of material recovered helped guide her choice about which four-by-four-meter patch of jungle to dig next. Scooping up handfuls of assorted debris—stone, burned plastic, wood, any object that to our untrained eyes resembled bone—she quickly filtered the significant from the "noise."

On the surface, much of dig's day-to-day labor and archaeological practice seemed counterintuitive to members of the military team on their first excavation, as it did to the Vietnamese farmers who worked land of their own. When instructed to push cleared brush *up* the steep incline rather than down, many of the local workers shook their heads in disbelief and frustration. It made no sense, and the Vietnamese American linguist Le, an augmentee also from the navy, had to battle their skepticism. He tried to lead by example, to model the work required. Straddling the language divide between the Vietnamese and Americans, Le had a knack for reading people and smoothing out cultural frictions that served officials on both sides well. But the dig logistics were often challenging to explain, especially when they didn't yield ready results. Sifting seven tons of soil and debris daily through quarter-inch mesh screens in search of wreckage and remains surely appeared excessive, if not futile, as days passed without any remains recovered.

After the first week of excavating, tensions began to build and divisions emerged among the Vietnamese workers. Apart from Bác Thuận ("Old Man Shovel")—who in reality looked to be in his mid- to late 40s—the older members of the group had staked claim to the positions closest to and up at the screening station on the mountain ridge, leaving the younger men to work the lower sections of the bucket line. The difference was significant: those toward the bottom of the line stood in the direct sun for hours, stuck with the most tedious work of the dig. The sole US team member who understood both the language and the cultural dynamics, Le ended up running interference between the two camps, on the one hand asking the elders to compromise or, in turn, exert their own authority, and on the other hand pushing the younger men to work harder. For him, the difference in work ethic had to do with the war itself. He rationalized that the older workers felt a kind of sympathy for the Americans. "Knowing, you know, that Americans died there, helping them. 'Cause they fought in the war also, you know? . . . And we have to travel so far and work so hard to recover our fallen soldiers. So they sympathize a lot. . . . The older people actually have to think about it more, but the younger worker, maybe is just there . . . It's good money."[28] Eventually, the Vietnamese officials stepped in and fired some of the younger men. Many were replaced the next day with the older workers' relatives, immediate and extended. Bác Hùng soon had six members of his family working at the site, Bác Thuận brought his wife and daughters. Kin ties proved a stronger labor incentive and the mood gradually lightened along the bucket line, despite the disappointing lack of results.

Finally, on day nine, a single tooth and then another appeared in the screens, to the surprise of the entire group. One was a pre-molar and the other a molar with restorations, an important feature to compare later against dental records on file. The day had started slowly, with the digging especially hard because of the unit's tough terrain. And so just after the lunch break, when one of the US team members called out from his screen that he had found a tooth, those of us on the ridge erupted in cheers. The Vietnamese at the screening station beamed; they too seemed to take joy in the discovery. "It was like finding gold," explained Le. The news traveled quickly down the bucket line to the excavation site itself. The effort and strange methods of the past several days finally had brought results and a boost to morale.

Objects of curiosity for the team, the teeth drew close inspection. I hadn't expected their color: a bluish-green tint that made them look almost fake. But to hold them in your hand, you sensed their worth, their particular power—the potential to recognize individual identity of one or more of the missing service members whose remains had lain undetected on the mountain slope for four decades despite Vietnamese and American efforts otherwise. As one of the team members reflected, "At the least, somebody's loved one would eventually get part of them back." Later that day, back at the base camp, some of the US team studied the photographs of the five missing men, searching for clues as to which of them might have just been recovered. Doc hoped aloud that the teeth might belong to one in particular, a missing navy medical corpsman whose photograph coincidentally he had seen over and over during the course of his career with the navy, displayed on POW/MIA remembrance walls in naval hospitals and medical training facilities. For him, the prior encounters had infused the recovery mission with special meaning.

As I had already learned at the laboratory back in Hawaii, finding teeth and not bone is hardly unusual. The acidic soil of Southeast Asia tends to erode bones more quickly than teeth. The discoloration too has its logic—the blue-green tint was likely due to the oxidation of materials in the metallic dental restorations as the teeth decomposed in the soil for over four decades. I was struck by the way teeth could become a signpost for a person's identity. On the surface, teeth are not something we typically associate with someone's individual identity, at least not in an era in which DNA, our genetic "fingerprint," dominates understandings of unique biological markers. We tend to think of teeth instead as commonplace, expendable, even replaceable. But in this particular context, the teeth offered a chance to resolve absence, to know definitively who died where and to return some portion of a missing person to surviving kin. Elusive relics of the war, they mattered as proof of identity after death in ways they never did in life.

Invigorated by the initial discovery, the excavation efforts went on to yield an additional five teeth and three minuscule potential bone fragments. In the days that followed, my eye became increasingly sharpened to the shape of rocks and my fingers to their feel, surface, and weight. At the beginning of the mission, Laurel had spoken about the rocks' "warmth," the sensation of their relative temperature as they lay in her hand. For her, bone generally feels warmer than rocks, which have a cooler and damper feel. I struggled to understand what she meant at the time, but after holding the teeth in my own hand, her explanation made more sense. There was something different, or at least I felt myself to be more attuned to their singular texture and weight. Nevertheless, like Doc, I continued to fret about the responsibility of screening the dirt and debris. In fact, finding teeth and then bone, actual human remains, had added a new dimension to the day's work. It made searching alternately burdensome and thrilling— burdensome in the worry that I would flip the screen and empty its contents without being absolutely certain that I hadn't overlooked some fragment of bone, tooth, or wreckage; thrilling in anticipating that I too might happen upon remains, that we might find another fragment of one of the missing men.

Gradually, however, finds became less frequent. Our efforts unearthed fewer pieces of wreckage, as the excavation followed the principle of digging units until a buffer zone, an outer, so-called sterile edge, was created through an absence of recovered objects. The occasional attention-grabbing piece of material evidence still popped up, including a Zippo lighter that the team leader spent over an hour pursuing, bucket after bucket of soil removed, until half of his torso stretched into the hole he'd dug following the lead of telltale discolored earth. Even still, momentum tapered off as we neared the end of the month, and team members began talking about home, about meals they craved and family they missed. Signs of fatigue and impatience surfaced.

For two of the US team members, however, the ethos of exceptional care ran especially deep, connecting this excavation to their experiences in Iraq and at Dover Air Force Base as mortuary affairs specialists, or 92Ms. Each had served at the different ends of the contemporary conflict's care for its war dead—from receiving bodies fresh from the conflict to assisting with their embalming process back at Dover. Both states are disturbing, for different reasons, as one of them, the team sergeant, explained:

> For me, the remains that you first get when you're in Iraq are so— either they're still smoking because they're burnt to a crisp and they have that smell to it, or just the disgusting, been-in-the-heat-forever, the metallic blood smell. But then in Dover, you know, where they see the remains when they first come in . . . [and during] the embalming process where the remains are cleaned up. You still see how disfigured they are, but then at the end you see how perfect they are. It's so crazy.[29]

For these two members of the team, recovery missions with JPAC fell under this same ethic of care—caring for the missing in action from past conflicts followed the same creed as caring for the bodies of fellow service members killed in action. Indeed, in their view, faith in the mission itself was paramount; it kept people centered when the conditions became more challenging, when base camp got old and the physical labor too much. The other 92M added, "You've got to have work ethic. That's something you can't learn out here. . . . When times get tough, it's important to have some kind of belief in the mission." For him, the assignment with JPAC was "one of the more gratifying things I think I could do with myself."[30] Through it, he also honored his grandfather, who served in the US Navy for over thirty years, including as a corpsman in World War II. This particular mission was his last before leaving the military, and he was determined to appreciate it, whatever the conditions.

THE FINAL TWO DAYS OF THE MISSION broke with the routines we had developed over the month, and in their own ways offered lessons in the practice and politics of MIA accounting. The second to last day was dedicated to documenting the mission's archaeological results. Just as the start of the dig unfolded deliberately, from locating and clearing UXO to staking the units, it closed with a methodical, if odd, task: to prepare the site for final photographs, we needed to "sweep" it clean, removing any debris or soil that had since fallen into the excavated units. Awake at daybreak, the US team split into two groups—a smaller team remained at the base camp to dismantle structures, haul equipment up the slope to the landing zone, and coordinate the airlift test run, while the rest of us hiked to the dig site for the final clean-up session. Among our tools, we carried five brooms.

Once there, we quickly cleared the site of debris and set up a rudimentary screening station at the base of the grid in the draw. The anthropologist remeasured her units, replacing stakes where they had come loose, and then directed us in sweeping the entire site, its so-called floors. It seemed a silly exercise: whisking away loose dirt and small rocks on the side of a mountain that we had so unceremoniously (if systematically) ripped apart in search of remains and wreckage. While some of us swept, others gathered the scree into buckets to send down to the screening station to make sure no bit of remains or wreckage had escaped notice. Within three hours we finished, and the anthropologist and the photographer began recording the site in its final, preternaturally pristine state. The photographs, like the sealed and marked evidence bags, were part of the scientific record being assembled through the recovery efforts; they documented the terrain as an archaeological space from which we had extracted teeth, bone, munitions, fragments of life support, and other material evidence.

The exercise of final photographs also illustrated just how much the dig had changed the landscape and how much physical exertion was required to recover the few, minute pieces of human remains we did locate. From the base of the site, in the corner unit where the scavenger witness once crouched to give us directions, a massive area of denuded jungle extended upward, a stretch of rust-orange earth interrupted only by a few solitary trees, too big to be removed. The view from across the draw was even more striking; there you could take in the angle of the slope, its dips, the change in soil, the niches that the workers on the bucket line carved into the mountainside to have solid ground beneath their feet. Though the landscape had altered and grown familiar through the excavation's rou-tinized labor, it was a transitory change. The jungle would soon reclaim the site. In this regard, the photos served as an important resource for future digs. The site would not yet be officially closed as additional units needed to be dug. In fact, two more recovery mission teams would re-turn over the following two years as the search for remains continued, and the photographs would help guide their efforts.[31]

This final sweep took place just before another major event of the mis-sion. We had known for several days already that a member of Congress would be coming to the site at some point toward the end of the dig. To our frustration, the delegation didn't appear until the very last day, keeping us at the base camp for another twenty-four hours, though the excavation had ended and, for all intents and purposes, the mission was over. The poli-tics were not lost on the US team members, especially those who had served multiple tours in Iraq and Afghanistan: the congressman wanted to visit a site, regardless of whether that entailed visiting work in progress.

With final photos complete and the base camp organized for our departure, we had little to do but wait for the delegation's arrival by helicopter. The local workers were scheduled to come after lunch to assist with the final stage of breaking down the site, but by mid-morning, a small group, many of those who were part of the lunchtime exchanges, assembled by the creek just beyond the base camp. They began pre-paring an elaborate meal: a vat of *bún bò* (a beef broth with vegetables, meat, and congealed blood dumplings) and piles of rice noodles. Along with the large pots and the food itself, they had carried in special porcelain dishes for the occasion, as well as more decorative chopsticks, not the simple wooden ones they lent us up at the screening station.

Eventually, the helicopter arrived, and the congressman and two others, a staff member who had served in the Vietnam War and another female congressional staffer, picked their way down the steep incline from the landing zone, the woman holding tight to the arm of one of the military personnel accompanying the group. Immediately it was clear—she wouldn't be visiting the excavation site. There was simply no way she could make the trek up the slope. The congressman and his aide, however, were determined to tackle the mountainside and view the excavation, or what remained of it. The aide was former special forces, with almost two hundred "jumps" during his service in Vietnam, leaving him with 50 percent disability in both of his knees. But he didn't complain; he would make the hike up without a word about the steep grade.

During the brief tour of the base camp, the recovery team leader steered the delegation toward a large wooden board where the photographs of the five missing men were displayed. In truth, the board had been set up in anticipation of the congressional visit, a fact that irritated Doc. In his mind, it should have gone up earlier, at the beginning of the mission. Standing before the photos, the congressman, a member of the House Committee for Veterans' Affairs, seized the opportunity to press the team, in particular the anthropologist, about when the military members of the mission would be informed if their efforts eventually led to an identification. Though seemingly out of place, the question hinted at tensions within the Command, about which the congressman had obviously been briefed. It spoke to concerns about the flow of information and charges of territorialism or obstinacy, alternately levied by the MIA accounting community's military and civilian leadership against one another. His line of inquiry was a harbinger for things to come: one year later, the various agencies within the Department of Defense working on MIA recovery and identification would undergo intense scrutiny regarding the efficiency and transparency of their collective efforts (recall Senator McCaskill's hearing testimony), with the scientific and military components often pitted against one another.

With the tour of the base camp over, the delegation and members of the US team headed up the slope to the excavation site, where the anthropologist assumed the task of explaining the archaeological protocols—the processes of digging, screening, and recognizing remains. There, the congressman's attention turned to scavenging and concerns as to whether local

Vietnamese would try to dig up remains after the US team had departed. He voiced his skepticism of the local workers, without whose labor remains could not have been recovered in the first place, as well as of the VNO—the Vietnamese officials—particularly in their capacity to secure the site. A few minutes later, seemingly oblivious to the irony of his request, he asked in a roundabout way about wreckage and whether there might be something for him to take home. An article from the excavation "sitting on your desk sure is a conversation starter," he explained to the anthropologist. Laurel politely but firmly declined his request. JPAC's (now DPAA's) position was clear on this point: recovery leaders do not allow souvenir collecting on sites such as these, where US service members have died.

After we returned to the base camp, a contingent of the US team offered to take the congressman and his staffer to the swimming hole where we cleaned up at the end of each day—what we called the "pool"—and to a waterfall farther up. It was a pleasant hike and would be a good end to the tour. The route would take us past the workers, who were eagerly awaiting us to join them for the lunch they had prepared. A few members of the US team dashed ahead while the delegation lingered at the base camp, and we sat down on the rocks to enjoy the steaming bowls of *bún bò*. They measured out heaping portions with meat and blood dumplings for us and then for the congressman, when he and the others arrived. Urged by his staffer to try the food being offered, he turned to ask, "Do these people know who I am?"

The meal was rushed to fit his pace. Leaving behind half-finished bowls, we guided the delegation along the creek toward the pool; a smaller group then continued with him up to the waterfall, where he and one of the US team members lost their footing, coming close to slipping off the precipice in an attempt to get a good photograph of the congressman on his site visit. On the way back, he again passed by the workers at the creek. They offered him slices of pungent jackfruit, but he joked to his staffer that they should push on before he was forced to eat "more crap." Those of us within earshot cringed, grateful that the Vietnamese hadn't understood his words—or so we hoped.

Once the delegation finally departed, other scenes of gift giving and leave taking unfolded. Part of a larger system of exchange at work, they were tied to the site's history and MIA accounting writ large. For example, when the US team left at the end of the recovery mission, the base camp's tarps and plywood would go to homes and businesses, a bit like the downed helicopter salvaged for parts and scrap so many years ago. But there were also more purposeful items bequeathed. Surreptitiously, beyond the view of the Vietnamese officials, on these last two days of the mission, US team members had assembled special packages, rice bags stuffed with goods, to give to the villagers with whom they had labored most closely over the past month. To the most respected of the workers, Bác Thuận, the man whose tireless exertion outstripped everyone on the site, team members gave their own prized possessions—assorted equipment, trowels, a utility knife, the base camp's microwave in need of repair. He would return later that day to present the team with a handwritten letter expressing his own gratitude. In it, he addressed the two linguists: "I know we spent a lot of time together sharing stories and feelings. . . . We are sharing a little of our belongings and a lot of our heart as gifts. It's almost one o'clock now and I cannot sleep because I am still thinking. Because I cannot control my greed and accept your gifts for memories. That's why I write this letter to give to you tomorrow." To the rest of the American team ("Please forgive me for not knowing everyone's name") he ended with "a few words to say goodbye. I would like to represent the workers to wish you all to be happy to return to your country with your families. . . . We can shake hands and wait for the day we meet again."

Bác Thuận also brought a live chicken that he offered for our final dinner at the base camp. Flabbergasted at the notion, the team leader hesitated: "What the fuck will we do with a chicken?" But others, in urgent, hushed tones, pushed him to receive the gift with the proper decorum. They understood that to refuse to accept it was to reject the bonds that the past month's hours of intense, communal labor had forged—in Bác Thuận's words, "so much love and emotion" felt at the mission's end. The chicken spent the rest of the afternoon tied up in a bag under the kitchen hooch, until one of the team members, who beneath his veneer of grit and bravado honed in the forward operating bases of Iraq, took pity on the bird and, simultaneously cursing it for its incessant squawking and gently pulling at the knots that bound its leg, untied it. Already dusk, he carried the chicken up to the landing zone and walked it into the jungle, leaving it to its own fate. Like the others, he couldn't bring himself to kill the bird, but didn't want Old Man Shovel to return the next day to see what could only be perceived as the team's ingratitude for his gift. A willful beast, the chicken followed him back out of the jungle and under the bright stars wandered about the barren landing zone.

As the gifts given and received made clear, the bonds of reciprocity that arose among members of the two groups were temporary and asymmetrical.

The asymmetry stemmed from the war itself, part of the imbalance of the US-led enterprise—a recovery mission for American remains in a land scarred by US bombs and whose own numbers of missing dwarf the US MIA toll by hundreds of thousands. And yet these exchanges, especially the gifts between the American team members and Vietnamese workers, offered a means for expressing gratitude and for saying goodbye in the absence of a common language.

The next morning, we woke up early, broke down our tents, and packed our footlockers. Within hours the site was dismantled and the equipment flown out by helicopter. Then we hiked out, just as we had hiked in. With one exception.

June 17, 2012: Laurel and I are walking up the last incline of the dirt logging road, and she's handed me the black pelican case that contains the seven precious teeth, the three bits of bone, and the scraps of the wreckage that constitute material evidence. I take it in my hand and feel its weight as it swings by my side—the metaphysical weight of at least one of our five missing men now recovered. It's the lightest and heaviest thing I've carried in or out of the site; it's our collective achievement, resting in the grip of my hand. The main road nears, and I pass the case back to Laurel, the proper custodian. It's hers to walk out, her charge—and honor—to fulfill.

From start to finish, symbols and rituals marked the mission and the various transformations that it spurred, with the most important among them centering on the remains themselves. Once back in Đà Nẵng, where all the teams (six recovery teams and one investigation team) had reassembled, these teeth and fragments of bone became the objects of a final display of expertise and authority: the joint Vietnamese and US scientific examination at the conclusion of the mission, known as the Joint Forensic Review. Laurel had handed over the recovered "possible human remains" to the VNO once we left the site, and they remained in the Vietnamese officials' custody until this formal joint review. The event took place at the resort hotel where we stayed on our arrival to the country. In one of its conference rooms, American and Vietnamese forensic anthropologists and odontologists convened to examine and debate the status of the remains— whether they were human (and not animal); whether they were American remains (and not Vietnamese). If the experts agreed with one another that the osseous material might indeed be human, and likely American, the

Vietnamese would grant the permission necessary for repatriation—that is, to be transported back to the United States.

On this occasion, the teeth recovered from our site offered the Vietnamese and American odontologists an opportunity to compare methods; subtle corrections to mistakes in identifying the precise kind of tooth were followed with equally courteous words of gratitude and praise. Extracted from sealed plastic evidence bags, examined and photographed, and again stored according to the chain-of-custody protocol, the remains entered the realm of scientific analysis, where they would reside until they yielded enough data to restore individual identity and allow for individualized commemoration. In short, before they could belong again to a human being, one or more of the MIAs from the crash site, they belonged to the nation and, specifically, to its military forensic guardians. The following day, the Vietnamese authorities formally handed over the black evidence cases filled with the possible remains before the repatriation ceremony on the tarmac of the Đà Nẵng airport.

The occasion illustrated how scientific practice and military ritual worked in tandem to redefine the recovered remains as sacred objects, ushering them from one state of existence (unrecovered remnants of a helicopter crash) and one sphere of meaning (biological material) to another (a revered, symbolic object of the nation). This is one of the most important aspects of rituals—they allow social groups to signify and set apart the sacred from the everyday and the mundane. Rituals also help usher objects and people through liminal space, that ambiguous position "betwixt and between."[32] More often than not, we tend to think of rituals as religious acts—prayers, hymns, rites, and so on—but rituals arise in the most secular of contexts as well, where they assign and protect meaning. The screening station at the top of the mountain slope, for example, was a space governed by ritual; there was something deeply transformative in the act of picking out bits of metal, cloth, glass, tooth, and bone from countless screens of nothing other than rocks, sticks, and leaves. We changed the most ordinary artifacts into the sacred, turning them over in our hands and then dropping them into the bucket designated for recovered wreckage, for vestiges of the air crash and its human losses. We had recognized something special and set it apart. For "sacredness as an attribute is not an absolute; it is brought into play by the nature of particular situations."[33] Indeed, it was the ritual act of screening that prompted one of the most powerful moments of the mission: when the first tooth was recovered and its consequence rippled through us, the assembly of

American team members and Vietnamese workers on the ridgetop. We had found someone, one of them, in a tiny fragment of a human being. In that instant, the entire mission changed.

So too the repatriation ceremony that marked the first leg in the long journey home toward identification and commemoration turned on ritual. Its symbols and scripted motion transformed the remains into something more than simply bits of bone found on a mountainside or objects of scientific examination. It was there, in this public celebration of recovery, that they first became sanctioned emblems of national sacrifice.

Military ceremony enabled this "rite of passage," this transformation in the meaning ascribed to the remains.[34] Here we see how rituals also entail performance and require audiences, whether present or imagined, to achieve that transformation. Just as the month-long recovery efforts, the daily rites of digging and screening, performed American care for its dead to both current service members and the Vietnamese laborers and officials, the ceremony on the tarmac that day performed the ritual of repatriation to American and Vietnamese audiences alike. The team members stood at attention in their Class B uniforms, sharp and polished. Some served as guards. Others were assigned to carry the remains and place them gingerly within the silver transfer cases—the same kind used to transport US bodies back from Afghanistan and Iraq to Dover Air Force Base and into the care of mortuary affairs specialists, like the two on our mission. Once secure inside those cases, the remains were covered in the American flag—brought under the aegis of US control. Those tasked with the flag draping had practiced over and over the snap that unfurls the cloth; their motion perfectly synchronized, the flag hung taut above the case. In that single instant of suspense before the nation's literal and figurative reclamation took place, everyone's attention was riveted. Then, finally, with the flag tucked securely around it, the coffin was lifted and carried into the gaping belly of the awaiting aircraft and the next destination, the Central Identification Laboratory in Hawaii.

The Time in Between

FOR ALL THE TIME I have spent researching the recovery and identification of missing persons—first in Bosnia and Herzegovina, and now in the United States—I still struggle with one particular act: contacting surviving families to ask them about their lives and about their missing loved ones. However I might justify it with grander aims of understanding the experiences of those most intimately connected to the processes of caring for war dead, the request is an intrusion. It comes from a stranger, who asks to tread upon a realm of memory and emotion that is quite private and, for many, still raw, no matter how many years have passed since the news of loss or disappearance. Sometimes, the request is met with wariness, sometimes with polite but tacit refusal. More often than not, I have benefited from the generosity of families who, without knowing exactly what anthropology is or ethnographic research entails, have answered yes.

Their stories inform my exploration of "homecomings," when identified remains are finally returned to their surviving kin. In these homecomings, we see yet another side of exceptional care, a more localized, private version than the pageantry on the tarmac in Đà Nẵng or the celebration of First Lieutenant Michael J. Blassie's identification presented in the Memorial Room at the Tomb of the Unknowns. Not that the nation is absent or these homecomings don't involve military rituals of remembrance. They do. But homecomings expose the layers of grief sedimented in the lives of those left to contend with uncertain loss for decades on end; they also evoke forms of commemoration that have as much to do with a local "home," defined by family and community, as with the *patria* to which the remains have been returned. Finally, through these stories of homecoming, we see how even the tiniest fraction of a body, located, identified, and returned through the myriad labors of accounting, can do the magical, powerful work, in Laqueur's words, of settling safely the missing in action or killed in action/body not recovered into memory and into a proper place of posthumous belonging.[1]

Dwayne Spinler was one of the MIA family members who shared his experiences and memories with me. Son of an air force pilot shot down in 1967, Dwayne was just five years old when his father, Captain Darrell John Spinler (the same Capt. Spinler of REFNO 0738 in Chapter 2), left for the war. His last memory of his dad is riding in the car with him to the airport. Dwayne cried the whole way there and the whole way back because he was scared that his father wouldn't come home.

"And he didn't."

Dwayne and his wife, Dawn, were among the families who came to JPAC in 2011 to take custody of identified remains and escort them home. I accompanied them as they toured the facility and watched as they stepped into the family visitation room to behold all that now remained of Dwayne's father—three scant teeth, bluish in color, a rusted pocket knife, and a pair of nail clippers. I also looked on when, earlier in the visit, he spoke with Marin Pilloud, the anthropologist who had helped recover his father's remains. This too was an intrusion of sorts, or so it felt to me as part of the small group of JPAC staff who stood nearby as their conversation unfolded. Its intensity had filled the hall outside the forensic anthropology examination room.

Dwayne is a tall, sturdy-looking man. As I would learn later, he takes after his father, who at six feet four was strikingly handsome, with broad shoulders and chiseled jaw. Dwayne explained that in flight training school, his father was "almost too tall to qualify, because there was a concern that he wouldn't fit in the cockpit." Perhaps that frame, the son's physical stature, was what made the next few moments so arresting. As Marin was wrapping up, having given the tour and talked briefly about the recovery mission she and veteran archaeologist Greg Fox had directed at his father's crash site, Dwayne asked if he could hug Marin. He leaned down—he was much taller than she—and as they embraced, he began to cry, at first softly and then his whole frame shook with muffled sobs. Marin's eyes filled with

Captain Darrell John Spinler with his wife, Darlene.

tears as he whispered to her "thank you" over and over. As she explained to me later, she was twelve weeks pregnant with her own son at the time and felt Dwayne's loss all the more keenly for it. The rest of us stood transfixed and silent, as if even a shift in weight would pierce the bubble of solace that had enveloped them.

When he stepped away, Dwayne once more thanked her for finding his father.

As I would with several of the cases I researched at the laboratory, I followed Capt. Spinler's story of homecoming from afar. Newspaper coverage helped sketch a portrait of his momentous return:

> Now tiny Browns Valley, population 600, expects to double its size for a day this month, when Darrell Spinler's remains return home for a full military funeral.
>
> Spinler's parents have since passed away, and no close relatives remain in Browns Valley. But the town, a farming community in Traverse County on the border with South Dakota, is bracing to accept a long lost hero back home.
>
> "We've just been trying to do what we can. If we get 600 visitors, it could make a real mess in town. We're just trying to coordinate traffic control and making sure everybody's got a place to go," said Jeff Cadwell, the city administrator.[2]

Dwayne himself went on to publish an essay online recounting his family's experience. In "Bringing Dad Home," he chronicled the various events—from the first phone call he received to his father's burial in Browns Valley—interspersing his reflections with photographs of the journey, its way-stops, and the people who gathered to welcome his father home. A modest work on the surface, it encapsulates the experience of MIA accounting from a family member's perspective. Among other things, Dwayne Spinler concludes, "family is not limited by genetics or marriage. You can find family anywhere."[3] Marin was part of that expanding, if ephemeral, web of familial ties. "When I first learned who she was," he wrote, "I remember wanting to reach out and touch her arm, this person I did not know, so intimately linked to my father."[4]

While the notion of kinship forged through the return of remains arose repeatedly in the course of my fieldwork with MIA families, Dwayne's essay—alongside the poignant encounter between him and the anthropologist who "found" his father—crystallized the unique memory work that advances in forensic science have enabled. But to understand fully that work requires an intrusion into the most personal of recollections—those associated with someone loved and lost. Would Dwayne be willing to speak with me about his father's life, his loss, the years of ambiguity, and finally that homecoming to Browns Valley, Minnesota? Would he be willing to allow an outsider access to those memories?

And so, six years after watching Dwayne come to the lab to receive his father's remains, I sent him a letter: *"Dear Mr. Spinler, I hope you won't mind me reaching out to you."*

EARLIER I ARGUED THAT MIA HOMECOMINGS, though the celebrated endpoints in the longer journey of recovery and identification, necessarily have their beginnings. So too they have their middles, the time in between, a time of survival and endurance. I am speaking here not of the missing in action, but rather the parents, spouses, and children left behind. For those families who await news of their loved one, ambiguity and uncertainty disturb memories and color imaginings with shades of confusion, hope, grief, anger, and fear. Dwayne Spinler's outpouring of sorrow, I soon came to learn, grew out of that "time in between" as much as it did from the unexpected return of his father's remains. This was one of the lessons I learned when we finally spoke—one that the narrative of exceptional care often sidesteps—namely, the profound imprint that prolonged and ambiguous absence leaves on those who wait and wonder about the "what ifs" of their loved one's fate and their own life's course. A couple of weeks after I sent it, Dwayne answered my letter, and not long afterward, he told me about his life after his father's death and before the return of his remains.

As is the case for many of the MIA children I've spoken with, when he lost his father, Dwayne lost a piece of his innocence. But he was also burdened with a responsibility of care few young children ever come to know. On the day of the "initial" funeral service in 1967, when relatives gathered to mourn Captain Darrell John Spinler's loss, a close family friend, one of his father's mentors from the air force, instructed Dwayne to take up that burden:

> When I was a kid I remember him very clearly telling me this. I think it was at the initial funeral, 'cause they didn't find any of my dad's remains at that time. This was up in Minnesota. I actually have some newspaper clippings of a picture of my dad's father, my grandfather, my mom, me, and my brother, as they were giving my mother either the flag or purple heart or something like that. And I remember

Colonel Tudor telling me "Ok, you got to be the man of the house, you got to take care of your mom," and, you know, my dad died when I was like six and a half years old. And I'm sure his intentions were good, but, you know, for me, as a kid—it's no mistake I got into the mental health field as a profession—that he didn't know how seriously I took that. And for me, I didn't tell anybody, I had nobody really to talk to, and I kind of assumed, ok, because my mom really struggled with my dad's death for many years. Which eventually turned into depression, then she was on medication. Her first suicide attempt was when I was eight.[5]

At the time, Dwayne didn't know the full story. The adults in his world decided it would be better to shield him, to tell him that she had slipped in the bathroom and hit her head against the sink. But even then, he recalled, "it still didn't feel like they were telling me the truth." Years later, hospitalized once again for attempting to take her life, his mother acknowledged what had happened on that first occasion. If her admission shed light on a confusing, troubling episode from his childhood, it also underscored what Dwayne had long witnessed firsthand—his mother's daily battle to survive her husband's loss. Her emotional fragility introduced another layer of precarity into his life. "As a young kid, I had the sense that, well, Dad's gone, he got killed in the war, and I'd seen Mom struggling with her sorrow and grieving and it turned into depression, and I think, well, I got to take care of Mom, because if something happens to Mom, what's going to happen to me?" In her bereavement she sought comfort in private rituals of remembrance, ones that Dwayne took care not to trespass. "There would be times," he explained, "where she'd pull out this suitcase that would be in storage which would have a lot of the letters that my mom and dad would send back and forth when he was in Vietnam. I never read a single one for a reason. It's like it's not my business. That was between my dad and my mom. And you know that would contribute to her feeling sorrowful and sad."

Then early one morning, when Dwayne was in graduate school, he got a call from his father's mentor, Colonel Tudor.

I thought, who the hell is calling me at 8 o'clock on a Monday? And I just had this gut feeling, and it's like, well, it's probably not good news. And it was Colonel Tudor on the phone. And he said, "Dwayne, this is Colonel Tudor, and I don't know how to tell you this other than to just tell you, but your mom has committed suicide the previous night." She had been drinking alcohol, and took an overdose of medications, and on top of that she was in her car in the condo garage with a hose attached to the exhaust pipe, so asphyxiation. And my half-sister, who's like eleven years younger than I, she was asleep in the condo, down in her basement bedroom, and fortunately my mom turned the ignition off on the car. Otherwise the fumes probably would have killed my half-sister too. So my half-sister found her and called the police.

Grief has a way of churning up guilt, warranted or self-imposed, forcing it to the surface of even the stillest waters. When Dwayne spoke to me about his mother's struggles with depression, he did so alternately as a son and a professional counselor, recounting his own frustrated attempts to support her through the tools of mental health care he himself was in the process of learning at the time. "What was hard for me was for a lot of the years my mom was alive, she'd call me up, I'd be in school, college, undergraduate or graduate school, she'd be sad, depressed, sometimes intoxicated, and I'd talk her down. My mom wasn't a bad person, she just had a bad illness, and she never got over my dad's death." Without him, without even the solace of his returned remains, Dwayne's mother suffered, and there was little Dwayne could do to lessen that suffering, try as he might, including through one final, touching gesture to comfort his mother by honoring his father.

About a week before the call I got from Colonel Tudor saying that she had committed suicide, I had had a conversation with my mom, to let her know that I was about to be a father and that my girl-friend, we were going to get married, and we already knew the sex of the baby. It was going to be a boy. And I told my mom that we were going to name him after my father. And it was met with about fifteen seconds of just silence on the other end of the phone. And I'm just thinking, "Oh crap, this is going to upset her or something."

My mom never got to meet my son. She died before he was born. A week after was when she committed suicide. And so I struggled with feelings of guilt. You know, here I am studying this profession, and I've talked her down numerous times on the phone, and it's like I'm a graduate student, I'm not an expert in this field, I'm trying to become an expert. But it felt like I had failed my job.

Eventually I came to the realization that I didn't cause my mom's suicide. I didn't do it to her. She didn't do it to me. . . . She did it to herself, and it hurt. It was a really sad situation.

As his mother's unabated, and ultimately debilitating, grief brought an end to her life, it also predominated Dwayne's "in between," stretching across his childhood and adolescence and inflecting his relationships in marriage and fatherhood, well after her death in 1985. And then he got a call out of the blue in February 2011, forty-four years after the news of his father's air crash. Captain Darrell John Spinler—the three teeth Marin and the JPAC team excavated on the bank of the Xe Kong River in Laos—had been accounted for, and Dwayne would serve as the special escort to shepherd those tiny fragments back to Browns Valley to be buried alongside his father's parents, grandparents, and grief-stricken wife.

One of the striking features of his essay, "Bringing Dad Home," is Dwayne's attentiveness to those around him and the spontaneous acts of remembrance his father's remains spurred. Though he insists that "you can find family anywhere," a particular kind of familial bond—that born of military service—stands out among the myriad encounters he chronicles along the journey from Hawaii to Browns Valley. On one of the flights, he spotted a man with a Vietnam Veterans baseball cap, and, after the pilot announced that Dwayne and his wife were escorting his father's remains home (to the applause of fellow passengers), Dwayne got out of his seat and approached the veteran. He wanted to thank him for his service. "I knelt down on one knee and we shared a firm handshake while exchanging mutual heartfelt tears together." In his work, Dwayne has counseled numerous veterans. "I have always recognized the unique pain seen in the eyes of a veteran." He and the older man "shared a moment" and then he returned to his seat. A few minutes later, the man reached up to his overhead bag, removed his Vietnam Veterans cap, and walked down the aisle toward Dwayne and his wife. Tearing up again, the man asked, "Would you place this in the casket for me on behalf of all our Vietnam brothers?" Dwayne told him he would be honored to do so.[6] The gift of a seemingly mundane article—a baseball cap—from a total stranger—a man Dwayne had never met before and would likely never see again—would come to rest in that most sacred of spaces: the coffin. It would lie nested next to the full Class A uniform, meticulously ironed and fixed with medals earned in war, and atop the traditional wool blanket, itself pinned securely around

Family and friends assembled at Captain Darrell Spinler's graveside, including Dwayne (center, dark suit), his brother David (to his right), wife Dawn (to his left), and son Darrell John (behind him).

three teeth. Having been plucked from the banks of a river halfway around the globe, those tiny remnants of a human life, along with the cap, the uniform, an MIA bracelet worn in remembrance, and the bundle of letters that Dwayne never read, the ones exchanged by his mother and father while the war raged on, would all be lowered into the hollowed-out plot of a cemetery in a small town on the border between Minnesota and South Dakota.

IF DWAYNE SPINLER TAUGHT me about the knotted grief that can grow in the spaces and years between loss and homecoming for MIA families, Jeff Savelkoul helped me understand what MIA absence might mean for a veteran. Their experiences likewise affirmed the powerful event of a homecoming, when the living and the dead become entwined in a project of national belonging that nevertheless unfolds according to local traditions of remembrance and recalling specific histories of loss. They also helped me appreciate how such remains could invite new configurations of family, when kith and kin and strangers alike convene to remember not just a distant war, but a life lost and, decades later, returned to a particular community of mourners.

A survivor of the CH-46 helicopter crash that killed radio operator Lance Corporal Merlin Raye Allen, Jeff Savelkoul came back to the United States in 1967 a physically scarred man with a battered, broken, and burned body—to say nothing of a psyche that in the aftermath of the fiery crash on the mountain slope also had to absorb the fact of his best friend's death. That fact eventually brought him to the driveway, the top of the gravel lane, of the Allen family property in Bayfield, Wisconsin. He felt he had to visit them but feared their reaction, especially to his physical appearance; a significant portion of his ears had been burned off when the rear fuel tank was struck and flames had shot through helicopter. "If I looked this bad, what would they think their son endured? I made four trips from Minneapolis to Bayfield—a four-hour trip. I'd get there and turn around at the end of the Allens' driveway and go back home. I just couldn't face them. Finally, after sixteen years and four tries, I got up the courage and walked up to the house. It turned out to be one of the greatest things I've ever done in my life."[7]

Merl's mother, Eleanor, opened the door. She was taken aback, but not for the reasons Savelkoul had feared. Rather, his story defied everything she and her husband knew of the helicopter crash that killed their son. They had been told by the military that no one had survived. And yet there at their doorstep stood this stranger, claiming not only to have known their son, but to have served with him in Vietnam and to have survived the very same crash. To hear Jeff and Merl's sister, Marilyn, tell it, Skip Allen, Merl's father, didn't believe a word of it. He was immediately suspicious of Jeff's claims. Not until Marilyn arrived—her husband Ralph was on the Bayfield police force, and the Allens called him to tell Marilyn to rush home—did the truth begin to sink in. Marilyn knew of Jeff from her brother's letters home and had even exchanged letters with Jeff herself. He was who he said he was, a member of Team Striker, and Merl's best friend during the months of war they lived through and waged in 1967.

From that day forward, Jeff became a part of the Allen family, growing close to Merl's parents and five siblings, especially his brothers, Casey and Sean Allen. They'd go hunting and fishing together, and over time, Jeff shared details about Vietnam and about the helicopter crash. For Sean, who was twenty-two years old when they met, Jeff allowed him the "chance to know my brother as an adult." Among his family, he explained, "We didn't talk about Merle too much." (Merl's childhood nickname was

"Merle," pronounced Merlie, but as he grew older, he preferred Merl.) "I was the youngest of six kids—three boys and three girls—I was the baby of the family. I remember my mom crying a lot, but I never really knew why. It was later on, years later, that I understood. But it was hard not knowing the details of Merle's death. It helped to know what happened."[8] For Eleanor too, Jeff's arrival provided some modicum of relief. Years later, just before her death, she summoned Jeff to her side and told him what a difference his coming to the door that day meant in her life. And she left him with a final request: "Jeff, you go find the other mothers and tell them—you tell them the truth, that's what they want to know."[9] However painful the prospect, it was a charge Savelkoul embraced. "I was afraid to share that story again, so two of the members of Team Hawk [another team from the marine corps' Third Reconnaissance Battalion, Alpha Company] dropped what they were doing, left their jobs, and went with me. We went around [the country] and visited the family members and the headstones, and monuments, of my teammates on Team Striker. Just as Eleanor had requested."[10] By that time, the Allen family had already erected their own stone-and-concrete memorial marker for Merl out at York Island in Lake Superior; both Eleanor and her husband, Alden "Skip" Allen, would be laid to rest beside it, but before their son returned home.

2004 proved a monumental year for Jeff, though in our conversations, first over diner fare and later over the phone, he only mentioned one part of the story. That was the year when Jeff got the promising news of a breakthrough in the military's efforts to locate the site of the helicopter crash. A joint investigation team had recovered a few articles that appeared to be associated with the loss incident, among them a full deck of fifty-two playing cards—all aces of spades—still wrapped in plastic, and Jeff's own rosary. The cards, Jeff explained, had an important story behind them, one directly tied to Merl and the brutality, both psychological and physical, of jungle warfare:

> Merl was always scheming up something, and constantly writing letters. Recon's trademark was the ace of spades. It had a significant PSYOP [psychological operations] value. The NVA [North Vietnamese Army] were very superstitious and terrified of them and we left them in "very significant" places in the bush.[11] We were handmaking our own cards there in country and getting the company clerk to copy them for us. Merl got this idea and wrote to Bicycle

Merl Allen.

Playing Card Co. He explained our situation and the next thing we know Bicycle sent Merl 52 decks of 52 aces of spades each. Merl was our hero. The rest of us carried a few to the bush, but Merl carried a whole deck.[12]

While the cards evoked Merl's memory, for Jeff the rosary had an especially powerful, proliferating symbolism. Through its recovery—from the very site and soil of the mountain slope—he felt his connection to the lives left behind: "Along with it came a little bit of dirt and, I feel, the souls of my lost teammates." Conjoining the places of war (and death) with the places of home (and birth), he took six of the rosary beads, "one for each of the lost, some dirt from each of their markers and some dirt from the Khe Sanh airstrip [part of the marine corps combat base where he first met Merl]," and left them, along with an account of the crash, at the foot of Merl's memorial on York Island. At last, he wrote, "the team is back home together, at least in spirit."[13]

What he didn't tell me was that in August of that very same year—2004, thirty-seven years after the crash—Jeff Savelkoul was awarded a bronze star for his efforts to save fellow members of Team Striker. The delay in the medal's conferral resulted from both the catastrophic event and the conditions of the war itself, which was in the middle of one of its most lethal years—at least in terms of American casualties.[14] In the military, medal recipients can only be nominated by persons higher in the chain of command, and in this case, they had all died; or so it was believed, until decades later, when it was discovered that an officer had been transferred into the battalion three days before the crash. He was still alive and thus still able to put in for the award. The official citation notes, "Realizing that other members of his patrol and the crew were still trapped inside the helicopter, Lance Corporal Savelkoul tried to assist other members but was not successful." Even this singled-out merit he deflected back onto Merl and the others who died in the crash. "It's nice to be recognized, but more importantly, it recognizes the guys who didn't come home. . . . This is for them," he insisted.[15]

In February 2013, when the Marine Corps Casualty Office contacted Marilyn and her siblings with the news of Merl's recovery and identification, it was decided among them that Jeff, for years already considered a member of the family, would travel to Hawaii to serve as the special escort, accompanied by an active duty marine corps escort. By that time, the Department of Defense had ceased its program to fund family members' travel to the island to take custody of remains and escort them home, as Dwayne Spinler had. So the duty—in Jeff's words, the honor—fell to him. On the phone from Honolulu to a reporter in Wisconsin, he explained how he had dreamed every night for forty-six years of Merl's return. "Some days it's not real—but it is now. I just closed his coffin, I'm getting ready to board the aircraft. He's coming home."[16] Once en route, Jeff shared a letter with the pilots of the flights from Honolulu to Los Angeles and Los Angeles to Minneapolis/St. Paul in which he described Merl's service and the helicopter crash and explained that he was escorting home the remains of his "teammate, best friend, and hero, from the jungles of Vietnam, 46 years later." "I thought you'd like to know."[17] During the five-hour lay-over in Los Angeles, the Delta Air Lines ground crew supervisor "didn't think an American hero should just sit on the tarmac" and so arranged for a space in an adjacent warehouse where Jeff could wait with Merl. "We drove all the way around LAX. I rode with Merl and couldn't hold back the tears. As we passed, every truck, every plane (!) stopped. Every ground crew stood at attention, hands on hearts. When we finally got Merl settled, the ground crew all pitched in and bought us a pizza."[18]

As Jeff's descriptions underscore, homecomings such as Lance Corporal Merlin Allen's are both highly public and intensely private affairs. Out of respect, though I was aware of his identification, I waited until one year had passed before contacting the Allen family about my research and my role in the recovery mission. What follows is an account gleaned from various perspectives—from members of the Allen family and Jeff Savelkoul, veterans at the Duwayne Soulier Memorial VFW post in Red Cliff, attendees of the memorial service, media coverage, and from Amanda Wilmot, the professional photographer whose keen eye captured the homecoming's route, events, and above all, the people assembled in the work of remembrance that began at the Minneapolis/St. Paul airport on June 28, 2013, and ended on York Island, Lake Superior, the next day, June 29—one day shy of the forty-sixth anniversary of the helicopter crash. Her photographs, which the family shared with me, shed light on this public/private dynamic of LCpl Allen's homecoming, often providing a visual corrective for scenes I could only imagine based on conversations with those who had gathered to bring Merl home. Though she would explain to me later that "most of the photographs that day were taken blindly because there were constantly tears in my eyes," she understood the gravity of the task as "documenting a part history," indeed a history that was "continuing to unfold."

When the plane touched down at the Minneapolis/St. Paul airport in the early morning of June 28, people were ready. Members of the Allen family, Jeff Savelkoul, and Mariano "Junior" Guy, the one other Team Striker survivor of the CH-46 crash, the funeral director from Bratley Funeral Home in Washburn, Wisconsin, and the six members of the marine corps honor guard detail, in their crisp uniforms and white gloves, were waiting on the tarmac. The Minnesota Patriot Guard Riders had already assembled at their nearby staging site and been debriefed by 5:45 a.m. "Bring your 3×5 flag and pole, water, and everything you need to be self-sufficient"—that is, prepared to show their "respect and honor, and finally say 'Welcome Home' to this Vietnam War hero."[19] Once the honor guard had lifted the flag-draped coffin from the aircraft cargo container and placed it in the black hearse, Merl's siblings drew close to touch it, one by one, reunited with their brother (his single tooth) at long last. Shortly thereafter, the convoy departed, met by the Patriot Guard Riders just outside the airport, to begin the two-hundred-mile journey to northern Wisconsin. After crossing the St. Croix River, the Minnesota riders passed the baton of escort to the Wisconsin chapter. They too were at the ready, eighteen bikes in total, joined by Wisconsin State Patrol, county sheriffs, and local police from towns along the way. Formed in 2005 in response to the Westboro Baptist Church and its shameful, bigoted protests staged at military funerals, the Patriot Guard Riders' mission is two-fold.[20] As invited guests of the family, they are to "show our sincere respect for our fallen heroes, their families, and their communities" and "shield the mourning family and their friends from interruptions created by any protester or group of protesters," doing so through "strictly legal and non-violent means."[21] For especially charged scenes, the thunderous revving of their engines works to drown out the protesters' hate-filled chants. In this instance, however, the Allens needed no shielding. On the contrary, from the Twin Cities, where well-wishers gathered on overpasses to glimpse the procession of cars and motorcycles, to Washburn, where local residents lined the streets, children included, saluting and waving flags, Merlin Allen was restored to his family and his home state with respectful, solemn fanfare.

His first place of temporary rest was the Bratley Funeral Home in Washburn, where friends and family gathered for a visitation from 6:00 to 8:00 p.m. Patriot Guard Riders in their black leather and jean-jacket vests, armbands, and ball caps stood vigil on the sidewalk outside the building. Their row of three-by-five flags mirrored the sea of red, white, and blue across the street, where scores of handheld flags had been stuck in the boulevard grass and others fluttered in the breeze atop the several dozen flag poles—one for each fallen soldier from Washburn, from WWII onward—in the American Legion memorial flag park across the street. Inside in the funeral home, LCpl Allen's remains sat on a small table covered in white cloth. The family had traded out the military's standard wooden urn in favor of a polished box wrought by Casey Allen's own hands; he picked cherry, a hardwood that Merl had used in most of his own woodworking projects. A display of flowers, artifacts, and photographs surrounded it, including a tripod bearing a framed collection of the medals LCpl Allen had earned in Vietnam, as well as a mounted copy of Executive Order #106 by Wisconsin's governor Scott Walker. On the occasion of Allen being "laid to rest forty-six years after sacrificing his life on behalf of his nation, far from American soil"—a faint echo of Merl's own prescient words back in 1967 when he lodged his protest of the proposed national lakeshore park—Walker decreed that "the flag of the United States and the flag of the State of Wisconsin shall be flown at half-staff at all buildings, grounds, and military installations of the State of Wisconsin equipped with such flags beginning at sunrise on Saturday, June 29, 2013, and ending at sunset on that date."[22] While the executive order signaled the official recognition of Merl's return, the visitation marked the start of a series of localized—both communal and familial—rituals that drew him closer and closer into the intimate sites of his hometown and his youth before war.

The following day, people from Bayfield, Red Cliff, Washburn, and neighboring townships and cities of the North Woods assembled in the gymnasium of the Bayfield High School for a memorial service. Veterans from the region, their branch and membership telegraphed by legion hats, pins, and patches, had arrived to pay their respects. Children and adults filled the folding chairs and packed into the bleachers, many of them wearing yellow ribbons—an emblem of military absence and plea for swift return—pinned to their shirts. To a slideshow projecting images of Merl and scenes from their youth, siblings Cindy, Marilyn, and Casey each recalled their brother, to laughter and tears. So too did "Junior" Guy, who had assumed the role of special escort upon Merl's arrival in Washburn. Standing before the podium's microphone, flanked by fellow Team Striker member Jeff Savelkoul, Junior recounted the fateful day and his anguish at losing Merl and the others. He wept openly before the family and the crowd.

"Grief is a state of mind; bereavement a condition," historian Jay Winter writes. "Both are mediated by mourning."[23] In tracing mourning's pathway

Members of the Minnesota Patriot Guard Riders await LCpl Allen's arrival.

Sean Allen reunited with his brother.

Before the memorial service at the Bayfield High School.

On the dock at Little Sand Bay (front row), Mariano "Junior" Guy, Marilyn Neff, Sean Allen, and Jeff Savelkoul.

Carrying Merl home, Mariano "Junior" Guy and Jeff Savelkoul.

The memorial stone on York Island where Merl Allen is buried, alongside his parents, Eleanor and Alden Allen.

Impromptu tributes on York Island.

Cindy Hawkins sprinkling sand on her brother's final resting place.

from initial discovery to eventual commemoration undertaken by communities during and after World War I, he notes how "kinship bonds widened"—what we might see as foreshadowing Dwayne Spinler's "you can find family anywhere" or Jeff Savelkoul's bond with the Allen siblings and his charge from Merl's mother. In the case of the Spinler and Allen families, rituals of mourning so delayed seemed to widen these bonds of kinship, however fleeting or enduring, even further. The return of a long-absent fallen service member invited a sense of communion that others were eager to share in; as the flag-festooned streets of Washburn, Bayfield, Red Cliff, and Russell Township announced, the news of homecoming tapped into notions of national belonging and obligation. Dwayne Spinler homes in on this aspect of mourning's generative effect in his essay: "We met many people who knew my father as a child, in high school, or college. We were grateful for the stories they shared of their time with him. We also met people from the area who had never met him but knew of him. Others had never heard of him until recently. Many came to pay their respects while some just knew they needed to be with us but did not really know why."[24]

To be sure, such a response to identified and returned MIAs is by no means exclusive to the Vietnam War. I once attended a funeral at Arlington National Cemetery for a service member who had been missing in action (unaccounted for) from World War II. Though on a smaller scale than the memorial service held in the Bayfield High School, men, women, and children had gathered at the graveside in Arlington to witness the interment. The three-volley rifle salute, taps, the folded flag handed over to next of kin—there didn't seem a dry eye among the group of mourners in those moments of ritualized military burial. Only later did I learn that not a single person among the assembled had a firsthand memory of the deceased. None had known him in the sense of ever shaking his hand, sitting around the same kitchen table, or hearing his voice. And yet his marked return had drawn people, total strangers and distant relatives, into the orb of protracted mourning. Here we can see the capacity of missing war dead to foster and stretch bonds of kinship, so much so that acts of mourning the decades-absent fallen come home can leapfrog generations and stir sympathies both phantasmal in origin and immediate in force.

But the unique memory work enabled by the return of MIA remains— "fullest possible accounting" come to fruition—isn't just about widening bonds of kinship. It's also about the capacity for those remains, even a single tooth recovered and repatriated, to foster both personalized narra-

tives and localized (rather than strictly national) rituals, and this is where
the particular history of the Vietnam War comes into play more explicitly. In his book *Remembering War the American Way,* historian G. Kurt
Piehler argues that the "federal government, by neglecting rituals and memorials, contributed to the alienation of those who fought in this
struggle."[25] That alienation extended to the memory of MIAs and their
surviving kin as well. Eventually, alienation yielded to the pressures of national memory politics, when demands of "Bring 'em home or send us
back" and "Until the last man comes home" gave way to a sophisticated
scientific enterprise of MIA accounting.

If the ensuing ethos of exceptional care sought to rehabilitate the nation's
record in war—among other ways, through the bodies of its unaccounted
for—then their return offered local communities a chance to redress that
alienation—proof positive of the POW/MIAs slogan, "You are not forgotten." Four and five decades on, homecoming from a war whose stained
history had stained its combatants by association in the immediate
postwar years, shifted the focus away from the nation and back onto a
single life—a youthful life, a family left behind, and a hometown that could
now simultaneously celebrate and mourn his return. Such celebrations,
however cut by sorrow, centered on stories. As Jeff Savelkoul explained
just before he escorted his best friend home from Hawaii, "The world needs
to be told his story. Because then people don't die in vain and then get forgotten."[26] And so the newspaper coverage of the memorial service for
Merlin Allen told his story, and told the story of that storytelling:

> Before Allen, whose nickname was Merl, enlisted in the Marines he
> was a kid with an infectious smile who liked girls, cars and hanging
> out with his friends. His room was messy. He snuck *Mad* magazines
> into the house. He liked to sleep late, somehow managing to listen
> for the school bus before leaping out of bed, dressing and catching
> the bus to school, said his younger sister Cindy Hawkins.
>
> Sometimes when he drove his younger siblings to church he talked
> them out of the money they were supposed to put in the collection
> plate and instead of going to Mass, he and his brothers and sisters
> bought chocolate milk and doughnuts, stopping to pick up a church
> bulletin to take home as "proof". . . .
>
> During the funeral, a montage of photos was shown to the
> crowd—pictures of Allen as a baby, posing for school pictures,
> swimming, smiling with his siblings, wearing his high school letter

sweater, proudly showing off his Marine dress blues uniform. The pictures showed Allen growing older, growing up, then stopping at the age of 20.

People in the crowd sniffled and fought back tears as the final photo showed his name on the Vietnam memorial wall.[27]

The details of the war itself come in bits and pieces in these articles, with allusions to the helicopter crash, the injuries sustained by Jeff, Junior's (the other survivor's) valiant efforts to assist the evacuation.[28] But depictions of war as war—the violence Merl and Junior and Jeff were trained to track and unleash, symbolized by that pack of fifty-two aces of spades, hardships Merl faced during his twenty months of service, even his frustration at sacrificing for his country when that country was taking away his family's land and his home—are strikingly absent. "True war stories," Viet Thanh Nguyen writes, riffing on Tim O'Brien's *The Things They Carried*, "acknowledge war's true identity, which is that while war is hell, war is normal, too. War is both inhuman and human, as are its participants."[29] And yet, by the logic of Nguyen's more expansive ethical memory, a public accounting that encompasses the inhuman alongside the human is a lot to ask of families for whom the "time in between" has already inflicted such pain, and who have just been reunited with their missing loved one after so many years of uncertainty.

Moreover, to read depictions of Merl's "infectious smile" or the portrait of a teenager with a "messy room" and a penchant for chocolate milk and doughnuts as merely a willful erasure of war's destruction or an intentionally partial memory misses an important facet of these stories. They are an inherently local act of reclamation, a different kind of exceptional care. That is to say, they move beyond the lofty, but often flattening, category of the "fallen hero," and instead return him, Merl, to the grounding details and relationships of his life before the war, in addition to his service in it. In doing so, stories help return him to his family as the proper guardians of that memory. It was the public telling of such stories, stories invited by the Allens and told by friends, relatives, former classmates, neighbors, local veterans, news media, and even strangers, that helped the Allen family traverse that final leg of their brother's journey home.

Before he could finally come to rest at home, first there would be a military send-off. Following the memorial service, the long stretch of vehicles, again escorted by the Patriot Guard Riders, wound its way up Highway 13 from Bayfield to Red Cliff. Past the Duwayne Soulier Memorial VFW post on the left, past Buffalo Bay on the right, named after the Chippewa elder who secured the Red Cliff Band territory on the Bayfield Peninsula a century and a half before, and past the Legendary Waters Casino and its marina, they eventually turned onto Old County Highway K and headed north to the campground at Little Sand Bay. Somewhere along Highway K, the column encountered a homespun billboard nailed to a hickory tree: "Now Entering ALLEN Country" it announced in red and blue lettering. Beneath it, on a separate white board, was a blown-up, grainy photograph of Merl in his utility uniform, framed on three sides by the marine corps seal. For those who knew the particular history of the Allen family's fight to hold on to their property back in the 1960s and 70s, the sign defiantly confronted the dispossessions of land, home, and child/brother, all sacrificed to the nation's domestic and foreign agendas. If only for this day, Merlin Allen's homecoming returned that stretch of sandy beach and the island he so cherished to his surviving family, especially his five siblings.

Part of Russell Township, Little Sand Bay is a public campground right on the edge of Lake Superior. I camped there for a few days during one of my visits to Bayfield and Red Cliff. Each morning I would wake up and head to the beach to walk along the narrow strip of dry sand. I'd find a spot, a piece of driftwood, where I'd leave my towel, and then I'd swim out a few yards. I didn't stay long in the water. Even in the height of summer the Great Lakes can be pretty chilly. I'd return to the main dock to dry off and warm up in the sun, its bright rays by then glinting off the water's surface. In some small way, I wanted to gain a sense for the *place* of Merl's homecoming—not just the flag-lined streets and the tourist-filled shops of Bayfield, but the more enduring spaces of his youth. "I, Merl Allen, will my beach at Sand Bay to the future senior class for their swingers next summer." The lake and its beaches were one of them; they were also the site of his official military funeral service, where the marine corps honor guard performed its ritual of gifting a folded flag to the fallen's next of kin. In fact, there would be two flags gifted, twice over, in a display of the widening bonds of kinship that the return of MIA remains had prompted.

The ceremony took place on the dock, where a clutch of black folding chairs had already been set up in neat rows. In front of them stood the same small table draped in white cloth and now flanked by two bright bouquets of red-white-and-blue-themed flowers. Following the honor guard and escort, Jeff and Junior passed between columns of saluting veterans from the region, including the Red Cliff VFW post members, Randy and Butch among them. Junior carried Merl. He placed him on the table, where two folded flags already rested. The family filed onto the dock and took their seats on the chairs, Junior, Marilyn, Sean, and Jeff in the first row, Cindy, Casey, and Sheila, along with spouses and children, behind them. It was a stunningly beautiful summer day, where the vibrant colors of a military funeral—the marine corps dress blues, the honor guard flags, the polished brass, and the gleaming wood of shouldered rifles—were all set off by the lake, sky, and shoreline. The rituals that followed centered on the flags, the material conduit between the military and the family as guardians of the dead. One by one, the honor guard detail unfolded the cloth from its tight triangle and un-furled it above Merl's urn, holding it aloft for the duration of the three-volley rifle salute. Among the hundreds of photographs that Amanda Wilmot snapped that day, there is one that captures the essence of the unique memory work enabled by Merl's homecoming: there on the dock, sitting together before the urn, before the single fragment of his recov-ered remains, the two siblings—the eldest and the youngest, Marilyn and Sean—and the two survivors, Jeff and Junior, hold each other's hands as they behold this final public tribute to Merl. They are the closest of kin in this instant. Once the honor guard detail had refolded the flags, they presented them one by one to Marilyn. She passed the first to Sean and held on to the next. And then they stood together, turned to Jeff and Junior, and gifted each with a flag.

Dwayne Spinler writes about this very moment in his essay, "Bringing Dad Home." For him, though the words spoken upon the presentation of the flag were haunting—"On behalf of the President of the United States, the Department of the Air Force, and a grateful nation, we offer this flag for the faithful and dedicated service of your father, Captain Darrell John Spinler"—they represented the first time in the whole process that he felt a "profound sense of peace." So too, Marilyn described her gradually shifting emotions. When she first learned Merl's remains had been recov-ered, she was elated. "But then reality set in. I felt pain, the same pain I felt when Merle was killed. As the days got closer to Merle coming home, the pain lessened. I felt peace in my heart the day we buried Merle on our beloved York Island."[30]

IN HIS QUIRKY TREATISE ON SPACE, place, and memory, *Species of Spaces*, Georges Perec writes, "I would like there to exist places that are stable, unmoving, intangible, untouched and almost untouchable, unchanging, deep-rooted; places that might be points of reference, of departure, of origin: My birthplace, the cradle of my family, the house where I may have been born, the tree I may have seen grow." But, he tells us, "such places don't exist," because just as time wears away at them, our memories also betray us. "Space melts like sand running through one's fingers. Time bears it away." For Perec, the writer, there is only one recourse—to write and thus to "leave somewhere a furrow, a trace, a mark or a few signs" of these fragile places.[31] But he overlooks other possibilities for keeping sites alive in our memories, as points of not only reference and departure, but also spaces of communion and commemoration. The Allen family crafted their own possibility the day they brought Merl home to York Island.

Once the military rites had been rendered at Little Sand Bay, the family and a select group from among the attendees boarded the *Outer Island,* a World War II navy vessel (a landing craft, tank) that had helped ferry troops, armor, and supplies to the beaches of Europe in 1944.[32] It was an ideal boat for the occasion, both for its historical significance and logistical reasons. It's about two and a half miles from the Little Sand Bay dock to the southern tip of York Island, where shallow waters and a sandy shoal prohibit other larger vessels from landing. The former amphibious assault craft could drop its ramp directly onto the island beach, allowing its passengers, from little children to more senior attendees, to disembark easily.

As special escort, Junior was entrusted with carrying Merl, the wooden box around which all activity now focused, to the burial site. The group made its way from the boat onto the island, threading through light brush to arrive at a small clearing several yards in from the water's edge. This place, too, I had visited, two years after the funeral, again to get a sense for where Lance Corporal Merlin Raye Allen finally rested. It is a serene place, bordered by a mix of northland woods—birch, fir, aspen, and pine—and with a carpet of island grass and wild flowers as ground cover. At its center stands the memorial to Merl. In the late summer of 1970, Casey and his father had hauled material over from the mainland, picking a calm day to tow a concrete mixer on their floating swimming dock behind their fourteen-foot Starcraft. Once there, they used beach aggregate to make the concrete and gathered stones from the island. "All the concrete had to be hauled up the steep hill in buckets," Casey explained, an act of commemoration that would be echoed some forty years later in the bucket chain that moved the soil up to the ridge at the excavation of Merl's crash site.[33] A few weeks later, their uncle Tom, Eleanor's brother, the son of a stonemason himself, layered the rocks and set the bronze plaque in the center:

IN MEMORY OF
MERLIN RAYE ALLEN
WISCONSIN
L CPL 3 RECON BN 3 MAR DIV
VIETNAM PH

OCT 22 1946   JUN 30 1967

In the intervening years, other markers have been added to the clearing. You can see the more informal "furrows" and "traces"—to borrow from Perec—left behind to punctuate private and collective journeys of commemoration. A tree trunk near the center of the space bears witness specifically to military memory, where various pins and patches are affixed to the bark, the majority of them marine corps emblems. When I visited there, a weathered ace of spades was tacked to the tree. But there are also permanent markers that attest to the intertwined military/family memorial significance of this spot on the island: in 2009, a stone placed by the Alpha Recon Association to honor its brothers "missing and fallen"; in 2007, on the fortieth anniversary of the helicopter crash, a monument to the five members of Team Striker killed, including Dennis Perry, who perished from his wounds two days later, as well as the pilot, Captain John House, with the inscription "Never Returned—Never Forgotten"; and most intimate of all, at the foot of Merl's memorial, the headstones of his parents, Eleanor Allen, who died in 1999, and Alden Allen, who died in 2001. At that same base, on June 29, 2013, Sean and Casey prepared to bury their older brother beside their parents.

At first, the island wasn't quite as willing a recipient as planned. The deep, narrow plot had filled with water overnight; though the sky was nearly cloudless that morning, it had rained heavily in the preceding days, leaving the ground saturated. Casey and Sean together had to press their weight onto the urn vault to submerge it. At last the vault settled into place, and the attendees, one by one, took a small handful of sand to sprinkle over the water-filled hole, bathing Merl in the grains of that beach he had so loved. He was finally at rest. From the mountainside in central Vietnam to the examination table in Hawaii to the clearing on

York Island, Merlin Raye Allen had traveled a long way to come home from war.

WHEN I ASKED THE ALLEN SIBLINGS—who, importantly, include Jeff Savelkoul—about whether it mattered to them that so little of their brother's physical remains was recovered and repatriated, they uniformly told me no. As Casey explained, "I was thrilled if one bone chip came home; I knew it was my brother, I finally knew his fate, and he was coming home."[34]

Their responses echoed Dwayne Spinler's. He too understood and accepted why more remains could not be found beyond the three teeth that Marin and the recovery team unearthed from the banks of the Xe Kong River; he trusted the validity of the science that correlated the loss incident with the excavation site and later identified the teeth; and, having escorted him back to Browns Valley, he considered his father home. Dwayne begins his essay, "Bringing Dad Home," recognizing the good—the exceptional—fortune of that homecoming made possible by a nation bent on returning its fallen to surviving kin: "I am not sure how you are supposed to feel when you find out that the remains of your father, who died in 1967 at age 29 during the Vietnam War, have been found 44 years later. I only know what I felt—shock . . . confusion . . . joy . . . sadness . . . all of the above. But mostly I was struck with the feeling that my family was extremely fortunate."[35]

✦ 1970 ✦

She kept them all. The sheaves of yellow Western Union telegrams, with their staccato barrage of block letters, announcing, one by one, her son's death and the stages of his body's transport home. On May 26, 1970:

> MR & MRS FRANCIS R. HESSING, REPORT DELIVERY DON'T PHONE. . . .
>
> THE SECRETARY OF THE ARMY HAS ASKED ME TO EXPRESS HIS DEEP REGRET THAT YOUR SON, PRIVATE FIRST CLASS JAMES W. HESSING, WAS KILLED IN ACTION IN VIET NAM ON 23 MAY 1970. HE WAS IN AN ARTILLERY FIRING POSITION WHEN THE AREA CAME UNDER MORTAR ATTACK BY HOSTILE FORCES.
>
> PLEASE ACCEPT MY DEEPEST SYMPATHIES. THIS CONFIRMS NOTIFICATION MADE BY A REPRESENTATIVE OF THE ARMY. . . .

Over the course of seven days, the formal declaration of death and extension of "deepest sympathies" give way to typo-filled directives about funeral arrangements and the pending itinerary—a far cry from the surfeit of official care that heralded Lance Corporal Merlin Raye Allen's homecoming four decades later. But then again, it was a different time.

On May 27, 1970:

> THIS CONCERNS YOUR SON, PFC JAMES W. HESSING. THE ARMY WILL RETURN YOUR LOVED ONE TO A PORT IN THE UNITED STATES BY FIRST AVAILABLE MILITARY AIRLIFT. AT THE PORT REMAINS WILL BE PLACED IN A METAL CASKET AND DELIVERED (ACCOMPANIED BY A MILITARY ESCORT) BY MOST EXPEDITIOUS MEANS TO ANY FUNERAL DIRECTOR DESIGNATED BY THE NEXT OF KIN OR TO ANY NATIONAL CEMETERY IN

WHICH THERE IS AVAILABLE GRAVE SPACE. YOU WILL BE AD-
VISED BY THE UNITED STATES PORT CONCERNING THE MOVE-
MENT AND ARRIVAL TIME AT DESTINATION. . . .

On May 29, 1970:

REMAINS YOUR SON JAMES WILL BE CONSIGNED TOMERKKEL
[sic] FUNERALHOME [sic]

17 SOUTH 1ST STREEET [sic], BAYFIELD, WISCONSIN INAC-
CORDANCE [sic] WITH YOUR REQUEST. PLEASE DO NOT SET
DATE OF FUNERAL UNTIL PORT AUTHORITIES NOTIFY YOU
AND FUNERAL DIRECTOR DATE AND SCHEDULED TIMEE [sic]
OF ARRIVAL DESTINATION.

On June 1, 1970:

REMAINS PFC JAMES HESSING

ESCORTED BY MAJOR LEONARD MOE DEPARTING SAN
FRANCISCO NORTHWEST FLIGHT 152 900 AM FOR MERKEL FU-
NERAL HOME BAYFIELD WISCONSIN ARRIVING MINNEAPOLIS
MN 215 PM 2 JUN DEPARTING MINNEAPOLIS MN MID CONTI-
NENT EESNA [sic] APPROXIMATELY 315 PM 2 JUN ARRIVING
ASHLAND WI APPROXIMATELY 445 PM 2 JUN REQUEST FU-
NERAL DIRECTOR RECAIVE [sic] REMAINS AND ESCORT AT
ASHLAND NEAREST TERMINAL TO BAYFIELD . . .

Though the last of the three Bayfield High School graduates to
die—killed on May 23, 1970, three years after Duwayne "Wotsy"
Soulier and Merl Allen—James (Jimmy) Hessing was the first to
come home, and his family was thus the community's first initiate in
the funerary rites for the Vietnam War. I didn't meet the Hessing
family right away; in fact, it wasn't until a commemorative gathering
for Wotsy that I heard of relatives still living in the area. And there
wasn't much family left to meet.

Jimmy's father, Francis Hessing, had died of cancer on Easter
Sunday, April 1971, almost a year after his son perished. Jimmy's
older brother Gary died in 2012.

His mother, Florence Hessing, lived a long life. But it was a life
marked by loss. Shortly before Jimmy's death, both of her parents
and her sister had died; then her son, followed by her husband. Gary

Corporal James William Hessing.

would eventually relocate to Louisiana. Florence was ninety-eight years old when she passed away in 2015. Her obituary tells the story of a hard-working, kind-hearted woman: "She married Francis Hessing and together they made their home at the corner of Happy Hollow and Highway 13 where they raised their two sons, Gary and James. After Francis was diagnosed with cancer, Florence assumed his duties as mail carrier for the Star Route to Cornucopia route for a number of years, retiring in 1980. During Francis's illness, she ran the farm, milking cows, tending chickens, working and harvesting her large garden, as well as running the house. . . . Florence is best remembered for her favorite quote, 'One day at a time.'"[1]

You can glimpse some of that motto and much of her dedication to her family, especially her younger son's memory, in what she left behind—the boxes of newspaper clippings, photographs, letters, and, with their pages stapled together in the order they arrived, Western Union telegrams. "She always talked about Jimmy," her daughter-in-law Joanna explained. In the summer of 2017, I visited with Joanna and later her son, Jimmy's nephew, Bill Hessing. It's Bill who inherited Florence's informal archive, and he and his girlfriend Keeley were the ones to spread its contents out on their dining room table and pore over the clippings and photographs together with me. Bill told me what he knew of his uncle, what he had heard from his parents and grandmother. Four years old when his uncle died, he had no memories of his own. From their accounts, he knew that Jimmy was a shy, lanky kid; he was drafted into the army and ended up in artillery. His death came as a terrible blow to his parents, Florence especially. Two of Jimmy's friends from the army, guys he served with, came to visit Florence and Francis when they got out. They wrote letters to her over the years. When Bill talks about his uncle, the lines of his weathered face soften and his eyes grow watery. You get the sense that he inherited more than just his grandmother's archive of ordered grief.

The newspaper clippings chronicle Jimmy Hessing's brief career in the army: an account of him completing basic training in Fort Knox, Kentucky, logged under a column called "service notes"; and a letter he sent from Vietnam, addressed to the Bayfield County Press:

Dear Friends,

I would like to say thank you sincerely for the Christmas gift—a subscription to the Bayfield County Press while I am serving in the U.S. Army.

I am in the Ashion [*sic*] Valley area in Viet Nam. When the first issue reached me it was like a touch of home.

Also many thanks and much appreciation to all of the members of the Hyland Club for their thoughts of me. The can of goodies reached me in fine shape and was real yummie.

Also a fruitcake from the Salvation Army of Duluth came to me. A big thank you for them too.

PFC James W. Hessing

A few months later, Jimmy Hessing was dead, killed on May 23, 1970. Clippings of the dark news swell Florence's archive, their headlines moving from the local to the regional: "Rural Bayfield Soldier Is Killed in Vietnam"; "Cornucopia Soldier Is War Victim"; "James Hessing Killed in Viet Nam"; "Cornucopia GI Killed in Vietnam"; "State GI Killed"; "19 Honored Dead in This Area"; and "Identify 4 Midwest GIs Killed in S.E. Asia." Then come the articles about his funeral, about posthumous medals awarded and presented to the Hessings, including a Bronze Star and Purple Heart, and finally a piece about a memorial plaque gifted to the Bayfield High School. With her husband and older son by her side, Florence is pictured handing the plaque to the high school principal.

Among the news articles is also the Hessing family's published "note of thanks." On June 4, 1970, they wrote to their community, an echo of their son's gratitude expressed just a few months before:

> The family of Cpl James William Hessing wish to thank all of our wonderful friends and neighbors both in Bayfield and the endless areas around Bayfield who stood by with comforting condolences in so many ways during the shock of losing our dear son Jim in Viet Nam.
>
> These have been bitter hard days. But with warmth and understanding from Rev. Gee, Rev. Anderson and Rev. Wrobbel, it has helped.

A special thanks to the ladies of Faith Baptist Church who were so thoughtful to serve lunch and to the many who furnished food.

Another special thanks to Dolores Leafblad who sang so lovely and to Linda Pinckney who played the organ so beautifully.

Deep from our hearts we thank everyone.

Mr. and Mrs. Francis Hessing
Mr. and Mrs. Gary Hessing

Florence's collage of news, telegrams, and funeral mementos sketch the sudden rupture and reorientation of her life. As loss continued to follow her, she had little choice but to take it "one day at a time."

While a shock for the Hessing family, Jimmy Hessing's death was, by that point in the war, a tragically commonplace event for the region and the nation. Indeed, he was one of many from the state of Wisconsin to die in Southeast Asia that year (an estimated 141, according to a list published among Florence's newspaper archive), and one of its total 1,161 "fatal casualties" by the end of the war.[2] Thirty-seven of those casualties were missing in action/killed in action but body not recovered, and two of them were graduates of Bayfield High School. In a way, Jimmy Hessing became the cornerstone of the community's sacrifice to the nation and to the war—the lanky kid who was drafted into the army—the last to die but first to come home and the first to be buried, six months after he left for Vietnam.

Called its "Wall of Faces," the Vietnam Veterans Memorial Fund website hosts a virtual page for each of the service members memorialized at the physical monument on the National Mall. Below the page's individual profile there is a space to leave a remembrance. Jimmy Hessing's page has a few such remembrances, two that provide the location of his grave in Bayfield's Greenwood Cemetery, one of his photograph at the Red Cliff VFW post, a couple of well-wishes from strangers, and then this:

You cooked a mean porkchop, Jim
Posted on 10/15/08—by David Soumis
I met Jim in 1968 while working at Kohler Co. We lived in the company dorm.

After hitting off pretty well, we got an apartment together with a couple of other guys, and had some real good times.

Jim always said he was a pretty good cook, so we left him be the first to cook dinner. He charcoaled the pork chops to a crisp. The potatoes weren't too bad.

I have never forgotten him, and he pops up in my mind often.

I, too, ended up in Nam . . . so as a friend and fellow nam Vet . . . I salute you, and will never forget you.

Thanks for the time we had.[3]

It's the kind of message that in a different era might have become part of Florence's archive, and maybe even prompted a posted note of thanks for the remembrance itself.

· 6 ·

In Absentia

IF YOU'RE NOT LOOKING FOR IT, the Duwayne Soulier Memorial Post in Red Cliff, Wisconsin, is easy to miss. Though the sign out front announces, "VFW and Auxiliary Post 8239—Public Welcome," the unassuming single-story building sits atop a gently sloping lawn, slightly elevated from the road. A pair of picnic tables and some wrought iron chairs crowd a narrow stretch of concrete patio just outside, spillover seating when they fire up the grill for a fundraiser or veterans gathering. The interior matches the exterior. Nothing fancy or flashy, unless you count the neon Green Bay Packers sign in the front window.

While I don't have many other VFW posts to compare it with, it seems to me that the Duwayne Soulier Memorial Post is a pretty special place, for all its ordinariness. Cans of beer and pop are cold and cheap. Though they volunteer their hours, the bartenders know what they're about, as do the customers; or, more to the point, they know each other—who drinks Budweiser or Miller Lite or Diet Coke and when they're ready for another. There aren't really tabs, as people arrange dollar bills and quarters on the bar as they go. Randy, the post's quartermaster, doesn't talk much; Diane, an auxiliary member and regular behind the bar, doesn't put up with cursing. The barstools are comfortable, and the place is always clean. Sunday afternoons in the fall draw a crowd for the football game and a potluck meal, and on a good day, that brings its own tradition. Every time the Packers score a touchdown, a bottle of Sour Apple Pucker Schnapps comes out, and someone makes the rounds, filling up each person's thimble-sized Dixie cup. A shout rings out—"Let's Go Packers!"—and down the hatch goes the bright-green, Jolly-Rancher-sweet liquor. On Applefest weekend, the peninsula's fabled harvest celebration, the post hosts a pancake breakfast fundraiser. For a few dollars a plate, you get two apple pancakes and two links of sausage, fresh off the griddle, with a side of homemade brown-sugar butter.

Though people of all ages from the community come to the post—as Randy put it, "this place has been used for everything from baby showers to funerals, birthdays and weddings"—there was a time when it almost folded. Post 8239 was originally chartered in June 1969, and its founding members were mostly World War II veterans, not all of whom embraced veterans of the war in Southeast Asia. For decades they lacked a permanent meeting site, moving instead from bar to bar in the area. By 2003, "with depleted membership and a tiny, wood-framed clubhouse with few amenities, the organization appeared near death, and remaining members were informed by the national organization that because of the post's inactivity, its charter would be canceled."[1] Spearheaded by its commander at the time, Danny Gordon, a friend of Merl Allen and one of the first Vietnam War veterans I met in the community, the post pushed to revive its numbers, to find a new home, and, most importantly, to rename the Red Cliff VFW in memory of Duwayne "Wotsy" Soulier. They eventually settled on the current property, which had been gifted to the post for a dollar by another vet, Joe Pascale. People like Randy Bresette and Butch Kuepfer, its commander, rejoined after a lapse of several years; with their children grown up, they had more time on their hands. In 2006, the members decided to gut and expand the existing structure, what had been a little hamburger joint, eventually doubling it in size. They wanted to remain debt free, so everything came from donations, either individual gifts of money or material, or through the numerous fundraisers they held. Randy did the lion's share of the work on the building's construction. Though he himself was not a veteran, Larry Soulier (known by everyone in the community as Bootin or Boot) also donated hundreds of dollars in labor and material. Given its namesake, Randy explained, "He's got an affinity and an affection towards this post."[2]

We often think of commemorations for war dead as highly orchestrated events—that is, the kind of eye-catching, ceremonial fanfare that marks national holidays like Memorial Day, July 4th, or Veterans Day or that is on display for special occasions like Lance Corporal Merlin Allen's or Captain Darrell Spinler's homecoming. But commemoration can take more mundane shape; it can come in the form of everyday acts or more gradually accruing communal gestures, like a rehabilitated VFW post, whose windows are bought one by one, or flooring laid and siding hammered through the gift of labor. Akin to the monuments and ceremonies Jay Winter describes in the wake of the Great War, within such gestures and gifts, the living dedicate themselves to "good works among their fellow men and women. Grief and indebtedness, sadness and personal commitment are the pillars of local commemoration."[3] These quotidian forms and places of remembrance reveal a side of the MIA accounting process that tends to go less noticed—what families, veterans, and communities do when the missing haven't yet returned, or may never return. In appreciating these commemorative practices, we can see how local memory reckons with unfulfilled obligations, just as rituals at sites like the Vietnam Veterans Memorial (the "Wall") in Washington, DC, grapple with the unfinished work of MIA accounting on the national stage.

These less scripted modes of remembrance necessarily grapple with unresolved absence, and in doing so, they expose a particular friction within the US military's MIA accounting efforts: despite the state's fervent pledges of "fullest possible accounting," some—even beyond those already considered unrecoverable (for example, those lost at sea)—will remain missing in action or killed in action/body not recovered indefinitely, perhaps permanently. There may be no homecoming. For obvious reasons, this fact fuels frustration; measured against its cultivated ethos of exceptional care, the state has effectively reneged on its end of the social contract with the service member and thus also with his or her surviving kin. By no means exclusive to the conflict in Southeast Asia and its missing war dead, such a perceived abrogation of responsibility nevertheless compounds the particular sting of that war's betrayals and thus demands action. When raised expectations go unmet, official attention turns to ferreting out failure and assigning blame. Congress ups the ante, expands the mission, insists on greater efficiency.

But if nothing else, we can glean from the examples of Merl Allen and Darrell Spinler that caring for missing war dead is never strictly the purview of the state. The missing service members belong to grieving families and communities just as much, if not more, than to a "grateful" nation. Thus, the Vietnam veterans slogan, "Bring them home or send us back," finds it echo in the Patriot Guard Riders' pledge to honor the fallen and help escort remains home. Or the Delta Air Lines honor guard. Or the flag-lined streets of small Midwestern towns. Or a family's decision to bury their loved one next to his parents in a hometown cemetery rather than

Arlington National Cemetery. So when the unaccounted for remain unaccounted for, it comes as no surprise that families, veterans, and their communities take memory matters into their own hands. In doing so, they push back against the problematic assumptions of "closure"—that byproduct of a therapeutic culture so often invoked by mainstream media in their coverage of the accounting mission. When decades have since passed and there is no resolution in sight, closure doesn't fit. MIA families already know well the phrase's limits.

In the face of prolonged and likely permanent absence, some relatives instead improvise their own rites of reclamation, their own ways of welcoming home those who will never return. Occasionally folded into larger commemorations, such events may also acknowledge the fraught homecoming for veterans who returned alive but not to the pageantry afforded the missing war dead recovered four and five decades later. They may make use of existing memorial spaces, like the Vietnam Veterans Memorial in the nation's capital or a VFW post in northern Wisconsin. Whether bigger or smaller in scale, public or private, planned or impromptu, these memorial practices offer a modest corrective to the expected end, the aim and destination of MIA accounting. They hint at an alternate vocabulary, distinct from the science-inflected language of remembrance embraced by the state and mainstream media.

"Join us to honor and remember"

Earlier I described a feature at the Duwayne Soulier Memorial Post that materialized the community's experience of military service and loss, particularly from the Vietnam War. There is a wall—it's actually spilling onto a second one these days—covered with the photographs of veterans and members, living and deceased, from World War I to active duty. In the very center, at the threshold between the two sides—the living and the dead—is Duwayne "Wotsy" Soulier's framed collage with his photograph, service medals, and a pencil rubbing of his name from the Vietnam Veterans Memorial. Lost over sea and thus deemed unrecoverable, he is the one "who will never come home." To his left are photographs of Merl Allen and Jimmy Hessing—the one who came home forty-six years later and the one who came home right away, respectively. For Butch, the VFW post commander, it was only right that their photos were grouped together. "It's just that this little community having three veterans killed over in Vietnam, it just ties all the families together."[4] When Casey Allen addressed the crowd assembled at his brother's memorial service, he too made sure to note that the Bayfield community sacrificed not only his twenty-year-old brother, but also twenty-year-old Private First Class Duwayne Marshall Soulier and twenty-one-year-old Corporal James William Hessing.[5] For his own part, Randy saw how the stories of the three young men had become braided into the fabric of local memory, across generations:

> When you think of one of them, the other two just automatically come to mind. My granddaughter when she was a junior in high school went on a trip to Washington, DC, and she had been here [at the post] enough times. And she ended up at the Wall. So the next time she came up here she said, "Grandpa, look what I got!" She said, "Here's the rubbings from the Wall." I said, "How'd you know that?" She said, "I just looked at it [the post's wall of photographs] every year and I remembered."[6]

A soft-spoken man, Randy didn't recount the story casually; his voice and expression telegraphed how much it meant that his granddaughter had remembered the three—strangers to her, but men whose lives—lost lives—affected her grandfather profoundly. Butch and others were quick to explain that the post ran in large part because of the countless hours Randy put in behind the bar and organizing events. He was the backbone of the place. And when he fell ill in 2017, those who stepped in to cover his shifts couldn't quite believe the commitment he had shouldered day in and day out over the years. It was also his idea originally to collect the photographs and arrange them on the wall, and to make the three Vietnam War dead the centerpiece of its recognition.[7]

More than just a space for the living veterans to gather and socialize, the post plays a specific commemorative role in Red Cliff and the wider community. Jimmy Hessing was buried in Greenwood Cemetery on the outskirts of Bayfield, where his father and much later his mother joined him; Merl Allen was buried next to his parents on York Island. Wotsy, on the other hand, has no gravestone. In its absence, Post 8239 has become his memorial site—a place where the public is welcome but also where local veterans, family, and friends keep an informal vigil through the clubhouse's day-to-day operations and activities. On April 30, 2017, one day shy of the fiftieth anniversary of his death, however, the family decided it was time to commemorate Wotsy publicly and explicitly through a modest ceremony at the post. "Join us to honor and remember Duwayne "Wotsy"

Soulier," the flyer read. At the invitation of Bootin and his wife, Rose, I traveled to Red Cliff to be there and take part in the day's events.

I arrived at the post early that morning to find one of Wotsy's sisters, Cindy, and his nephew Jimmy already spreading the thin plastic tablecloths over the banquet tables and strategizing about where to place the various crockpots, paper plates, and plastic cutlery. It was my first signal that the day's memorializing would entail more than just speeches and military rituals; remembering Wotsy meant sharing a meal together in his honor. And what a meal it would be. Within a few short hours, the serving tables were loaded up with huge warming trays of mashed potatoes, turkey in gravy, meatballs in gravy, sliced ham, fresh fried whitefish, rutabaga, wild rice casserole, coleslaw, fruit salad, and the like. To the side, on the dessert table, someone had placed an enormous white-frosted sheet cake decorated with Wotsy's photograph, the same headshot of him in his utility uniform and helmet that hangs at the center of the post's wall of photographs. Inside the fluted blue borders, red icing spelled out the phrases "In Loving Memory" . . . "You Are Not Forgotten" to frame the edible photo cake topper. A little red-icing heart punctuated the message. There had been some panic about the cake—a local bakery had taken the order but when the day drew near, no one returned the family's calls. And so in a pinch, they turned to the bakery department at the Walmart in nearby Ashland. Everyone was pleased with how it turned out. While we finished preparing the tables, outside on the lawn, Bootin, Randy, and others assembled another tent and set up a white tarp to shield the area from the gradually rising wind. The gray skies promised an unseasonably cold spring day.

With a couple of hours before guests would arrive, Jimmy and I headed over to the Red Cliff casino to grab some breakfast, and there we had a chance to talk more generally about his uncles, his family, and the contrast between Red Cliff and Bayfield, between the Native American community, the white residents, and the lopsided development, spurred by burgeoning tourism, of upscale restaurants, hotels, and boutiques. ("Who names a restaurant the Fat Radish?" Bootin once joked.) On our way back to the post, we drove through the old reservation, where Jimmy had spent summers as a child. At the time, he explained, he had dreaded coming north—he grew up in Milwaukee, where his mother had moved and eventually met his father; he didn't like the feeling that he was the "white" kid, the interloper from the city. These days, trips to Red Cliff are a welcome chance to spend time with his uncle, go golfing on the peninsula, and enjoy

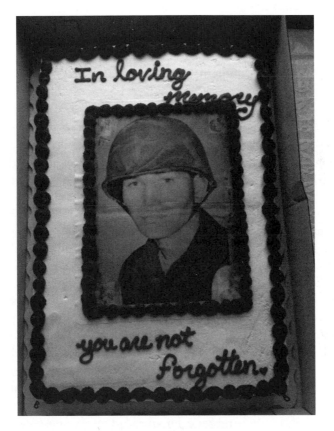

The cake for Duwayne "Wotsy" Soulier's remembrance
gathering.

Rose's "boiled" dinners (a local dish that involves a pot full of simmered
meat, vegetables, and fist-sized dumplings). Here was Bootin's old home,
he pointed out as we drove along; here was his grandmother's property;
here was the stretch of lawn that the kids would take to get down to the
shimmering lake. There was no indoor plumbing, he remembered. Instead
they relied on a communal pump and outhouses—dispossession of another
order, with a deeper historical grain. Later I would ask Randy and Butch
about the demographics of the post—that is, about its makeup in terms of
Native American versus white veterans. "About 90 percent Native," they
explained. While the number made sense given the post's location in Red
Cliff, it also intersected with larger national trends. In his pioneering study

of Native American combatants and veterans of the Vietnam War, Tom Holm argues that "factors of low economic and educational levels" combined with "a very youthful population (the average age of Native Americans in the period of the Vietnam War was between 19 and 21) virtually assured that most Indian males would be primary candidates for military service," and within that service "be very likely to become infantrymen and experience combat in Vietnam." Like other racial minorities who served in the war, they "bore a disproportionate share of fighting." Indeed, more than forty-two thousand Native Americans served in Southeast Asia between 1960 and 1973, with 250 of them dying there, Wotsy among them, killed in action/body not recovered.[8]

The conversation with Jimmy and the tour through the reservation helped contextualize the commemoration at the post that day, where tribal rituals joined military tradition in honoring the community's one remaining missing war dead. Though on a smaller scale than Merl Allen's homecoming—there were no Patriot Guard Riders, no remains to escort along Highway 13—the chance to "honor and remember" Duwayne (Wotsy) Soulier gathered people from near and far in similarly widened bonds of kinship. Among those who traveled from out of state was Wotsy's unit commander (team leader) Stan Pace, who had flown in from Kentucky the day before. As the post began to fill up with relatives, neighbors, and veterans, Stan talked with Marilyn Neff (Merl Allen's sister), who had come with her husband, Ralph, to pay their respects. As he recounted the events leading up to Wotsy's death, how the young man ended up on a medevac helicopter that had crashed into the South China Sea just a few hundred yards away from the hospital ship, he had to turn away and regain his composure. Marilyn reached out to touch his arm; she told him she understood how hard it was to talk about it.

At noon, the ceremony began with a rite of military homage. Filing in to the recorded strains of bagpipes playing "Going Home," members of the post, the American Legion in Bayfield, and the Apostle Islands Honor Guard, as well as other attending veterans, made their way, one by one, to stand before Wotsy's photograph. Once there, each saluted the image, turned, and walked on. There wasn't much room for maneuvering, with all the seats taken and people standing two rows deep toward the back. After an introduction by Butch and an address by the Bayfield County veteran service officer, it was time for the speeches. First came family—Bootin and his two sisters each taking a turn before the microphone to recount stories and reflect on who their brother was to them, not as a US

Marine, but as their sibling, a fun-loving teenager with a sentimental streak. Bootin told how Wotsy once had a job working alongside him in a metal fabricating plant. Wotsy kept tracing the name of a girl he liked— Linda—on the metal's surface. Finger oil leaves a mark, even when painted over, Bootin explained, and so he would have to rework and repaint each piece his brother had processed to get rid of "Linda." Eventually, he told his little brother to knock it off with Linda's name. The crowd laughed. Cindy followed suit with a story of how, when they were in high school, a new boyfriend had swung by their home to pick her up for a date. He walked right up to the house, something she had desperately *not* wanted him to do; her family was moving the outhouse that day, and the pit hadn't yet been dug. So the boyfriend pitched in for her. Wotsy gave his little sister a hard time—not just for shirking her duty, but for sloughing off the chore onto her hapless date. She chuckled as she recalled his scolding her, "You shit in it, you should help move it!" The last of the three to speak was Darlene, the oldest of the siblings but the smallest in stature, a petite woman with a quiet manner and quieter voice. She explained that she had already left the house when Wotsy was a young boy; her memories of him were more distant, both in terms of time and force. She peered out at the crowd, almost bewildered by the moment, and uttered her simple tribute. "He was my little brother." From there, others among the gathering rose to tell stories of Wotsy in high school, of a yearbook party when Merl Allen called out, "Wotsy, it's the Watusi!" and how each brother grabbed his sister, the two pairs cutting it up to the 1960s dance craze. Mary Defoe read aloud the poem she had written years ago, the beautiful reckoning of youth cut short and the disbelief that followed. At its end, she declared, and heads nodded in agreement, "Everyone loved Wotsy. Everyone loved Wotsy."

Making his way slowly to the front of the room, Stan Pace stood before the crowd as the sole voice from Wotsy's military service. Though there were plenty of Vietnam vets in attendance, Stan was the only one who had actually served alongside Wotsy. Recalling the young man he knew by the nickname of "Chief," a marine under his command in the Seventh Communications Battalion, First Division, he told the story of what had happened, of how Wotsy had sustained injuries and another marine was killed when their jeep ran over a mine while they were on a mail run. He took pains to stress that Wotsy had been thus wounded and was not sick with a fever, as some of the military records indicate.[9] "Don't let anyone tell you differently." Wotsy's condition was severe enough that he had to be transported—medevaced—first to the hospital in nearby Chu Lai, and then to a navy hospital ship anchored twelve miles off the coast of the Quảng Tín Province. He later learned that the chopper had crashed into the sea. On the edge of tears, he confessed that he had been "carrying around [Wotsy's] ghost for the last fifty years." There was a moment of stillness, of hesitation, and then Butch stepped forward to embrace him. Later, Stan would tell me that he wouldn't have missed the day, the chance to honor his fellow marine, for anything.

The speeches and words of remembrance tacked between the two profiles—Wotsy as a sibling, classmate, friend, even a high school crush, and Duwayne Soulier as a marine who died in service to his country but whose remains never came home. On the whole, remarks addressing the latter were long on a sense of sacrifice but short on breathless patriotism. Not that it wasn't a crowd that honored military service, or the nation, for that matter—far from it—but the Vietnam War's price of dispossession had left its particular mark. As one Vietnam vet pronounced with an edge of anger in his voice, "The US government cuts blank checks when it sends people off to war. And it cashed those checks with these three men." Here again, Wotsy's memory was inextricably entwined with Jimmy Hessing's and Merl Allen's—the three Bayfield youth lost to the war in Southeast Asia.

More than just sharing memorial space with a localized, personalized portrait of Wotsy, the notion of "national" sacrifice likewise encompassed dual meanings. Duwayne Soulier was a member of the Chippewa Nation, namely, the Red Cliff Band of the Lake Superior Chippewa, and the ceremony that followed the speeches paired military rites with tribal ritual in honoring both his memory and his spirit. After Butch read aloud a final dedication to Private First Class Duwayne Soulier, the honor detail of the VFW Post 8239, with white gloves and shouldered rifles, exited the building to perform the requisite rifle salute. Though they lacked the precision of the Old Guard sentinels at the Tomb of the Unknowns in Arlington National Cemetery, their deliberate movements echoed the salutes they each had given Wotsy at the ceremony's opening. The volleys rocked the air three times, and then off to the side a bugler played taps. It was a beautiful rendition, its clear notes muffled only by the tent tarps flapping in the biting wind.

Once the military ritual closed, the Native tradition began. Dressed in a gray track suit, a spiritual leader from the Red Cliff Band lit a ceremonial pipe and offered the smoke to the four directions. Then, speaking in the Ojibwe language, he said a prayer in honor of Wotsy, words of a different nation recognizing a warrior's sacrifice in its own terms. As soon as he finished, his partner, a younger man in a brightly embroidered black vest, began a song, his voice oscillating to the beat of the hand drum he played. To his right, the neon Packers sign remained unlit in the post's window. Once the ceremony ended, the spiritual leader invited us back into the building to begin the feast in remembrance of Wotsy. He blessed the food. Holding a plate aloft, he explained that he had prepared a spirit offering from the potluck fare, which he would take directly to Wotsy's mother's grave. Without a burial site for Wotsy, his mother's headstone was the next proper place to leave the offering. Then the meal began. The little building soon buzzed with voices and laughter as people fell into conversation over plates of food cooked in honor of Duwayne "Wotsy" Soulier KIA/BNR.

I PULLED OUT OF THE LITTLE SAND BAY CAMPGROUND with my headlights off, guided by the dark shapes of the trees bordering the road. I didn't want to wake the other campers. It was 4:20 a.m., and I had exactly twenty minutes to make it to Bootin's driveway—"look for the mailbox covered in ivy"—if I wanted to join him and his brother-in-law Junior out on the lake. Retirement for Bootin had meant returning to commercial fishing, a livelihood that once dominated the peninsula's economy and for members of the Red Cliff Band still drew on tribal rights tied to the sacred waters of their ancestors. During fishing season (from late November through early October), every other morning, he and Junior (Rose's brother) cast off from the dock at the Bayfield marina and headed out onto the lake to haul in their sometimes prodigious, sometimes meager, catches of whitefish and lake trout and then reset their hundred-yard-long gill nets in the deep channels off the shores of the Apostle Islands. The day before this particular morning, I had been sitting with Bootin and a few others at the casino bar, nursing a Coke and catching up on area news. I had returned to Red Cliff and Bayfield a couple of months after Wotsy's remembrance ceremony to follow up with some interviews about the VFW post, Merl Allen's homecoming, and the like. When Bootin mentioned that he and Junior were fishing the next morning, I asked if I could tag along.

In the shadows of that liminal sky, not yet morning but no longer night, we stepped onto the fish tug, and without a single word exchanged between them (as would be their habit for the majority of the day), Bootin and Junior set to work readying the gear and then guiding the boat out of the marina.

Lawrence "Bootin" Soulier with his lake trout catch.

The eastern horizon hinted at dawn; it was not yet 5:00 a.m., and the water was smooth as glass. As we gathered speed, I leaned into the frame of the open sliding door starboard side and took in the cool air. Theirs is a commercial vessel with all the attendant smells—fish guts overlaid with rusted steel, grease, weathered twine, and Pine-Sol. The minutes passed in relative silence but for the steady rumble of the diesel-fueled engine, and I watched the sky gradually gain its color. Bootin stepped over and pointed to a spot on the horizon; get ready, in a couple of seconds, he told me, the sun would rise there. And so it did, its pinkish-red orb piercing the line between the water and sky. I've thought a lot about that day on the boat, watching the two men in their wordless choreography of synchronized labor, pulling in and letting out the nets, untangling gills from the yards of unspooling mesh and tossing the slippery catch into the plastic bins, which they topped off with crushed ice, and later, homeward bound, flinging a few whitefish out the back to the bald eagles that had learned to chase the vessel in hopes of their just reward. There was a sad symmetry to Bootin's lifelong work on the lake, casting his nets deep into the water to see what they might ensnare, while halfway around the globe, his brother's remains lie on an ocean floor, as of yet undetected and likely too deep for a US military underwater archaeology team to recover. Bootin is not a man to complain or pontificate. When I asked him once what he thought of his brother's enlisting in the marines, he told me, "It was up to him." Did he know what he was getting into? He nodded his head, "I think so." He and his sisters have never actively pushed for answers or demanded action on their brother's case; they have never attended a government briefing or traveled to Washington, DC, for the National League of POW/MIA Families annual meeting. This doesn't mean that they don't care, or that they've forgotten, or that they wouldn't be thrilled if someday they picked up the phone to hear the words, "Your brother's remains have been identified." But in acknowledging the circumstances of his death and thus the likely impossible conditions of his recovery, they've made do with their own modes of commemoration. They've visited the Wall and taken rubbings of his name. Members of the auxiliary, they're staunch supporters of the local VFW post; beyond his help with the physical structure, Bootin has flipped pancakes and burgers as part of its charity work for the community. He spends an hour or two a couple of times a week visiting with friends at its bar. He and Rose, his sisters and their families, invited friends, neighbors, local veterans, and tribal members to join them in remembering Wotsy fifty years after his death. They do their best to keep his memory alive, and they share their gratitude with the Red Cliff community and especially the Vietnam War vets at the post who have helped them in that task.

Last Known Alive

Both in their more informal memory work and the support they enjoy (and appreciate) from their respective communities, Bootin and his sisters have a lot in common with Pam Cain, the daughter of an air force pilot missing in action since 1966, not yet recovered. And while they share the bond of grappling with five decades of absence, their experiences also differ in striking ways. Pam is an MIA daughter who lost her father at age twelve. His status for many years was carried as "last known alive," yet another subset within the government's "unaccounted for" category. Unlike Wotsy or Merl Allen or Darrell Spinler, there was evidence to suggest that her father may have survived his aircraft's being shot down. As a child and later the spouse of a service member, Pam has lived in different parts of the country, including in the Washington, DC, metro area, and she has been actively engaged in the POW/MIA accounting issue for over three decades, serving on the National League of POW/MIA Families' board of directors since 2007. Standing before the Vietnam Veterans Memorial on Father's Day 2012, she explained, "I do everything I can to remind the government that he needs to come home."[10] An articulate, determined advocate for the accounting mission, Pam doesn't cast herself as a policy wonk or Beltway insider on the "issue." Rather, her activism centers on the need to educate the public and support families who struggle with the effects of the Vietnam War, namely, the uncertainty inherent in the unaccounted-for category, what the league's former executive director Ann Mills-Griffiths calls the more "touchy-feely stuff." In fact, the first time I met Pam was at a workshop on "Dealing with Ambiguous Loss," which she chaired at the 2016 annual league meeting and government briefing.[11]

Perhaps more than any other case I encountered, the circumstances of Pam's father's loss and her family's experiences with the US government's MIA accounting efforts capture the thorny dimensions of an uncertain fate resulting from a deeply contentious war. Major Oscar Mauterer, posthumously promoted to Colonel Mauterer, was last seen alive on February 15, 1966, by the pilot of the lead plane in a two-plane mission flying cover over Khammouan Province in Laos: "He was observed to bail out, deploy a good parachute and descend to the ground in an area heavily populated with enemy forces."[12] A career pilot with the air force, he had volunteered to serve in Vietnam. "It was the old 'service to country,'" Pam explained. Though later he would express disillusion with aspects of the American campaign, nevertheless, "he felt the government had put a lot of money into him and his training, and he needed to be there." Pam remembers the day he left for the war; she recalls fondly how he insisted on coming home to Washington, DC, to spend Thanksgiving with his kids (rather than having her mother fly out to Hawaii for the usual allotted R&R); and then there's the day she learned he had been shot down:

> It's been fifty-one years, and I can remember it like it was yesterday. I was in junior high and I walked home, as I always do, and I got to my street and I saw my grandparents' car parked out front. Again,

Then Major Oscar Mauterer, Bien Hoa Air Base, Vietnam, 1965.

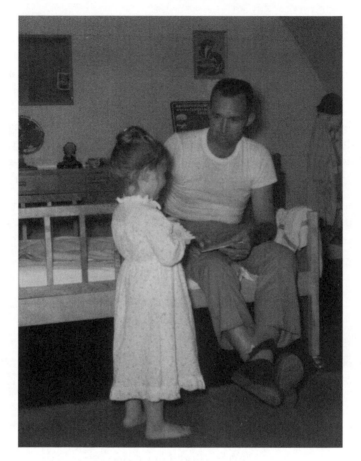

Pam Cain with her father, Oscar Mauterer, Chitose Air Base, Japan, July 1956.

we were going to go see them that same weekend so, "Why are they down here?" And I got to the front door and I walked in and my mother was at the top of the steps wearing sunglasses with tears streaming down her face. And my grandparents—her parents—were there. And I knew right away, and she said something's happened to Dad. And from that moment on, obviously, my life changed.[13]

With their family based in Washington, DC, at the time, Pam recalls how the tense circumstances in the nation's capital compounded her anxiety at the news of her father being shot down. "It was a really tumultuous time.

It really started hitting me with the riots and the protests, and then what was happening at home to me and to us. We were getting phone calls, really nasty, awful phone calls. 'Your dad, your husband, got what he deserved.' The whole baby killer thing.[14] Other calls saying, 'We know where he is. We have evidence.'" To not pick up the phone risked missing vital news, and so Pam's mother answered the calls. The family—namely her mother—had been told that he was shot down over Laos, notably, at a time when the United States was not officially "in" Laos. They were instructed not to share information with anyone; they were not to speak to the media, "because you're going to put your husband, your father, in possible danger." The isolation weighed heavily on the family, as did the sense of dependence on the US government. Pam's parents had had conversations before her father left about "what if." He had told her mother, "Listen to what the government tells you." He had had faith in its capacity to care for his family, if he himself should not return.

But that was the great uncertainty—would he return? Although he fell into the category of last known alive, Oscar Mauterer never "made it into the prison system"; his name never appeared on any official POW lists. Given the report that he parachuted to ground in an area controlled by enemy forces, to Pam's mind, someone should have known what happened to him. The fact of his purported survival also complicated the search and recovery process. "Then it became like looking for a needle in a haystack because they weren't just looking for a crash site," she explained. "They knew he wasn't there," at the site where the plane had gone down. "I'm growing up, and I'm going, well, if you're not looking for the crash site, what are you looking for? You're looking for one man in a country where we weren't supposed to be." Years would pass during which time Pam, her mother, and her younger brother heeded the government's directive to stay silent and await news. Periodically, with the war still unfolding, her mother was asked to come to the Air Force Casualty Office to look at POW photographs, to see if her husband's visage was among them. He never was.

It wasn't until her late twenties that Pam became mobilized as an MIA family member. Sitting in the chapel at Fort Myer, just outside the gates of Arlington National Cemetery, at the memorial service for her father—a service the family had decided to hold around the time the US government was declaring the presumption of death for its missing in action—for the first time, she felt deeply angry.[15] "We are doing this but not one damn thing has changed." She became actively involved in advocating for her father's case, joining the National League of POW/MIA Families; she traveled to

Washington, DC, (by then she lived in California) for the annual briefings; she met other MIA children and compared stories. It was an eye-opening experience. After the first league meeting, she called her mother to say, "We have to talk." Pam's engagement with the league led to her mother's own epiphany, albeit a painful one. "She was devastated, not only by losing her husband," but by her guilt over what she perceived to be her own passivity and naïveté in remaining quiet, in "believing what she was hearing," and in not joining the league sooner. For years, mother and daughter would attend the annual meetings and push for developments on Mauterer's case. Pam promised her mother she would bring him home to her, a pledge made that much more pressing when Pam's mother was diagnosed with leukemia in 2002.

Forty-four years after Colonel Oscar Mauterer parachuted to the ground in Laos, never to be heard of again, Pam received a text message, a request from the Joint POW/MIA Accounting Command (JPAC) for additional photographs of her father. "And I was smart enough at that point to keep my mouth shut and just say, yes, I'm sending you pictures. And I to this day travel with a thumb drive on which I have a lot of his stuff, photos, etc. And so ten minutes later they had their pictures. And very shortly thereafter—and again this is all kind of backchannel, it's not through a letter and an investigation—I got a report saying that the photo was Dad." Pam pressed to see the image for herself; several weeks later, she attended "The Ride Home," an event in Georgia marking National POW/MIA Recognition Day, where JPAC personnel were also present:

> They put it up on the computer, and we were all in a hotel room. And I saw the picture. And, um, it was Dad [her voice breaks]. Yeah, I didn't need any dental records, it was Dad. [In the photograph] He's reposed. He's in his flight suit, you can see part of the harness. . . . Do I know that somebody who's unconscious is dead? Do I know if that was a staged photo? Do we? So you know, you have all those questions. They did say and you can see there's a little, almost a little wound, kind of here [points at her temple] and you could see, and they said that they brushed away the blood. Well, that could be somebody shot him. I don't know how you get that bailing out. So again, a lot of questions.

While the discovery of the photograph definitively removed Colonel Oscar Mauterer from the "Last Known Alive" list, the field investigation that had produced it also yielded firsthand witnesses who claimed to know the precise whereabouts of his remains. Members of a North Vietnamese Army unit tasked with locating an American pilot who had bailed from his aircraft confirmed that Mauterer was dead (the witnesses claimed he was already dead when they found him) and that they had buried his body, all but his boots, which were too big; those they left nearby the hastily dug grave. In 2014, following a site survey, the 131st Joint Field Activity, carried out by US and Laotian personnel, excavated the area believed to be the burial location. To Pam and her family's great disappointment, no remains were recovered. Pam's mother died in 2015.

For Pam Cain, a tension exists between wanting to continue to push the US government to recover her father's remains—chase down every lead and bring even some small part of him home, to be buried in Arlington National Cemetery—and ceding those hypothetical resources to other families. "I find myself fighting a lot of emotions now about [whether I am] asking too much. Am I at the point where, you know, again, other families don't have what I have? And so I do fight that battle of whether I should—I can't let go—but should I be content with what I have so that other families have a chance?" There is one thing, however, very clear in her mind. No amount of time passed and not even the news of her father's recovery and identification will bring her that seemingly prized condition of "closure," a term, as psychologist Pauline Boss and poet Donna Carnes explain, that posits "not only a mythical, unobtainable goal, but also an especially unhealthy goal to expect of those who must carry ambiguous loss, for years or even a lifetime."[16] For Pam, a trained professional in social work who chose to specialize in grief, hospice, and senior care, the notion of closure fails to apprehend the range of hope that she and her family endured over the years: hope that he might have survived, but also hope that he wasn't tortured; hope that he died swiftly and painlessly; hope that his remains would be recovered and identified; hope that this would happen before her mother passed away from cancer; and now hope that it might occur while Pam and her brother are still alive. Undergirding it all is the recognition that her father's ambiguous absence has been a constant presence in her life since age twelve.

> Closure. I really hate that word. Even if my dad ever comes home, I will never have closure. I lost my dad at a time in my life and his life, the whole circumstances of the war. You know, just everything

about it. That will never be ok. If I can accept it, yeah. And I think in terms, I think, I know that I've accepted that he's dead. By now, I mean, he'd be an old old old man, and I hope that he didn't go through some of the torture. And I'm pretty certain that he probably died earlier on after his shoot down, rather than later, which for years, again, we didn't know. But that whole thing of ambiguous loss, it's all encapsulated in that, to me—that whole sense of ambiguous loss. That grief, that loss, stays with you, you know?

Some people go, oh well, you live in the past, or you need to move on. Well, I've grown up. I went to college. I had a career—I have a career. I have a family. I think I've kind of done the usual things that we do in life. I've been very happy in the things I've done. . . . But my dad will always always be that something that is not closed. It's just still an open thing.

Countering that gap, that "open thing," Pam has crafted her own rituals of remembrance.[17] In the most abstract sense, her advocacy within the MIA community itself serves as a way of memorializing her father; it connects her loss to something larger, to lives beyond her own and those of her immediate family: "Even if I get accountability for my dad, I'll never ever walk away from this." Like Bootin's gifts of labor at the Red Cliff post, indebtedness and grief, sadness and personal commitment, form the backbone of her commemorative activism. That said, she also has her more material rites and places of honoring her father's memory. Even though the earth below it shelters no remains, her father's headstone in Arlington grants her a "little bit of peace, a little bit of solace." Each year, on Christmas, February 15, Father's Day, his birthday, and National POW/MIA Recognition Day, she sends flowers to be placed at its base. It sits on a hill in a memorial section, surrounded by others—not just from the Vietnam War—for whom the headstones are likewise symbolic. Indeed, Pam knows several of the families whose unaccounted-for loved ones have markers there as well, and often when she visits her father's tombstone, she finds herself speaking to them. She's taken her grandson there; he placed a little rock on top of his great-grandfather's marker. "And because the cemetery doesn't like balloons," she explains with a mischievous smile, "I always put balloons."

At the Wall

On the bright, cold morning of Veterans Day, November 11, 2017, Maya Lin stepped to the podium before her black granite creation—once derided as a "black gash of shame and sorrow"—to give special remarks at the thirty-fifth anniversary of the dedication of the Vietnam Veterans Memorial.[18] "I envisioned cutting open the earth and polishing its open sides. The walls would not be massive but instead thin and light, so the names alone become the object," she explained. But the names were also to do particular work—to conjoin the living and the dead in the sociality of reflection. "The walls would be polished to a mirror's shine, so you see yourself reflected in the names. . . . And that as you descend, the names rise up to meet you. And that you would be able to find your time on the wall, and connect with your fallen colleagues. I was intently focused on creating a work that would talk to each one of you individually yet also to have you seam together as a family. So that you and your service would become a part of the very fabric of this country."[19] But what of those who inhabited (or continue to inhabit) that ambiguous state of missing in action, or, its subset, like Pam Cain's father, last known alive? How does the monument as a permanent testament to the devastation of war—albeit one side of it—address the uncertainty surrounding these individual service members within that social fabric and yet leave open the possibility for resolution of their fates?[20] With the design still in planning, the National League of POW/MIA Families waged a pitched battle to preserve not only the sanctity of, but also the critical political distinction between, the POW/MIA and KIA categories. By such logic, flattening the differences between the *missing* (even if bureaucratically presumed dead) and the *definitively dead* undercut the urgency to account for the POWs/MIAs— not unlike the league's initial resistance to interring an Unknown Soldier of the Vietnam War in Arlington National Cemetery because the act might signal the end to concerted POW/MIA accounting efforts.[21] At first, the league rejected even the MIA names' inclusion on the Wall; but if they were to appear on its granite panels, the league refused to support the design's uniform listing of MIAs and KIAs, going so far as to obtain a restraining order to stop the memorial's construction.[22] "We explained to them, 'We will stop you because we will not put our missing men's names on the wall as killed in action.' Just won't do it. We're working too hard, so we've got to find a way."[23] Eventually, the two sides agreed on a symbol of two equidistant intersecting lines to be etched next to the names of the missing in action, in contrast to the diamond symbol beside those killed in action. "It's not a cross," Ann Mills-Griffiths is quick to point out because "not all missing in action were Christians."[24]

Once an individual MIA is accounted for, the equidistant lines are filled in to create a diamond. If an individual were to return alive, the lines would be surrounded by a circle. To date, no circles have been drawn.[25]

For many MIA families, in the absence of a grave, the Wall with its names and its equidistant lines has become over the years the primary site of mourning for their missing relative. Each time Pam Cain visits the memorial, she leaves an object of some sort for her father—"a flag or a yellow rose, something"—an act that, according to American studies professor Kristin Hass, the memorial invites, as people come to it with their recollections and object gifts to grapple with the war's own "restive memory."[26] Pam also takes pains to find and trace her fingers over the names of other MIAs, in support of friends from the league. She participates in the reading of the names, an event held by the Vietnam Veterans Memorial Fund on certain anniversary dates (e.g., tenth, thirty-fifth, etc.); it spans four days, the last three of which run from 5:00 a.m. to midnight, rain/snow or shine, in the run-up to the official Veteran's Day ceremony at the memorial. Others light a candle at dusk to place at the base of their missing service member's panel on National POW/MIA Recognition Day. Still others forge their own traditions, bringing some artifact of home to the Wall to bridge the gap between absence and presence.

Deanna Klenda used to bring wheat. Every year but one since the Vietnam Veterans Memorial's dedication, she'd gather a little bundle of grain from her family's farm outside of Marion, Kansas, and take it to her older brother, Dean, at the Wall. They were four years apart and came from a close-knit family, part of the local Czech community in central Kansas. True to their heritage, all four of them loved to polka dance. When Dean and Deanna came in from their chores, just before dinner, "my mom would put on a polka, and instead of eating right away, we would polka dance around the house." They'd dance at weddings and to the Lawrence Welk show. "My mom and dad were fantastic polka dancers," and so Deanna and her brother would sweep past them on the dance floor, teasing them, "'We're better than you are.'" As much as he enjoyed polkas and their life on the farm, Dean Klenda also loved to fly. Having enrolled in the Reserve Officers Training Corps at Kansas State University, upon

Deanna Klenda's annual tribute to her brother at the
Vietnam Veterans Memorial.

graduation he joined the air force and went to flight school at Nellis Air
Force Base in Nevada, training on the F-105 Thunderchief, a one-person
fighter jet. "You don't know what a thrill is until you fly below the walls of
the Grand Canyon," he told his little sister. When he came home on break,
Deanna recalled, he would fly an aircraft. "He would buzz the farm, and
we knew we had to go to McConnell Air Force Base in Wichita. 'I'm here,
come get me.' Scared the crap out of all the farmers. One of my classmates
said, 'I dove off that tractor because a fighter jet was coming right over me,
right at my head.'"[27]

Married less than a year, Major Dean A. Klenda was shot down
on a bombing campaign over So'n La Province in North Vietnam on
September 17, 1965—his wife's birthday. Klenda was one of the war's
earliest MIAs.[28] Like Pam Cain and Dwayne Spinler, Deanna Klenda remembers the moment she learned the news of her brother's being shot
down. Though Dean Klenda was designated as missing in action, the
flight lead in the four-plane formation had observed what he thought was
an ejection seat, but no parachute, and then the Thunderchief slam into
the earth. Deanna was in college at the time, and after being notified
themselves by the local sheriff, her parents had driven up to Kansas State
University to tell her in person; she sensed something was wrong on the
phone, but thought perhaps it was about her grandmother. The three of
them sat in the car together. "I remember vividly. I sat in between my

Major Dean Albert Klenda.

parents. I put my arms around them. And I felt him there. I could feel my brother." She promised them, "I'll take care of you."

With her parents among the early members of the National League of POW/MIA Families, Deanna became actively involved with the group in the early 1980s. She accepted the knowledge of her brother's death but, along with her mother and father, pushed for the recovery of his remains; she attended regional family update meetings regularly, getting to know other MIA families from all over the country. Each summer when she made her trip to Washington, DC, to attend the league's annual national meeting, she visited the Vietnam Veterans Memorial to pay her special tribute. Her brother had always looked forward to that time of year—the harvest with its colors and smells. The wheat harvest marked the start of the harvest season, the bread and butter of their life on the farm. It also brought its "wheat stories," from sitting in the back of the wheat truck, careful not to spill any of the precious grain, to running down to the creek to cool off before returning to work in the wheat field. And so she thought, "'Why would I take a bouquet of flowers to my brother at the Wall? What would he love more than a handful of wheat?' So I went out and gathered wheat, a ribbon, and stuck a card with it." The gift of the family's livelihood and the grain of their youth became her memorial tradition, just as the Wall became the principal place marking his absence. Even that gesture had its own history. Right before Dean left for flight school, Deanna and her parents threw him a party. She made him a big, beautiful bouquet of weeds—a joke between them but also a reminder of the farm (and its wheat) in Kansas even as his Thunderbird flew over landscapes of places, countries, far removed.

To this day, Deanna prefers to visit the memorial at night. "It's beautiful. It's serene. There's fewer people," she explained. "I like to be the only one there." Sometimes she'll stop at the Lincoln Memorial first, to lean against one of its pillars and take in the view. And then she'll head to the Wall. On one visit, several years ago, she stepped out of the cab to the sounds of polka music. It was about 10:00 p.m., and she couldn't believe her ears—nearby were four musicians playing away. "When I looked at the Wall that night, when the music was playing, at the panel, I felt my family there. I could feel them," much like the day she sat between her parents, wrapped her arms around their shoulders, and comforted them over the news of him missing in action. "There was Mom, Dad, and Dean. What are the odds of a polka? And so I went over to [the musicians] and told them my story and what it meant to me. Playing the polka down there. And I thought they just had to know how much that meant."

On September 17, 2016, after fifty-one years of absence, Deanna Klenda buried her brother's remains in the small cemetery of Pilsen, Kansas, bordered on one side by wheat fields.[29] "Remains" in this instance meant a small piece of tooth enamel and a crown with restoration. From a forensic scientific perspective, it was an extraordinary case. Klenda's remains had originally been recovered by a Vietnamese farmer who had taken them to his property five kilometers away from the crash site; he had intended to melt the crown for its gold, but didn't succeed. Instead, he discarded the tooth in a garbage pit on his property. In 2011, the farmer led a joint US-Vietnamese investigation team to the site where he originally came across the tooth and where he discarded it. Three years later, another US

Siblings Deanna and Dean Klenda with the bouquet of weeds.

team returned to excavate the garbage pit and discovered both the crown and the tiny enamel fragment.

Tom Holland, former JPAC scientific director and now director of the Defense POW/MIA Accounting Agency's Strategic Partnerships program, traveled to Kansas to attend the funeral; over the years, he and Deanna had become good friends. He explained the unusual methodology involved in the identification. "We conducted a series of tests on [the dental remains] including a rather novel technique using different types of isotopes. We were able to map the enamel of the tooth recovered to somebody who spent the first 10 years of [their] life in either Nebraska or Kansas."[30] There was a second striking feature to the identification, a material anomaly that dovetailed the isotopic evidence. Deanna Klenda's uncle, Dr. Harry Klenda, was a well-established dentist, serving as president of the American Dental Association from 1969 to 1970. In his practice, he had experimented with making his own filling materials, including devising his own formulas for gold alloy fillings. Holland recalled that the "dental gold crown that we recovered from the same area as the tooth fragment—and which was a radiographic match to a gold crown documented in Dean Klenda's dental record—was a dull gold color (almost brass colored). It may have been the color and the higher melting point that convinced the Vietnamese villager who recovered it that it wasn't real gold." When Holland first described the gold crown to Deanna over the phone, he mentioned its dull gold color. She responded immediately, "I know just what it looks like. I have the same filling [material] in my mouth. Our uncle made it."[31] Perhaps more than any other detail, the crown confirmed for her that indeed her brother had been found.

Every year, from the time she started attending the league meetings, when Deanna looked out from the airplane window over the National Mall and its memorials as she headed home, she always felt that she was taking her leave from her brother, who remained there at the Wall. "I was usually sitting there with tears running down my face." In 2017, the first time she visited the city after her brother's recovery and identification, she felt something entirely different—relief. "I knew I was going home to him," back to Kansas, where he's buried next to their parents and an infant brother who died at childbirth, just a few miles from their farm and surrounded by wheat.

Welcome Home

On the podium with its empty seat honoring the war's missing in action, Maya Lin concluded her Veterans Day address on November 11, 2017, by saying that "if this memorial has helped to welcome you home, . . . then I am deeply honored to have played my part in your story."[32] Her remarks capture two of the dominant themes within MIA accounting, particularly surrounding the instances when "fullest possible accounting" has yet to occur: the notion of homecoming, in particular a delayed "welcome home," and that of stories both told and still playing out, almost a half-century after the end of the war in Southeast Asia. In my conversations with MIA families and veterans, the notion of "home" was regularly invoked— whether as the geographic object of repatriation (home to American soil), or the more metaphorical locus of loss and return ("he's finally home" or "until he's home"). The term also arose in discussions of Vietnam veterans' sense of national belonging, or rather exclusion, on their return from Southeast Asia. For example, in learning about the Wisconsin "hero bike"—the motorcycle left at the Wall in 1995 and dedicated to the state's thirty-seven MIAs—I reached out to two of the veterans who helped create it, Ken "Polack" Pezewski and Bob "Hogman" Thompson. They prefer to call the sleek, intricately detailed chopper the "memorial bike" or the "MIA bike." Hogman came up with the idea because of Washington, DC, traffic. Having traveled to the capital for the "Run to The Wall" Memorial Day commemorative gathering, he had become separated from Ken and the other Wisconsin bikers one evening. As he was rumbling through the city, trying to get his bearings, he got to thinking about the various things left at the memorial. And then it came to him: that's what they should do—build a bike from scratch and ride it to the Wall. As he and Ken recounted how they assembled the parts and organized the design competition and fundraisers, Hogman spoke about the discomfiting sense of alienation he felt when he got back from Vietnam. "Every place I went, I never felt I was home."[33] The bike, in some small measure, grew out of that disorientation; roaming around the streets of DC on his motorcycle, the idea of memorializing those who never came home through the craftsmanship of those who did—and yet never really felt at home—seemed a fitting tribute.

In the absence of state-led forms of remembrance and recognition in the immediate postwar years, historian G. Kurt Piehler explains that Vietnam veterans "created their own belated parades."[34] Similar to MIA families grappling with "ambiguous loss," they devised their own memorial objects and rituals of remembrance. In recent years, Vietnam veterans have gotten some help; they've started to receive more commemorative attention, as local, state, and national efforts to thank them and welcome them home proliferate—or, as the celebrated Anishinaabe writer Jim Northrup once put it, "It's getting popular to be a Vietnam vet." In 2009, Wisconsin Public Television staff floated an idea to some local Vietnam veterans, an initiative to document and memorialize the Vietnam War experience: what about a "welcome home" event, with a parade, a chance to gather veterans from all around the state? For the most part, the plan was met with skepticism. Producer Mike Derks recalled, "One guy said, 'I wouldn't cross the street to be welcomed home. People had their chance.'"[35] Eventually they pitched another idea—instead of a parade, the event would take place at the fabled Green Bay Packers stadium, Lambeau Field. Eyes lit up, interest grew, and veteran groups got behind the idea, what eventually became LZ (as in landing zone) Lambeau 2010.[36] Those killed in action and missing in action would take center stage, literally: in the middle of the football field, 1,244 empty white chairs marked the number of service members "who did not make it home," and Rolling Thunder Chapter 3 put on a Missing Man Table ceremony. Many of the veterans from northern Wisconsin, including those from the Red Cliff VFW post, made the trip south to attend, often accompanied by their spouses and children. As one veteran recalled, "As soon as I saw the advertisement on TV, I knew I wanted to go." When he got there, he was struck by how fellow veterans greeted one another: "Welcome home, brother, welcome home." After years of silence, that masculine code of mourning that kept stories—and, for some, memories—under tight wraps was finally given room to remember the war out loud and in public.[37]

Among the various highlights of the three-day event, Wisconsin's Native American traditions helped guide the belated homecoming rituals. Representatives of eleven tribes, five rows deep, led the color guard for the grand entry ceremony, with five drum groups singing honor songs to the veterans as they passed by. "Before the posting and retreat of the colors, Emcee George Greendeer, Oneida Nation Vietnam veteran, asked veterans to forgive the country that did not treat them well upon their return home and offered a prayer and a moment of silence for the soldiers lost in the Vietnam War."[38] Wearing a black "Marine Veteran" baseball cap and holding an eagle feather, Jim Northrup stepped to the podium to address the stadium later that evening. He introduced himself first in Ojibwe and then in English as being from "the Fond du Lac Reservation, in what is now called Minnesota."[39] That got some laughs and whistles. But what set the crowd roaring with delight was his description of his writing. He warmed up by explaining, "I'm an old Ojibwe warrior. My goal is to be the last surviving Vietnam veteran." Then a smile, "So far, so good."[40] He continued, "I write about Vietnam in the form of poetry, short stories, and I do it because it's helped with trauma of combat. I sometimes call it my brain takin' a shit."[41]

But then Northrup grew more serious and recited a poem about his late brother, Rodney Charles Northrup, one of three he would share that evening:

wahbegan

Didja ever hear a sound
smell something
taste something

that brought you back
to Vietnam, instantly?
Didja ever wonder
when it would end?
It ended for my brother.
He died in the war
but didn't fall down
for fifteen tortured years.
His flashbacks are over,
another casualty whose name
will never be on the Wall.
Some can find peace
only in death.
The sound of his
family crying hurt.
The smell of the flowers
didn't comfort us.
The bitter taste
in my mouth
still sours me.
How about a memorial
for those who made it
through the war
but still died
before their time?[42]

Northrup acknowledged the belatedness of the nation's care for the war's living—that is, the unexceptional, even absent, care that allowed his brother, who served in the US Army "in country 1968–69," to return damaged and haunted by the experiences of combat.[43] His poem touches on the same concern Mary Defoe expressed in her letter to the Department of Veterans Affairs after her husband Ken's death in 2013. She explained that it wasn't until 2007, through a casual conversation with his brother, that Ken learned that he was eligible for PTSD compensation—after struggling with it for forty years. "He and other vets have expressed their belief that the VA is just waiting for them to die." And yet for her husband, she explained, his identity as a Vietnam veteran was a "huge part of his legacy, and even though he didn't say this, I know he didn't want to be forgotten when he died."[44]

If being forgotten crystallizes the absence of care on a national level—the failure to rehabilitate the battered bodies and psyches of living veterans or to account for the remains of the missing war dead—the acts, gestures, and gifts of remembrance on more intimate, local scales remind us that veterans and war dead, missing or accounted for, belong just as much to families and communities as they do to the state. In Bootin and Rose's invitation to "join us to honor and remember" Wotsy Soulier is the tacit acknowledgment that the nation cannot care for his remains as they would wish—he will likely never be returned—and thus they as his family and the Duwayne Soulier Memorial VFW post as their proxy are the intimate guardians of his memory. The photo-topped sheet cake and the plate of food blessed and offered before his mother's grave—like Deanna's bundle of wheat at the Wall—welcomed him home in absentia. The family marked the occasion, an end of sorts, for an accounting mission that will never be full and never be complete.

· 2018 ·

Funeral Announcement For Marines Killed During Vietnam War (House, J., Killen, J., Runnels, G.)

Release No: 18-148 Sept. 21, 2018

The Defense POW/MIA Accounting Agency (DPAA) announced today that the remains of three U.S. servicemen, accounted for from the Vietnam War, are being returned to their families for burial with full military honors.

They are Capt. John A. House, II, 28, of Pelham, New York; Lance Cpl. John D. Killen, III, 18, of Davenport, Iowa; and Cpl. Glyn L. Runnels, Jr., 21, of Birmingham, Alabama, all U.S. Marine Corps. These men, accounted for on Dec. 22, 2015, will be buried as a group Sept. 27, 2018 in Arlington National Cemetery, near Washington, D.C.

Partial remains of two other servicemen who were lost in this incident and were individually identified in 2013, are also represented in this group. They are Marine Lance Cpl. Merlin R. Allen, 20, of Madison, Wisconsin, and Navy Hospital Corpsman Michael B. Judd, 21, of Cleveland, Ohio.[1]

The press release was standard Defense POW/MIA Accounting Agency (DPAA) practice. The video, on the other hand, was a special production. Opening with a birds-eye view of a mountainside covered in dense forest but for a patch of barren earth, a caption appears in the far-left corner, typewriter style, letter by letter: "Actual Recovery Site." Strident strings give way to a distant beeping and whining pitch. We hear its sounds before the image of the metal detector arrives. Scenes of a recovery site shuffle amid frames of black screen and white lettering: "OUR EFFORTS" . . . "RELENTLESS" . . .

The three-and-a-half-minute clip featured on the Department of Defense FY2019 Budget webpage in the fall of 2018 chronicled the story of Mrs. Amy House and her son Eric as they took part in a chain-of-custody ceremony at the DPAA facility on Oahu, Hawaii— that is, when they encountered, after fifty years of absence, the remains of Captain John A. House II, the pilot who died trying to save the men of Team Striker on June 30, 1967.[2] "We are as confident as we can be within the limits of our science that those remains at least in part represent your husband," explains Laurel, the anthropologist from the 2012 recovery mission, to the mother and son on their tour of the facility before they enter the family visitation room.

It's an earnest production in its attempts to harness the visit's poignant moments of recognition and ritual and thus attest to the exceptional nature of the MIA accounting mission. With the family's individual biographies of dispossession unveiled along the way, we learn that Captain House's son was only twenty-eight days old when his father went missing in action and that Amy House never remarried. Family loyalty and loss become enfolded into the video's larger national narrative.

"OUR DEDICATION" . . . "RELENTLESS" . . . "UNTIL THE NATION'S PROMISE" . . . "FULFILLED."

In the visitation room, we hear Mrs. House remark, "It's so minuscule," and we witness her and her son place the top layer of the blanket gently over the plastic evidence bag and fasten its edges with the traditional golden safety pins. Whatever is left of Captain John A. House II, it's such a tiny fragment that it disappears into the flattened bundle. Set on the funeral home stretcher, the remains are wheeled outside the building and between two rows of civilian and military staff, hands on hearts and saluting respectively. We watch mother and son as they look on.

What the captions don't tell us is that that "minuscule" piece will be interred together with the other fragments of remains that helped account for Lance Corporal John Killen and Corporal Glyn Runnels in Arlington National Cemetery. Nor does it mention that previously identified Lance Corporal Merlin Allen and Corpsman Michael Judd are also considered part of this group burial. A single flag-draped casket, containing the single securely-pinned blanket, will be lowered into the earth, and a single tombstone will eventually mark the collective grave. In the interim months, five temporary markers will crowd the head of their common plot. Although all five men are now officially accounted for, the tiny bits of bone and teeth to be buried cannot be definitively, exclusively associated with any one individual from the group. That aspect of their story is too complicated for a compact portrait such as this.

Instead, one more black-and-white frame draws a line under the message: "END OF A MOURNFUL TALE."

Conclusion

THE CHANGES ARE BOTH STARK AND SUBTLE. In the wake of the "failed science" critiques and the 2014 reorganization of the MIA accounting mission, the US military's forensic anthropology laboratory had relocated by the summer of 2015. Moving from one end of the Joint Base Pearl Harbor–Hickam to another, the lab and the other operational wings of the former Command, known now as DPAA West, settled into the Senator Daniel K. Inouye Defense POW/MIA Accounting Agency Center of Excellence.[1] Every detail of the new three-story facility—the wing-like span of its roof and waist-high wall of cascading water that runs along the entrance portico to the atrium garden, the light-filled corridors, the expansive examination rooms and state-of-the-art equipment—telegraphed the pivot toward a sleek, efficient, and above all, goals-driven mission.

In April 2018, I returned to Hawaii to visit the lab, now called the Scientific Analysis Directorate, to see firsthand how the reorganization had affected the work of recovery and identification. From my first steps into the building, it was clear how much anxiety hovered around the question of quantifiable outputs; the "accounting-for" goal set by the National Defense Authorization Act of 2010—two hundred identifications per year—still loomed large, literally. In the lobby, a massive, three-panel monitor projected the agency's image to the visiting public. Names, narratives, and numbers combined to showcase individuated and collective success. The panel on the left had a split screen: the lower half profiled a recently identified service member, complete with a headshot and the individual's name, rank, branch, conflict, and date of identification; on the top half, photographs cycled through scenes from recovery missions and repatriations. The middle panel had an interactive touch screen that allowed visitors to search for an individual case, a "service member profile," calling up its details, including photographs and text. But most telling of all was the panel on the right, whose screen displayed the "FY [Fiscal Year] 2018 Tracking," with a line graph charting the monthly target number of identifications against the to-date number of identifications.[2] The midyear 2018 numbers tacked well below the insistent line mapping the diagonal path to two hundred. Thus far, the lab was trailing its FY2017 pace, which had for the first time ever cleared the two hundred threshold—201 identifications for the year, thirty-four of which were made in the final month (September).[3] As Lab Director John Byrd explained, with the complex variables of recovery and identification, the achievement was "the equivalent of putting a man on the moon." And with that threshold met, they were now expected to make a successful lunar landing each year going forward.

The United States military's MIA accounting mission sits at a critical juncture. To meet the congressional benchmarks (rumored to be recalibrated to 350 identifications per year by 2020) and the raised expectations of families, veterans, and the media, the idea has been broached—though repeatedly rejected—of shifting the focus of energy and resources away from the Vietnam War's missing and increasingly toward the Korean War and World War II unaccounted for. The numbers from FY2017 themselves tell an incongruous tale of input and output: of the 201 identifications, only sixteen were from the Vietnam War, and of those sixteen, six were identifications of additional remains for individuals previously accounted for; yet 70 percent of DPAA resources are allocated for the Vietnam War.[4] There are other more tangible harbingers of gradually shifting focus and energy as well. One need only walk among the examination tables on the third floor of the new building to witness the change underway: you are met with row after row of complete or nearly complete skeletons, a far cry from the characteristic handful of bone fragments or teeth recovered from a Southeast Asia air crash site. They are instead the remains of Korean War unknowns disinterred from the Punchbowl, the nearby National Memorial Cemetery of the Pacific, along with World War II unknowns from the Manila American Cemetery in the Philippines, from the USS *West Virginia* and *California* of the Pearl Harbor attack, and the Battle of Tarawa, as well as the less complete elements of the Korean War

K208 cases and the fifty-five boxes of remains repatriated from North Korea in July 2018.[5] These bones, much more so than the scant recoveries and the unilateral turnovers from Southeast Asia, represent the "path to two hundred."

If numbers of annual identifications are the chief metric of the state's capacity to fulfill its obligations to its missing war dead, then Southeast Asia will gradually, necessarily, take a backseat to the two other conflicts. The more feasible recoveries from the Vietnam War have all but dried up, and in their place, the thousands of unknowns from the battlefields of the Korean Peninsula and the islands and atolls of the South Pacific will be unearthed in this project of exceptional care. But it is a contested evolution, one that does not sit well with some of the core members of the Vietnam War POW/MIA movement. Recall Ann Mills-Griffiths's statement at the 2009 congressional hearing: "It all started with the Vietnam War. If it wasn't for the Vietnam War, we wouldn't have the organization, the personnel, the assets and resources devoted that are today." There are battles ahead that will likely pit one conflict's set of mourners against the other in a climate of scarce resources and under the pressures of tabulating and demonstrating success before Congress and the nation. Distinctions are already being drawn. "We are losing the witnesses, and in Southeast Asia the soil is such that it's acidic, and it just eats remains," Mills-Griffiths argued recently. "And literally the remains are disappearing, so sure, there's a greater urgency."[6] Yet staking claim to the urgency of accounting for one's *own* absent war dead risks creating a hierarchy of both sanctity and suffering. Whose unaccounted for merit more attention, more money, more time? Within the calculus of individuated sacrifice, the missing may end up further dividing, rather than uniting, families in their advocacy for fullest possible accounting—or so it seems from the more concentrated centers of power and information dissemination within the MIA accounting mission—from the laboratory in Hawaii and the DPAA annual briefings to congressional hearings, media reports, and commemorative events at sites like the Vietnam Veterans Memorial on the National Mall.

APPLEFEST, OCTOBER 2017. The smells of the food stalls mixed in the cool morning air: kettle corn, apple bratwurst, deep-fried cheese curds, and corn dogs on a stick; apple crisp, apple pie, caramel apples, apple butter and apple jam, apple cider, and apples themselves, stand after stand of Cortlands and Honeycrisps. The orchards I had driven past the day before, along Highway J in the hills behind Bayfield, were well represented among the vendors that lined the town's main street. After sampling enough sticky, sweet food for the day, I walked up the hill to Diane's house where Butch and others were gathered to prepare the combined VFW and American Legion float. In fact, I arrived too late to do much helping, and so for the next hour or so, a small group of us sat in the shade of the driveway and talked, watching the cars pass by in search of parking, as Bayfield's streets and lawns gradually began to overflow with vehicles. The float for the Grand Parade consisted of a trailer decked in red, white, and blue metallic fringe, with six American flags adorning the sides. In the flatbed of the trailer, they had placed a picnic table, where Butch and another vet would sit for the duration of the event. Rich backed his shiny red truck into the drive and they hooked up the trailer. Eleven men would represent the two veterans organizations from the region, carrying honor guard flags and dressed in their VFW and American Legion jackets. The sole WWII veteran arrived and, clasping the arm of a younger vet, was helped into the truck's front passenger seat. Six women, including a mother-daughter duo from the pancake breakfast at the post the day before, comprised the Women's Auxiliary contingent, plus me and two young girls. The ladies from the auxiliary were to walk behind the trailer, tossing candy (bubble gum and Tootsie Rolls) to the crowd and handing out small American flags to children. I got to do the latter, which gave me a chance to interact with kids and their parents.

I took two bundles of flags to start with and looked down the hill at the crowds gathered on either side of the street, scanning for my first set of kids. I'd never done anything like this before. In junior high, I'd been in a marching band; maybe I had even tossed candy out as part of some small-town parade, but I'd never passed out flags. I wondered whether this is what happened—flags distributed curbside—right before Lance Corporal Merlin Allen's homecoming. Is this how symbols of a nation become imprinted into a child's sense of being and belonging? Something as simple as a flag handed to you, like a prize, from a stranger in the middle of brilliant fall day, as decked-out cars and trailers pass by and bubble gum rolls to your feet? For the past decade, I had studied how the accounting mission made the nation something real, something tangible, in people's lives—how it touched them and they it. As the parade started to take form, I knew I was glimpsing not the memory of missing war dead at work, but rather a hometown ritual that drew from the deep well of the nation, an artifact of both war and peace, and yet felt—and looked and smelled and sounded—profoundly local.

Ours was the first float, just behind the Bayfield fire truck that led the procession. Despite the slow march down Rittenhouse Avenue, those of us tasked with the flag distribution kept falling farther and farther behind; people really wanted the flags—kids of three or four stretched out their hands to accept my gift, their eyes registering wonder, bafflement, sometimes eagerness. Occasionally I would miss one and a parent would get my attention, motioning for a flag. Sometimes I ran out and had to race to catch up with the trailer, missing stretches of the crowd (and children) in between. Halfway down the main block, I heard someone call out my name. Merl Allen's brother-in-law, Rick, waved from crowd. He and his wife, Sheila, Merl's younger sister, had come from nearby Washburn to watch the parade led by the veterans, their numbers one fewer for her family's loss and her brother's absence.

Later, when I asked Butch whether he thought the parade and specifically their float went over well, he nodded. Sitting on the picnic table in the trailer, he had a good view of the crowd assembled. He was impressed with how people reacted, how they stood for and applauded the float as it went by. The signs on the side of Rich's truck announced that the vets marching and riding in the float were from the Gulf Wars, the Vietnam and Korean Wars, and World War II. And yet the effect wasn't one of sacrifice parsed out by conflict. Instead, walking side by side, the veterans represented the local contribution to the nation, which the crowd honored collectively through their applause, and the children, however inchoately, with their flags.

In the celebratory air of a small-town parade, the flags, the veterans, and the float called forth a stirring medley of ideals—sacrifice, honor, duty, obligation, and gratitude. The veterans were recognized that day as being from *there*—from the region and its small towns that dot the shoreline along Lake Superior—and yet having fought *over there*, on some foreign country's soil. They could be grandfathers or uncles, fathers, brothers, cousins, classmates, fellow churchgoers, or barstool mates. For some among the small group, years or injury denied them the possibility of walking the parade route; others, like Merl Allen, Wotsy Soulier, and Jimmy Hessing, were altogether absent. But if that hint of war's toll registered, it was fleeting. The Applefest Grand Parade celebrated military service in its hometown fashion, cleansed of the horrors that war may have introduced into those veterans' lives, the lives of their families, and the lives of those whose loved ones never came home. The sweet autumn air, brilliant blue sky, apples and candy, flags and fire truck all urged a different set of reflections, sentiments far from the ghastly scenes of Wilfred Owen's "Dulce et Decorum Est" or the memories that so tortured the brother of the "old Ojibwe warrior" and writer Jim Northrup.

And yet those scenes are mutually constituting: Merl Allen's death in the fiery helicopter crash on the mountainside in central Vietnam ("Is this the reward for serving my country?") is not so separate from the pageantry of a local harvest festival parade as we might think. In defining the nation as an "imagined community," Benedict Anderson argues that however beset with inequality or exploitation, "the nation is always conceived as a deep, horizontal comradeship." While he dispenses with stratifying aspects such as class, race, and gender too easily, he notes an important consequence of the sense of shared belonging. "Ultimately it is this fraternity that makes it possible, over the past two centuries, for so many millions of people, not so much to kill, as willingly to die for such limited imaginings."[7] That willingness to die—or, in American military parlance, to "make the ultimate sacrifice"—represents one of the defining features of a nation, however fragmented and instantiated it may be in its local rituals of belonging.

Less clear, however, is what flows from that sacrifice. What *is* Merl Allen's reward, then, if he must die on enemy soil, halfway around the world? How should a nation acknowledge the hundreds, or thousands, or millions of deaths on its behalf? What does it owe those dispossessed of its children, spouses, parents, and fellow service members? Running the gamut from small-town parades to the war monuments on the National Mall, spaces and practices of public commemoration in the United States answer—or evade—the chaos of violence through the ordering symbols of the nation. In this way, the Applefest float echoes the work of remembrance that unfolds daily at one of the nation's most sacred sites—Arlington National Cemetery and its celebrated monument, the Tomb of the Unknowns. The tomb is a space, above all, of clean lines and polished surfaces, where war's destruction gives way to ordered memory. Even more than the unknown buried there, the contemporary military takes center stage, as the visiting public, disembarking from tour buses on the hour and the half-hour, comes to witness the Changing of the Guard ceremony. Synchronized steps and heel clicks, shouldered rifles and white gloves, the ceremony performs military perfection before the backdrop of the Unknown Soldiers from World War I, World War II, and the Korean War. The Vietnam War crypt has already been emptied, but that story becomes one of cutting-edge science restoring individual identity.

The grit and muck and blood and tears of combat can only be intimated. For as Viet Thanh Nguyen explains, "beautiful, quiet war cemeteries mask the certainty . . . that these dead died in heaps, in fragments, in piles, in pieces, their limbs bent at impossible angles and their muddy clothes sometimes ripped from their bodies by the velocity of the man-made force that took their lives."[8]

But when bodies don't come home and fates remain unsettled, such order is even harder to craft; the absent war dead cannot be so easily "eased out" or "settled safely."[9] They require different rituals. Through their stories and the stories of those who mourn them and seek their return, I have explored how forensic science has itself become part of a complex ritual response, changing the way the United States as a nation remembers and honors its war dead. Its precision and promise have raised expectations of what is due and what is possible. In doing so, the science of MIA accounting has generated its own politics and obstacles of exceptional remembrance.

"It may be that forensic science has reached the point where there will be no other unknowns in any war."[10] Although an off-the-cuff response at a press briefing, when Secretary of Defense William Cohen uttered those words, he forecast a different modality of remembering men and women who die in service of the nation—one that precludes the possibility of *not* knowing, or *not* determining, an individual service member's identity, due in large part to advances in scientific knowledge and practice. He was correct. In the context of US military engagement in the Middle East since 2003, there are no unknown—meaning unidentified—American war dead. The numbers of US missing in action and killed in action but unrecovered are astoundingly low: from Iraq and Afghanistan combined, there are three missing individuals, and all three are Department of Defense contractors captured in the opening years of Operation Iraqi Freedom.[11] Myriad factors explain these numbers, from changes in how the nation wages war to its increased capacity to recover the bodies of its war dead and to identify those remains, especially through DNA testing. In the legacy of the Vietnam War's fraught accounting mission, families of current service members—like Myeshia Johnson—have come to expect the speedy recovery, repatriation, identification, and return of their loved ones' remains—that is, fullest possible accounting.

What are the effects writ large of this shift from anonymous and aggregated unknowns to individuated remains and MIA homecomings? The identification of First Lieutenant Michael Joseph Blassie as the Vietnam War's Unknown introduced a new dynamic of expectation into national commemoration and, with it, a new language of remembrance, one in which science simultaneously offered families and veterans some respite from otherwise unabated grief and the state a means to demonstrate its singular capacity to recover and send home its fallen service members. In that ethos of exceptional care, the memory of a contentious war could be redirected and exceptionalism reasserted years later through the proxy bodies—bones—of the formerly missing, now recovered and identified, war dead. The "work of the dead," to borrow from Thomas Laqueur, is not limited to the past. Caring for absent fallen, like performing military perfection at the nation's most hallowed ground, can also animate more contemporary and future-oriented projections of national belonging. As Nguyen warns, "The memories the living create of the dead—and the dead themselves—are strategic resources in the campaigns of future wars. Once the dead seemed to cry out against war, but now, just as plausibly, the dead seem to cry out in support of our troops who wage new wars."[12]

And yet such instrumentalism fails to capture fully the memories the living create of the dead far removed from the ambit of exclusively national commemoration. When the Allen siblings assembled on York Island to bury their brother next to their parents, they returned him to—literally submerged him in—the water-filled plot of the family's last vestige of their cherished island. When Bootin and his sisters shared their memories of their still absent brother, they did so within the melded traditions of the military and the Chippewa nation. When Deanna Klenda buried her brother Dean in the church cemetery surrounded by wheat fields, she drew him back into the embrace of her farming community, with its immediate and extended family. Though the nation is never entirely removed from these sites and rituals of remembrance, it does not define the memory work at hand. Rather, those were acts of distinctly local reclamation—be it of land, physical remains, or shared memories of a long-absent relative. Similarly, in the face of enduring absence, a Walmart cake with a tiny frosting heart to punctuate a message of remembrance and love or an archive of yellowed newspaper clippings and Western Union telegrams are also acts of exceptional care in and of themselves, prompted by the nation but enacted by families and their communities of fellow mourners.

If Secretary Cohen's 1998 projection of no other unknown from any (future) war continues to hold true, then the United States military's MIA accounting mission can only ever be a finite endeavor. The arc can only stretch in one direction—backward, into the past. And yet at the pace currently set by existent technology, expertise, funding, and political will (two hundred identifications annually), it would take 205 years to identify half of the total eighty-two thousand unaccounted for—the forty-one thousand individual service members who were not presumed lost at sea or otherwise deemed non-recoverable. At 350 identifications per year, that number drops to 117 years.

Having quantified the sacred, the mathematics mask the fundamental conundrum of the MIA accounting mission. At some point, the bonds of fictive kinship may stretch so far that the ties lose meaning. A century from now, the unaccounted for will be five, six, seven generations removed from their "primary next of kin." Who among them will remember Wotsy? Perhaps the Duwayne Soulier Memorial Post will still be standing; perhaps local veterans of future wars will know his story; perhaps his memory will find its way into the Red Cliff Band of Lake Superior Chippewa rituals of remembrance that have no need for underwater archaeology and DNA testing.

If he never comes home, perhaps his family's descendants and his community will take some measure of comfort that the nation that sent him to die on its behalf once tried to find him and bring him home.

Notes

Homecoming

1. According to the US military's formal system of categorization, Allen's precise status was killed in action/body not recovered, but until his recovery in 2012, he was listed in less formal contexts as missing in action, for example, as one of the state of Wisconsin's thirty-seven MIAs.

2. Adam Rosenblatt uses this phrase to capture the communal side of mourning and advocating for the dead, especially the missing. Rosenblatt, "International Forensic Investigations and the Human Rights of the Dead," *Human Rights Quarterly* 32, no. 4 (2010): 934. Similarly, Jay Winter writes of the expanding bonds of bereavement and "communities in mourning" after World War I. Winter, *Sites of Memory, Sites of Mourning: The Great War in European Cultural History* (Cambridge, UK: Cambridge University Press, 1995), 29–53.

Introduction

1. Émile Durkheim, *Elementary Forms of Religious Life,* trans. Karen Fields (New York: The Free Press, 1995), 215. His son's death was "a blow from which Durkheim did not recover." Joy Damousi, "Mourning Practices," in *The Cambridge History of the First World War,* vol. 3, *Civil Society,* ed. Jay Winter (Cambridge, UK: Cambridge University Press, 2016), 369.

2. Durkheim, *Elementary Forms of Religious Life,* 34–38.

3. Robert Hertz, "A Contribution to a Study of the Collective Representation of Death," in *Saints, Heroes, Myths, and Rites,* eds. and trans. Alexander Riley, Sarah Daynes, and Cyril Isnart (Boulder, CO: Paradigm Publishers, 2009), 145.

4. Chapter 1 examines the American response to mass death in war, beginning with the Civil War, whose "work of death" redefined the nation and its

culture. Drew Gilpin Faust, *This Republic of Suffering: Death and the American Civil War* (New York: Knopf, 2008), xviii. Both that chapter and the book as a whole have been informed by a rich body of anthropological scholarship on missing persons as victims of state-sponsored violence and human rights abuses; see, for example, Isaias Rojas-Perez, *Mourning Remains: State Atrocity, Exhumations, and Governing the Disappeared in Peru's Postwar Andes* (Stanford: Stanford University Press, 2017); Adam Rosenblatt, *Digging for the Disappeared: Forensic Science after Atrocity* (Stanford: Stanford University Press, 2015); Francisco Ferrándiz, "Exhuming the Defeated: Civil War Mass Graves in 21st-century Spain," *American Ethnologist* 40, no. 1 (2013): 38–54; Layla Renshaw, *Exhuming Loss: Memory, Materiality and Mass Graves of the Spanish Civil War* (Walnut Creek, CA: Left Coast Press, 2011); Paul Sant Cassia, *Bodies of Evidence: Burial, Memory, and the Recovery of Missing Persons in Cyprus* (New York: Berghahn Books, 2005); Victoria Sanford, *Buried Secrets: Truth and Human Rights in Guatemala* (New York: Palgrave Macmillan, 2003); and the edited volumes, Derek Congram, ed., *Missing Persons: Multidisciplinary Perspectives on the Disappeared* (Toronto: Canadian Scholars' Press, 2016); and Francisco Ferrándiz and Antonius C. G. M. Robben, eds., *Necropolitics: Mass Graves and Exhumations in the Age of Human Rights* (Philadelphia: University of Pennsylvania Press, 2016).

5. Arguing a similar point in his ethnographic study of Lawrence Livermore National Laboratory, Hugh Gusterson notes that "some of our most expensive scientific experiments are saturated with elements of myth and ritual." *Nuclear Rites: A Weapons Laboratory at the End of the Cold War* (Berkeley: University of California Press, 1996), 152.

6. By 1973, with the signing of the Paris Peace Accords, the US government aggregated not just prisoners of war (POWs) and MIAs, but also those killed in action/body not recovered into this collective group of the "unaccounted for." See H. Bruce Franklin, *M.I.A or Mythmaking in America* (New York: Lawrence Hill Books), 96–98. In his discussion of the three "wartime categories" of unaccounted for—namely, POW, MIA, and KIA/BNR—Thomas Hawley notes "the acronym *MIA* has become a sort of cultural shorthand for the entire issue of unaccounted-for [service members], a fact which, among other things, has effaced the evidentiary differences that formerly sought to distinguish the three categories with as much precision as possible." Thomas M. Hawley, *The Remains of War: Bodies, Politics, and the Search for American Soldiers Unaccounted for in Southeast Asia* (Durham, NC: Duke University Press), 45.

7. In identifying science as a language of remembrance, I am building on Jay Winter's argument that language (which he defines through the "different creative arts") frames memory and thus our "meditations on war." Winter, *War beyond Words: Languages of Remembrance from the Great War to the Present* (Cambridge, UK: Cambridge University Press, 2017), 2.

8. Ariel Garfinkel, *Scofflaw: International Law and America's Deadly Weapons in Vietnam* (Sunnyvale, CA: Lucità, 2018), 10–11; Ben Kiernan and Taylor Owen, "Making More Enemies than We Kill? Calculating U.S. Bomb Ton-

nages Dropped on Laos and Cambodia, and Weighing Their Implications," *Japan Focus: Asia-Pacific Journal* 13, no. 17 (2015): 1–3.

9. Edwin A. Martini, *Agent Orange: History, Science, and the Politics of Uncertainty* (Amherst: University of Massachusetts Press, 2012), 2–3; see also, Susan Hammond, "Redefining Agent Orange: Mitigating Its Impacts," in *Interactions with a Violent Past: Reading Post-Conflict Landscapes in Cambodia, Laos, and Vietnam*, eds. Vatthana Pholsena and Oliver Tappe (Singapore: NUS Press, 2013), 186–215. For an ethnographic study of the biomedical effects of dioxin, namely within the realm of prenatal screening and diagnoses, see Tine Gammeltoft, *Haunting Images: A Cultural Account of Selective Reproduction in Vietnam* (Berkeley: University of California Press, 2014).

10. Vietnam War US Military Fatal Casualty Statistics, Electronic Records Reference Report, National Archives, accessed December 13, 2018, https://www.archives.gov/research/military/vietnam-war/casualty-statistics. Viet Thanh Nguyen underscores the chasm between American and Vietnamese loss, noting that "the body count in Vietnam for all sides was closer to one-tenth of the population, while the American dead amounted to about 0.035 percent of the population." Nguyen, *Nothing Ever Dies: Vietnam and the Memory of War* (Cambridge, MA: Harvard University Press, 2016), 7.

11. Defense POW/MIA Accounting Agency, "Vietnam War Accounting: History," accessed December 13, 2018, http://www.dpaa.mil/Our-Missing/Vietnam-War/.

12. This figure is as of May 2019. The Defense POW/MIA Accounting Agency routinely updates the status of unaccounted-for Americans lost in the Vietnam War on its website: http://www.dpaa.mil/Resources/FactSheets/ArticleView/tabid/10163/Article/569613/progress-in-vietnam.aspx.

13. Heonik Kwon, *Ghosts of War in Vietnam,* 48–49; Shaun Malarney, "'The Fatherland Remembers Your Sacrifice': Commemorating War Dead in North Vietnam," in *The Country of Memory: Remaking the Past in Late Socialist Vietnam,* ed. Hue-Tam Ho Tai (Berkeley: University of California Press, 2001), 46–76; and Tâm T. T. Ngô, "Bones of Contention: Placing the Dead of the 1979 Sino-Vietnamese Border War" (paper presented, Radboud University, Nijmegen, the Netherlands, November 1, 2018).

14. Thomas Hawley notes that "even in 1973, the Vietnam War was the most accounted for war in US history." Hawley, *The Remains of War,* 34.

15. These numbers are approximations. See related discussions in Franklin, *M.I.A or Mythmaking in America,* 12; and Michael Dolski, "When X Doesn't Mark the Spot: Historical Investigation and Identifying Remains from the Korean War," in *Missing Persons: Multidisciplinary Perspectives on the Disappeared,* ed. Derek Congram (Toronto: Canadian Scholars Press, 2016), 149–50.

16. Faust, *This Republic of Suffering,* 102.

17. H. Bruce Franklin argues that the conflation of these two categories, embodied by the POW/MIA flag, served as a "myth" that, harnessed by consecutive administrations, not only worked to justify the war's extension but also profoundly influenced American foreign policy well into the 1990s (Franklin, *M.I.A or*

Mythmaking in America). Though he also draws on popular cultural representations, Franklin's analysis primarily concerns governmental policies, special reports, hearings, etc., "investigations" that, as Thomas Hawley notes, "are constrained by the rhetorical and representational milieus in which they are produced." Hawley, *The Remains of War,* 11–12. On this "myth" and its object of critique, see also Michael Allen, *Until the Last Man Comes Home: POWs, MIAs, and the Unending Vietnam War* (Chapel Hill: University of North Carolina Press, 2009), 158, 180.

18. Ann Mills-Griffiths, interview with author, November 17, 2017. On the military's MIA status determination process, see Douglas L. Clarke, *The Missing Man: Politics and the MIA* (Washington, DC: National Defense University Press, 1979), 13–25.

19. Allen, *Until the Last Man Comes Home,* 101–78; Franklin, *M.I.A. or Mythmaking in America;* Hawley, *The Remains of War,* 39–67, 218–19; and Clarke, *The Missing Man,* 2–3, 27–49.

20. Allen, *Until the Last Man Comes Home,* 140–48. The practice of presumptive findings of death was a particularly divisive issue within the POW/MIA movement, "often pitting wives who wished to get on with their lives against parents who told them it was 'easier to get a new husband than a new son.'" Franklin, *M.I.A. or Mythmaking in America,* 84; see also Clarke, *The Missing Man,* 42–45.

21. Hawley, *The Remains of War,* 14–15. On the statistical reporting of the body count, see Douglas Kinnard, *The War Managers* (Hanover, NH: University Press of New England, 1977), 8, 72–75; Edward L. King, *The Death of the Army* (New York: Saturday Review Press, 1972), 101, 105, 106; on body count production and performance, see Fred Turner, *Echoes of Combat: The Vietnam War in American Memory* (New York: Anchor Books, 1996), 26–27; and Susan Jeffords, *The Remasculinization of America: Gender and the Vietnam War* (Bloomington: Indiana University Press, 1989), 7–8.

22. Clarke, *The Missing Man,* 53. Richard Nixon, "Address on the State of the Union Delivered Before a Joint Session of the Congress," January 30, 1974, https://www.presidency.ucsb.edu/documents/address-the-state-the-union -delivered-before-joint-session-the-congress. The phrase has been part of the National League of POW/MIA Families' mission statement since its establishment: "The League's sole purpose is to obtain the release of all prisoners, the fullest possible accounting for the missing and repatriation of all recoverable remains of those who died serving our nation during the Vietnam War." Its voting membership extends to "wives, children, parents, siblings and other close blood and legal relatives of Americans who were or are listed as Prisoners of War (POW), Missing in Action (MIA), Killed in Action/Body not Recovered (KIA/BNR) and returned American Vietnam War POWs." See the organization's website: http://www.pow -miafamilies.org/.

23. Thomas Laqueur, *The Work of the Dead: A Cultural History of Mortal Remains* (Princeton, NJ: Princeton University Press, 2015), 10. See also Adam Rosenblatt's discussion of the forensic work that both enables and constitutes such care, *Digging for the Disappeared,* 167–98, and "Forensic Investigations and Human Rights of the Dead," *Human Rights Quarterly* 32, no. 4 (2010), 949; Jackie Leach Scully, "Naming the Dead: DNA-based Identification of Historical

Remains as an Act of Care," *New Genetics and Society* 33, no. 3 (2014): 313–32; and Layla Renshaw, "Forensic Science as Right and Ritual in the Recovery of World War I Soldiers from the Mass Graves at Fromelles" in *Un siècle de sites funéraires de la Grande Guerre. De l'histoire à la valorisation patrimoniale*, eds. Annette Becker and Stéphane Tison (Paris: Presses Universitaires de Paris Nanterre, 2018), 205–25. Often drawing on French philosopher Emmanual Levinas's ethics of responsibility, the concept of care in anthropology has become increasingly central to discussions of "biomedicine, biopolitics, affective states, forms of moral experience and obligation, structures of exploitation." Elana D. Buch, "Anthropology of Aging and Care," *Annual Review of Anthropology* 44 (2015): 279.

24. Thomas Laqueur, "The Deep Time of the Dead," *Social Research* 78, no. 3 (2011): 800; see also Laqueur, *The Work of the Dead,* 8–10.

25. Laqueur, *The Work of the Dead,* 10. In this passage, Laqueur summarizes Robert Hertz's seminal 1907 essay, "A Contribution to the Study of the Collective Representation of Death."

26. The National League of POW/MIA Families, "The Missing Man Table and Honor Ceremony," accessed December 13, 2018, http://www.pow-miafamilies.org/missing-man-table-and-honors-ceremony.html.

27. See the National League of POW/MIA Families, "History of the POW/MIA Flag," accessed December 13, 2018, https://www.pow-miafamilies.org/history-of-the-powmia-flag.html. Mrs. Mary Hoff was a member of the National League of POW/MIA Families at the time. According to Eldon Robinson, one of the six league founders and brother of Major Larry Robinson, a marine corps pilot shot down over Laos in January 1970, he worked with Hoff on the design, which originally was commissioned in three different versions—red and white, blue and white, and black and white. In the end, they settled on the black and white version, which they felt was more evocative of the POW/MIA experience.

28. Franklin, *M.I.A or Mythmaking in America,* 4. For a careful critique of the flag's symbolism and commemorative politics, see Hawley, *The Remains of War,* 202–10.

29. The figure of $130 million leaves out significant expenses associated with the MIA accounting mission. See Chapter 3, footnote 6. Other countries have undertaken efforts to recover and identify remains of their war dead, including Australia, Israel, Portugal, South Korea, Argentina, and France. On France's repatriation efforts after World War II, see Jean-Marc Dreyfus, "Renationalizing Bodies? The French Search Mission for the Corpses of Deportees in Germany, 1946–58," in *Human Remains and Mass Violence: Methodological Approaches,* eds. Jean-Marc Dreyfus and Élisabeth Anstett (Manchester: Manchester University Press, 2014), 129–45; and on their repatriation efforts after the Indochinese War, see Clarke, *The Missing Man: Politics and the MIA,* 55–58; and M. Kathryn Edwards, *Contesting Indochina: French Remembrance between Decolonization and Cold War* (Berkeley: University of California Press, 2016), 93–96. However, no other country has developed a comprehensive forensic scientific infrastructure comparable to the US MIA accounting mission. See Chapter 1, footnote 5.

30. Salman Rushdie, "Imaginary Homelands," in *Imaginary Homelands: Essays and Criticism 1981–1991* (New York: Penguin Books, 1992), 12.

31. Tim O'Brien, *The Things They Carried* (Houghton Mifflin Harcourt, 1990), 3, 7, 15, 21.

32. For an analysis of the objects left at Vietnam Veterans Memorial and their commemorative work, see Kristin Ann Hass, *Carried to the Wall: American Memory and the Vietnam Veterans Memorial* (Berkeley: University of California Press, 1998); and Paulette G. Curtis, "Filling in the Blanks: Discerning Meaning in the Vietnam Veterans Memorial Collection," *Practicing Anthropology* 33, no. 2 (2011): 11–15.

33. Stephen Greenblatt, "Resonance and Wonder," in *Exhibiting Culture: The Poetics and Politics of Museum Display* eds. Ivan Karp and Steven D. Lavine (Washington, DC: Smithsonian Books, 1991), 42.

34. "The Harley (from Wisconsin) Left at the Wall," *Vietnam Magazine*, April 11, 2012, history.net, http://www.historynet.com/the-harley-from-wisconsin -left-at-the-wall.htm; and "Wisconsin Hero Bike: The Motorcycle Left at The Wall," Vietnam Veterans Memorial Fund blog, "Your Stories. Your Wall," August 20, 2015, https://vvmf.wordpress.com/2015/08/20/wisconsin-hero-bike-the -motorcycle-left-at-the-wall/. See also John B. Sharpless, "Introduction," in Erin Miller, *Wisconsin's 37: The Lives of Those Missing In Action in the Vietnam War,* with John B. Sharpless (Jefferson, NC: McFarland, 2018), 7.

35. Jay Winter, *Sites of Memory, Sites of Mourning: The Great War in European Cultural History* (Cambridge, UK: Cambridge University Press, 1995).

36. For his definition of ethical or just memory that aspires to remembering both one's self and the other and their respective depths of humanity and inhumanity, see Nguyen, *Nothing Ever Dies,* 4–19.

37. See Miller's biographical sketches of those thirty-seven individuals, *Wisconsin's 37*. Of the original thirty-seven men, sixteen have been accounted for as of June 2019. Defense POW/MIA Accounting Agency, "US Accounted-For from the Vietnam War" (Reported For: Wisconsin)," http://www.dpaa.mil/portals /85/Documents/VietnamAccounting/pmsea_acc_p_wi.pdf.

38. "POW/MIA Recovery and Accounting, Panel 1, Part 2," April 2, 2009, C-SPAN, https://www.c-span.org/video/?285046-2/powmia-recovery-accounting -panel-1-part-2.

39. As Winter explains, "All the languages of memory bear traces of the different ways the wars of the twentieth century have changed our lives." *War beyond Words,* 208.

40. Horace Trauben, *With Walt Whitman in Camden: July 16–October 31, 1888* (New York: D. Appleton and Company, 1908), 88.

41. Stephen Jay Gould, *The Mismeasure of Man,* rev. ed. (1981; repr., New York: Norton, 1996), 53.

42. In this sense, sketching the forensic work of MIA accounting focuses on "science in action," both in the laboratory and as its facts circulate among wider publics. Bruno Latour, *Science in Action: How to Follow Scientists and Engineers through Society* (Cambridge, MA: Harvard University Press, 1987). Important models for this approach have included Alondra Nelson, *The Social Life of DNA: Race, Reparations and Reconciliation after the Genome* (Boston: Beacon Press,

2016); Kimberly Tallbear, *Native American DNA: Tribal Belonging and the False Promise of Genetic Science* (Minneapolis: University of Minnesota Press, 2013); Paul Rabinow, *French DNA: Trouble in Purgatory* (Chicago: University of Chicago Press, 1999); and Gusterson, *Nuclear Rites.*

1. Obligations of Care

1. Leah Thorson, "Feeding Deer Is a Growing Tradition at Jefferson Barracks," *St. Louis Post-Dispatch,* February 2, 2014, http://www.stltoday.com/news/local /metro/feeding-deer-is-a-growing-tradition-at-jefferson-barracks/article _0e6eeb7c-1ae3-54fc-b48d-8df1c70bc94c.html.

2. As the chief of the mitochondrial DNA section of the Armed Forces DNA Identification Laboratory, Huffine appeared at the Defense Department press briefing on the identification of the Vietnam War Unknown Soldier, held on June 30, 1998. US Department of Defense, News Transcript, Press Briefing, June 30, 1998, http://archive.defense.gov/Transcripts/Transcript.aspx?TranscriptID =1627.

3. See Micki McElya, *The Politics of Mourning: Death and Honor in Arlington National Cemetery* (Cambridge, MA: Harvard University Press, 2016), 1–2; and Sarah Wagner and Thomas Matyók, "Monumental Change: The Shifting Politics of Obligation at the Tomb of the Unknowns," *History & Memory* 30, no. 1 (2018): 40–75.

4. Ken Inglis, "Entombing Unknown Soldiers: From London and Paris to Baghdad," *History & Memory* 5, no. 2 (1993): 17. On the commemorative aspects of World War I monuments to unknown and missing soldiers, see Laura Wittman, *The Tomb of the Unknown Soldier, Modern Mourning, and the Reinvention of the Mystical Body* (Toronto: University of Toronto Press, 2011); Jay Winter, *Sites of Memory, Sites of Mourning: The Great War in European Cultural History* (Cambridge, UK: Cambridge University Press, 1995), 27–28, 78–116; Thomas Laqueur, "Memory and Naming in the Great War," in *Commemorations: The Politics of National Identity*, ed. John Gillis (Princeton, NJ: Princeton University Press, 1994), 156–58; George Lachmann Mosse, *Fallen Soldiers: Reshaping the Memory of the World Wars* (Oxford: Oxford University Press, 1990), 94–98; and Geoff Dyer, *The Missing of the Somme* (New York: Vintage, 1994).

5. "While other countries attend to their missing, the time, money, and importance attributed to this mission in the US far exceeds them." Michael Dolski, "When X Doesn't Mark the Spot: Historical Investigation and Identifying Remains from the Korean War," in *Missing Persons: Multidisciplinary Perspectives on the Disappeared,* ed. Derek Congram (Toronto: Canadian Scholars' Press, 2016), 164.

6. Historian Christian Appy argues that "the Vietnam War shattered the central tenet of American national identity," namely American exceptionalism. It is through Vietnam, he notes, that Americans learned "hard truths about themselves and their nation on the backs of a people they dehumanized and killed and whose country they wrecked. It was an expensive education and Vietnam bore by far its

greatest costs." *American Reckoning: The Vietnam War and Our National Identity* (New York: Viking, 2015), xiii–xiv.

7. Antoine Prost explains that the "primacy of increasingly powerful and available artillery dominated the effects of a war in which industry could produce seemingly unlimited torrents of steel to destroy the enemy." "The Dead," in *The Cambridge History of the First World War*, vol. 3, *Civil Society*, ed. Jay Winter (Cambridge, UK: Cambridge University Press, 2016), 563. In this same chapter, he discusses the challenges in calculating the war's military and civilian losses; table 22.1 provides estimates by country. "The Dead," 587–88.

8. Winter, *Sites of Memory, Sites of Mourning*, 2.

9. Jay Winter, *War beyond Words: Languages of Remembrance from the Great War to the Present* (Cambridge, UK: Cambridge University Press, 2017), 96–97.

10. Wilfred Owen, "Dulce et Decorum Est," in *The Great War Reader*, ed. James Hannah (College Station: Texas A&M University Press, 2000), 370. Owen was killed one week before the Armistice in November 1918. From Horace's *Roman Odes*, the Latin phrase of the poem's closing couplet—*Dulce et decorum est/Pro patria mori*—whose first line was taken as the poem's title, means "it is sweet and fitting to die for one's country." By quoting Horace, Hew Strachan argues that Owen placed himself "along a continuum that embraces two millennia," saying "little, if anything, about the peculiarities" of the war in which he served and died. *The First World War* (London: Simon & Schuster, 2006), xvii.

11. Thomas Laqueur, *The Work of the Dead: A Cultural History of Mortal Remains* (Princeton, NJ: Princeton University Press, 2016), 418.

12. Laqueur, "Memory and Naming in the Great War," 152; and *The Work of the Dead*, 417–20. On the "cult of the fallen" (war dead) manifest in the proliferation of military cemeteries and war monuments, including tombs for unknown soldiers, see Mosse, *Fallen Soldiers*, 70–106.

13. Laqueur, "Memory and Naming in the Great War," 162.

14. Winter, *Sites of Memory, Sites of Mourning*, 27.

15. Prost, "The Dead," 579. On Kipling's response to his son's disappearance, see John Horne, "The Living," in *The Cambridge History of the First World War*, vol. 3, *Civil Society*, ed. Jay Winter (Cambridge, UK: Cambridge University Press, 2016), 596–97.

16. Winter, *Sites of Memory, Sites of Mourning*, 95.

17. Laqueur, "Memory and Naming in the Great War," 158, 163. On this point, as well as on the tension between private mourning and public commemoration in France, see also David J. Sherman, "Bodies and Names: The Emergence of Commemoration in Interwar France," *American Historical Review* 103, no. 2 (1998): 463–66.

18. Winter notes that in their own "symbolic gestures of the return of the fallen," the United States, Italy, Belgium, and Portugal honored their own unknown soldiers the next year in 1921, with most countries following suit. *Sites of Memory, Sites of Mourning*, 27.

19. Mosse, *Fallen Soldiers*, 95.

20. Benedict Anderson, *Imagined Communities: Reflections of the Origins and Spread of Nationalism*, rev. ed. (1983; repr., New York: Verso, 2006), 9.

21. Michael J. Allen, "'Sacrilege of a Strange, Contemporary Kind': The Unknown Soldier and the Imagined Community after the Vietnam War," *History & Memory* 23, no. 2 (2011): 92.

22. Marin Pilloud, interview with author, July 26, 2012.

23. Michael Thompson, "Helping Guide Our Fallen Heroes Home," November 11, 2014. Delta Air Lines blog, accessed November 27, 2017, http://takingoff.delta.com/post/102360983798/veteran-s-day-2014.

24. Marin Pilloud, interview with author, July 26, 2012.

25. See David Finkel's candid look at the reflexive discourse of gratitude in his stories of US infantrymen returned from Iraq, *Thank You for Your Service* (New York: Picador, 2013).

26. Ben Fountain, *Billy Lynn's Long Halftime Walk* (New York: Harper Collins, 2012), 37. Fountain's fictional portrait mirrors the experience of historical figures, such as Ira Hayes and others from the flag raising at Mt. Suribachi during the Battle of Iwo Jima. "'How can I feel like a hero,' [Hayes] asked, 'when I hit the beach with two hundred and fifty buddies and only twenty-seven of us walked off alive?'" James Bradley with Ron Powers, *Flags of Our Fathers* (New York: Bantam Books, 2000), 12.

27. Andrew J. Bacevich, *The New American Militarism: How Americans Are Seduced by War* (New York: Oxford University Press, 2005), 24–25.

28. Katherine Verdery, *The Political Lives of Dead Bodies* (New York: Columbia University Press, 1999), 28.

29. Verdery, *The Political Lives of Dead Bodies*, 29.

30. Robert M. Poole, *On Hallowed Ground: The Story of Arlington National Cemetery* (New York: Walker & Company, 2009), 66. On US Quartermaster General Montgomery C. Meigs's plan to strip the Lee family of their plantation and create the cemetery, see McElya, *The Politics of Memory*, 96.

31. McElya, *The Politics of Memory*, 111–12.

32. On national differences in burials, cemeteries, and memorials to the missing, see Prost, "The Dead," 570–84; and Lisa M. Budreau, *Bodies of War: World War I and the Politics of Commemoration in America, 1919–1933* (New York: New York University Press, 2010), 47. In the case of France, families hired funeral undertakers to exhume and transport the remains of their fallen, a practice that eventually forced the state to recognize formally their right to the restoration and transport of the body.

33. Drew Gilpin Faust, *This Republic of Suffering: Death and the American Civil War* (New York: Alfred A. Knopf, 2008), 271. See also John R. Neff, *Honoring the Civil War Dead: Commemoration and the Problem of Reconciliation* (Lawrence: University Press of Kansas, 2005).

34. Notably, the repatriation of remains from military action on the continent (e.g., of US troops killed during the Plains Wars) was not always carried out.

35. Budreau, *Bodies of War*, 25, 27–36; G. Kurt Piehler, *Remembering War the American Way* (Washington, DC: Smithsonian Institution Press, 1995), 94; and Faust, *This Republic of Suffering*, 102–3.

36. Piehler, *Remembering War the American Way*, 95; and Budreau, *Bodies of War*, 43–44.

37. Piehler, *Remembering War the American Way*, 97; and Budreau, *Bodies of War*, 75–78.

38. Steven Trout, *On the Battlefield of Memory: The First World War and American Remembrance, 1919–1941* (Tuscaloosa: University of Alabama Press, 2010), 227. In 1955, Quentin Roosevelt's body was relocated to the Normandy American Cemetery and interred beside his brother Theodore Jr., who died of a heart attack during the Normandy invasion of World War II. Piehler, *Remembering War the American Way*, 132. See also, Elizabeth Borja, "The Grave of Quentin Roosevelt," National Air and Space Museum, https://airandspace.si.edu /stories/editorial/grave-quentin-roosevelt.

39. Piehler, *Remembering War the American Way*, 95. Antoine Prost argues that the cemeteries "constitute a manifesto of the United States on the old continent" ("The Dead," 574).

40. Budreau, *Bodies of War*, 21.

41. Piehler, *Remembering War the American Way*, 129, 130.

42. The four non-European permanent national cemeteries were located in the Philippines, the US territories of Hawaii and Alaska, and Tunisia. The American cemeteries in Europe and bodies of the dead buried thus became enlistees in projects of commemorative diplomacy meant to strengthen transatlantic unity in the decades that followed. Sam Edwards, *Allies in Memory: World War II and the Politics of Transatlantic Commemoration, c. 1941–2001* (Cambridge, UK: Cambridge University Press, 2015).

43. Edwards, *Allies in Memory*, 73.

44. The processing stations were located at Marbo on Saipan, Manila in the Philippines, Japan, and on Oahu for the Pacific Zone; at Fontainbleau (formerly at Strasbourg) and Carenton, France, and at Margraten near Maastricht in the Netherlands for the European Command; in Naples and Leghorn, Italy, for the Mediterranean area; and in Carthage, North Africa. There was also a mobile unit with headquarters outside of Paris. Mildred Trotter, "Operations at Central Identification Laboratory, A.G.R.S.," 1949, accessed January 29, 2019, http:// beckerexhibits.wustl.edu/mowihsp/words/TrotterReportpart1.htm.

45. Trotter, "Operations at Central Identification Laboratory, A.G.R.S."

46. Michael J. Allen, *Until the Last Man Comes Home: POWs, MIAs, and the Unending Vietnam War* (Chapel Hill: University of North Carolina Press, 2009), 129; Dolski, "When X Doesn't Mark the Spot," 137–70; Paul M. Cole, *POW/MIA Issues*, vol. 1, *The Korean War* (Santa Monica, CA: RAND, 1994), 55–56; and Michael Sledge, *Soldier Dead: How We Recover, Identify, Bury, and Honor Our Military Fallen* (New York: Columbia University Press), 39–42.

47. My thanks to Michael Dolski for providing this historical context.

48. Piehler, *Remembering War the American Way*, 155.

49. Piehler, *Remembering War the American Way*, 132.

50. Allen, *Until the Last Man Comes Home*, 129.

51. On the changes to US military recovery efforts and forensic practice introduced by the Korean War, see Cole, *POW/MIA Issues*, 62–74.

52. Viet Thanh Nguyen, *Nothing Ever Dies: Vietnam and the Memory of War* (Cambridge, MA: Harvard University Press, 2016), 119. The phrase "pure sex"

comes from a quotation in Michael Herr's *Dispatches* (New York, Vintage, 1991), 160; see Nguyen's analysis of the passage, *Nothing Ever Dies*, 117–19; as well as Fred Turner, *Echoes of Combat: The Vietnam War in American Memory* (New York: Anchor, 1996), 76–77; and Susan Jeffords, *The Remasculinization of America: Gender and the Vietnam War* (Bloomington: Indiana University Press, 1989), 9–10. On helicopters' role in the war, see Philip D. Chinnery, *Vietnam: The Helicopter War* (Annapolis, MD: Naval Institute Press, 1991).

53. Piehler, *Remembering War the American Way,* 168. In a related discussion as to why the Vietnam War produced so few unidentified remains (unknowns), see Allen, "'Sacrilege of a Strange, Contemporary Kind,'" 105.

54. Christian G. Appy, *Working-Class War: American Combat Soldiers and Vietnam* (Chapel Hill: University of North Carolina Press, 1993), 28. Between 7,500 and 11,000 women served in Vietnam, more than 80 percent of them nurses, and an estimated 55,000 civilian women worked in Vietnam. Heather Marie Stur, *Beyond Combat: Women and Gender in the Vietnam War Era* (New York: Cambridge University Press, 2011), 7.

55. Quoted in Douglas L. Clarke, *The Missing Man: Politics and the MIA* (Washington, DC: National Defense University Press, 1979), 52.

56. Article 21 specified that "the United States will contribute to healing the wounds of war and to postwar reconstruction of the Democratic Republic of Vietnam." Quoted in Clarke, *The Missing Man,* 53. On the linking of MIA accounting and reparations (Article 8[b], Article 21, and the February 1, 1973, letter from President Nixon to Premier Pham Van Dong in which he purportedly made an "unconditional" promise of reparations totaling $3.25 billion), see Clarke, *The Missing Man,* 62, 71–72; and Allen, *Until the Last Man Comes Home,* 87–91.

57. On the asymmetrical expectations surrounding MIA accounting and its role in normalization, see Christina Schwenkel, *The American War in Contemporary Vietnam: Transnational Remembrance and Representation* (Bloomington: Indiana University Press, 2009), 1–5; 182–85.

58. Allen, *Until the Last Man Comes Home,* 90.

59. Allen, *Until the Last Man Comes Home,* 84–87. See also, Paul D. Mather, *M.I.A.: Accounting for the Missing in Southeast Asia* (Washington, DC: National Defense University Press, 1994).

60. Clarke, *The Missing Man,* 53. The phrase was originally coined by members of the National League of POW/MIA Families (see Introduction, footnote 22).

61. On the divisions among Vietnam War veterans regarding how best to memorialize the war, including whether to inter a Vietnam unknown, see Patrick Hagopian, *The Vietnam War in American Memory: Veterans, Memorials, and the Politics of Healing* (Amherst: University of Massachusetts Press, 2009), 10–11, 18–20, 140–65; and Marita Sturken, *Tangled Memories: The Vietnam War, the AIDS Epidemic, and the Politics of Remembering* (Berkeley: University of California Press, 1997), 56–58.

62. Allen, "'Sacrilege of a Strange, Contemporary Kind,'" 105–7.

63. Christian Appy explains that "to revive proud faith in American exceptionalism required some serious scrubbing of the historical record," and that "Reagan

believed that antiwar memories of the Vietnam War posed an especially dangerous threat to his restoration project." *American Reckoning, 285.*

64. "Remarks at Memorial Day Ceremonies Honoring an Unknown Serviceman of the Vietnam Conflict," May 28, 1984, https://www.reaganlibrary.gov/research/speeches/52884a.

65. "Remarks at Memorial Day Ceremonies."

66. "Remarks at Memorial Day Ceremonies." See also, Allen, *Until the Last Man Comes Home, 239.*

67. Allen, *Until the Last Man Comes Home,* 239; see also, Hagopian, *The Vietnam War in American Memory,* 1–21, 181–83. It is worth noting that just over a week later, Reagan would deliver his famous D-Day/Boys of Pointe du Hoc speech in which he championed the "American-dominated response to restore moral order to the world." See Michael R. Dolski, *D-Day Remembered: The Normandy Landings in American Collective Memory* (Knoxville: University of Tennessee Press, 2016), 127.

68. Jim Garamone, "Vietnam Unknown Disinterred," DoD News, US Department of Defense, May 14, 1998, http://archive.defense.gov/news/newsarticle.aspx?id=41578.

69. Thomas Lynch, "Why We Must Know," *The Washington Post,* May 14, 1998, A23.

70. There are several detailed accounts of the selection process and 1st Lt. Blassie's eventual identification: Poole, *On Hallowed Ground,* 230–50; Allen, "'Sacrilege of a Strange, Contemporary Kind'"; Sarah E. Wagner, "The Making and Unmaking of an Unknown Soldier," *Social Studies of Science* 43, no. 5 (2013), 631–56; Robert Mann, *Forensic Detective: How I Cracked the World's Toughest Cases* (New York: Ballentine Books, 2007), 94–120; and Michael Sledge, *Soldier Dead: How We Recover, Identify, Bury, and Honor Our Military Fallen* (New York: Columbia University Press, 2005), 127–29. On the political import of 1st Lt. Blassie's identification, see Thomas Hawley, *The Remains of War: Bodies, Politics, and the Search for American Soldiers Unaccounted for in Southeast Asia* (Durham, NC: Duke University Press), 1–3, 190–99.

71. Public Law 93-42 was approved by Congress on June 18, 1973.

72. Though formed at the end of the war, the Joint Casualty Resolution Center didn't start from scratch; rather, it took over for the wartime casualty processing organization, the Joint Personnel Recovery Center (JPRC), which operated in-theater, with mortuary facilities at the Da Nang Air Base and Tan Son Nhut Air Base in Saigon. In 1973, US Army mortuary operations were relocated to Thailand, and three years later, the laboratory was transferred to Honolulu and reopened as the Central Identification Laboratory Hawaii (CILHI). (At the time of the relocation, with every plane headed from the mainland to Asia refueling in Hawaii and Camp H. M. Smith on Oahu, the headquarters of the United States Pacific Command [USPACOM], it made good sense to station the teams and equipment on the island.) In 1992, the Joint Task Force-Full Accounting (JTF-FA) was established as a finite entity with a finite mandate; nine years later, in 2003, the JTF-FA and CILHI merged to become the Joint POW/MIA Accounting Com-

mand (JPAC), which included the laboratory, now called the Central Identification Laboratory (CIL), located at Joint Base Pearl Harbor-Hickam, Hawaii.

73. Johnie Webb, interview with author, July 15, 2011. See also Poole, *On Hallowed Ground*, 240–41.

74. Report, "Status Review of Unidentified Remains from Southeast Asia (SEA) Now at the Central Identification Laboratory, Hawaii (CILHI)," n.d., attached to "Memorandum Thru [sic] Deputy Chief of Staff for Personnel Chief of Staff, Army," by Brigadier General Robert M. Joyce, 15 June 1981. J-2 Records Room, file 1998-078, JPAC, Hawaii.

75. In the vacuum of unknowability, the racial subtext of national belonging rose to the surface, a subtext that stretched back to the Tomb of the Unknowns dedication in 1921 and through the subsequent interments for WWII and the Korean War unknowns. As Micki McElya argues, though "framed as a universal body," all three unknowns "remained inherently male and white in popular and official understandings." *The Politics of Mourning*, 230.

76. Johnie Webb, interview with author, July 15, 2011. See also Mann, *Forensic Detective*, 106.

77. Donald Lunday, Joint Personnel Recovery Center, Memorandum for Record, Subject: Phonecon with Mr. Rogers, USA Mortuary, TSN, November 5, 1972, J-2 Records Room, file 1998-046, JPAC, Hawaii.

78. The formal decision to approve the deletion of the "Believed to Be" name association was taken on May 7, 1980.

79. Patrick Clifford, interview with author, August 4, 2011.

80. US Department of Defense, News Transcript, "Press Briefing Tuesday June 30 1998," http://archive.defense.gov/Transcripts/Transcript.aspx?TranscriptID=1625.

81. Ted Sampley, "The Vietnam Unknown Soldier Can Be Identified," *US Veteran Dispatch*, July 1994.

82. Sampley, "The Vietnam Unknown Soldier Can Be Identified."

83. Gonzales was required to file several Freedom of Information Act requests to obtain information about Blassie's case. The X-26 file had already been "purged" according to Pentagon directive, and thus documentary evidence pertaining to forensic anthropological analyses, material evidence, and intelligence reports was spotty and scattered at best.

84. CNN, "Soldier in Tomb of Unknowns May Actually Be Known," January 20, 1998, http://www.cnn.com/ALLPOLITICS/1998/01/20/unknown.soldier/.

85. The forensic anthropologists who evaluated the evidence (Thomas Holland, P. Willey, and Hugh Berryman) were board certified by the American Board of Forensic Anthropology. The certification "denotes the highest recognized level of professional qualification in the field of forensic anthropology." The American Board of Forensic Anthropology, accessed December 28, 2018, http://theabfa.org/.

86. Thomas Holland to commander, US Army Central Identification Laboratory, Hawaii, memorandum, "Proposed Identification of CILHI 1998-046-I-01," June 22, 1998, Central Identification Library, Hawaii.

87. Holland, "Proposed Identification of CILHI 1998-046-I-01." One of the nine families refused to provide a DNA sample, while another had no surviving maternal relatives from whom the lab could obtain a sample.

88. P. Willey, memorandum to Thomas Holland, "Proposed Identification of CILHI 1998-046-I-01 as 1Lt Michael J. BLASSIE, 490-52-6882, USAF," June 30, 1998, J-2 Records Room, file 1998-046, Joint POW/MIA Accounting Command, Hawaii.

89. US Department of Defense, News Release, "Secretary of Defense William S. Cohen's Statement Concerning the Identification of the Vietnam Unknown," Release No. 332-98, June 30, 1998, http://archive.defense.gov/Releases/Release.aspx?ReleaseID=1744.

90. National Museum of Health and Medicine, "Case Study: Michael J. Blassie." Past Exhibit, "Resolved: Advances in Forensic Identification of U.S. War Dead," accessed November 28, 2017, http://www.medicalmuseum.mil/index.cfm?p=exhibits.past.resolved.page_08.

2. The Science of Accounting

1. Ian Burney and Neil Pemberton explore this fascination with the forensic investigation and the broader cultural demands that led to it in *Murder and the Making of English CSI* (Baltimore, MD: Johns Hopkins University Press, 2016); see also Christopher Hamlin on the evolution of "forensic cultures," including within contemporary American popular culture, in "Forensic Cultures in Historical Perspective: Technologies of Witness, Testimony, Judgment (and Justice?)," *Studies in the History and Philosophy of the Biological and Biomedical Sciences* 44, no. 1 (2013): 4–15.

2. "Murder Is Her Hobby: Frances Glessner Lee and The Nutshell Studies of Unexplained Death," Smithsonian American Art Museum, Renwick Gallery, accessed December 29, 2018, https:/americanart.si.edu/exhibitions/nutshells.

3. Zoë Crossland, "Writing Forensic Anthropology: Transgressive Representations," in *Disturbing Bodies: Perspectives on Forensic Anthropology,* eds. Zoë Crossland and Rosemary A. Joyce (Santa Fe, NM: School for Advanced Research Press, 2015), 116.

4. The Defense POW/MIA Accounting Agency was established in 2015, and I visited its new facility on Joint Base Pearl Harbor-Hickam in April 2018 (see Conclusion). DPAA consolidated three of the previous separate entities of the MIA accounting mission—the Defense Prisoner of War/Missing Personnel Office, the Joint POW/MIA Accounting Command (which included the Central Identification Laboratory), and the Life Sciences Equipment Laboratory. For further discussion of this restructuring, see Chapter 3.

5. This figure has continued to expand. In 2018, the Defense POW/MIA Accounting Agency had a staff of approximately six hundred personnel.

6. Defense POW/MIA Accounting Agency, "Past Conflicts," December 14, 2018, http:/www.dpaa.mil/Our-Missing/Past-Conflicts/.

7. There were originally 867 unidentified sets of remains from the Korean War buried in the Punchbowl, and more than two thousand from World War II.

8. Such protocols, as Amâde M'charek notes in her study of a forensic laboratory in the Netherlands, are measures "aimed at the transparency and repeatability

of research, even after years have passed." M'charek, "Technologies of Population: Forensic DNA Testing Practices and the Making of Differences and Similarities," *Configurations* 8, no. 1 (2000): 126.

9. Trust in scientific knowledge production hinges on credibility. On the origins of such credibility and the experimental production of matters of fact, see Steven Shapin and Simon Schaffer's classic study of the seventeenth-century debate about pneumatics between Robert Boyle and Thomas Hobbes, *Leviathan and the Air Pump: Hobbes, Boyle, and the Experimental Life* (Princeton, NJ: Princeton University Press, 1985).

10. Michael J. Allen, *Until the Last Man Comes Home: POWs, MIAs, and the Unending Vietnam War* (Chapel Hill: University of North Carolina Press, 2009), 243.

11. Susan Sheehan, *A Missing Plane* (New York: Berkeley Books, 1986), 50–51.

12. On the Hart case and its fallout, see Allen, *Until the Last Man Comes Home*, 240–42; Thomas Hawley, *The Remains of War: Bodies, Politics, and the Search for American Soldiers Unaccounted for in Southeast Asia* (Durham, NC: Duke University Press), 108–14.

13. Josh Getlin, "Hearts & Bones: Thirteen Years after Lt. Col. Thomas Hart Disappeared in Laos, the Army Said It Had Found His Remains," *Los Angeles Times Magazine,* October 12, 1986, http:/articles.latimes.com/1986-10-12 /magazine/tm-2683_1_bone-fragments.

14. Madeline J. Hinkes, "Ellis Kerley's Service to the Military," *Journal of Forensic Science* 46, no. 4 (2001): 782–83. As one example of recurring errors, the external consultants noticed that estimations of stature consistently fell dead center of the predicted range, a virtual impossibility. There should be about 30 percent off, or outside, that range.

15. The Armed Services Graves Registration Office review board (later known as the Armed Forces Identification Review Board) was responsible for reviewing case files and either approving or disapproving an identification recommended by the CIL; prior to the 1985 recommendations, the board did not include scientific personnel. Appendix VI, "1985 Army Consultants' Recommendation of CILHI Operations and Army's Response," "POW/MIA Affairs: Issues Related to the Identification of Human Remains from the Vietnam Conflict," Report to the Chairman and Vice Chairman, Select Committee on POW/MIA Affairs, US Senate, United States General Accountability Office, October 1992, https:/www .gao.gov/assets/160/152704.pdf.

16. Hinkes, "Ellis Kerley's Service to the Military," 783.

17. In his ethnographic study of Lawrence Livermore National Laboratory, Hugh Gusterson notes that the WWII physicists' success in "penetrat[ing] the secrets of the atom" led to the pursuit of the hydrogen bomb, "an important milestone in the postwar militarization of American physics," one that scientists such as Leo Szilard and Albert Einstein fought to prevent. Gusterson, *Nuclear Rites: A Weapons Laboratory at the End of the Cold War* (Berkeley: University of California Press, 1996), 20–21.

18. Thomas Holland, interview with author, July 25, 2012.

19. Robert Mann, interview with author, May 9, 2012.

20. The National Institute of Standards and Technology, "Accreditation versus Certification," accessed December 18, 2018, https:/www.nist.gov/nvlap/accreditation -vs-certification. Lynch et al. explain that "administrative quality assurance/quality control (QA/QC) regimes are designed by associations of lawyers and scientists who advise government agencies on how to normalize a science that is not trusted to stand on its own feet." Michael Lynch et al., *Truth Machine: The Contentious History of DNA Fingerprinting* (Chicago University Press, 2008), 7.

21. In 2000, forensic anthropology and skeletal identification were not recognized as forensic disciplines for accreditation purposes. By 2017, because of the CIL's efforts, those fields became fully recognized, and in 2018, the CIL, renamed the Scientific Analysis Directorate, was accredited in five disciplines for forensic science testing: anthropology, which also includes archaeology, among other components; biology (specifically the collection of biological evidence such as DNA); crime scene investigation (related to aircraft wreckage and life support equipment); materials (trace), which includes recovered military equipment and individuals' personal effects; and odontology. ANSI-ASQ National Accreditation Board, "Scope of Accreditation to: ISO/IEC 17025:2005; ANAB 17025:2005 Forensic Science Testing Laboratories Accreditation Requirements: 2017," issued February 28, 2018.

22. In some respects, this tension between the civilian and military components within the Command reflected what scholars have characterized as the "widening gap" between civil-military spheres in American society. See, for example, Ole R. Holsti, "A Widening Gap between the U.S. Military and Civilian Society? Some Evidence, 1976–96," *International Security* 23, no. 3 (1998/99): 5–42; Samuel P. Huntington, *The Soldier and the State: The Theory and Politics of Civil-Military Relations* (Cambridge, MA: Belknap Press of Harvard University Press, 1957); Morris Janowitz, *The Professional Soldier: A Social and Military Portrait* (Glencoe, IL: Free Press, 1960); Elliot Cohen, "Why the Gap Matters," *National Interest* 61 (2000): 38–48; and Peter D. Feaver and Richard H. Kohn, eds., *Soldiers and Civilians: The Civil-Military Gap and American National Security* (Cambridge, MA: MIT Press, 2001).

23. William Belcher, interview with the author, August 3, 2012. The DOD's emerging emphasis on the importance of education has further widened this disconnect in experience and expertise. With educational opportunities available to its personnel through the use of online and correspondence courses offered by colleges and universities willing to offer credit for "life experience," coupled with an increasing number of enlisted personnel obtaining bachelor's degrees, there is upward pressure for officers to obtain graduate degrees—usually one-year, no-thesis master's degrees. As Holland explained, "If your only frame of reference is a one-year online MA, there is even less respect shown to civilian academics."

24. K. Phillips, interview with author, July 27, 2012.

25. Michael Dolski, "When *X* Doesn't Mark the Spot: Historical Investigation and Identifying Remains from the Korean War," in *Missing Persons: Multidisciplinary Perspectives on the Disappeared,* ed. Derek Congram (Toronto: Canadian Scholars Press, 2016), 161. JPAC (now DPAA) employs more than a dozen histo-

rians to cover historical analysis for the three major conflicts—World War II, the Korean War, and the Vietnam War. There are also full-time analysts and casualty resolution specialists working in Hawaii, Washington, DC, and in Southeast Asia, in addition to support from Defense Intelligence Agency staff assigned to regional offices in Cambodia and Laos.

26. Though the North Koreans "claimed that each box represented a single U.S. service member lost during the Korean War," the minimum number of individuals is estimated to be approximately six hundred, including at least twelve Korean nationals. Jennie Jin et al., "The Korea 208: A Large-Scale Commingling Case of American Remains from the Korean War," in *Commingled Human Remains: Methods in Recovery, Analysis, and Identification,* eds. Bradley J. Adams and John E. Byrd (Amsterdam: Academic Press, 2014), 409, 421.

27. While disinterments occurred on an ad hoc basis since the 1980s and a more formalized program emerged in 2009, it was not until April 2015 that the DOD began to coordinate efforts with the Department of Veterans Affairs to disinter remains from the USS *Oklahoma* and created explicit "thresholds for the disinterment of remains from any permanent U.S. military cemetery." Inspector General, US Department of Defense, Report No. DODIG-2018-138, "DoD's Organizational Changes to the Past Conflict Personnel Accounting Community," July 18, 2018, https:/media.defense.gov/2018/Jul/20/2001945039/-1/-1/1/DODIG -2018-138.PDF, 13. See also Dolski, "When X Doesn't Mark the Spot," 154.

28. See, for example, Debra Komar, "Patterns of Mortuary Practice Associated with Genocide: Implications for Archaeological Research," *Current Anthropology* 49, no. 1 (2008): 123–33. On the indexicality of the dead in archaeology, see Zoë Crossland, "Of Clues and Signs: The Dead Body and Its Evidential Traces," *American Anthropologist* 111, no. 1 (2009): 69–80.

29. In the case of fragmentary remains, each fragment "must share a unique landmark to ensure that fragments do not originate from the same skeletal element." Lyle W. Konigsberg and Bradley Adams, "Estimating the Number of Individuals Represented by Commingled Human Remains: A Critical Evaluation of Methods," in *Commingled Remains: Methods in Recovery, Analysis and Identification,* eds., Bradley J. Adams and John E. Byrd (Amsterdam: Academic Press, 2014), 195.

30. Microscopic analysis (such as histological analysis) is frequently used to determine whether the fragment is human or nonhuman osseous material. See Mariateresa A. Tersini-Tarrant, "Taphonomic Processes: Analysis of Fragmentary Remains," in *Forensic Anthropology: An Introduction,* eds. Mariateresa A. Tersini-Tarrant and Natalie R. Shirley (Boca Raton, FL: CRC Press, 2013), 386.

Ancestry refers to an individual's biological affinity with phenotypic characters that appear with greater frequency within human populations of a given geographic space, for example Europe, Asia, Africa, the Americas, and Oceania. In the field of forensic anthropology, ancestral background has generally supplanted race as an analytic category. As a case in point, in February 2013, the CIL revised its SOP for this aspect of the biological profile, replacing race with ancestry.

31. Assessing phenotypic expressions of human variation has been a source of significant, at times contentious, debate in the field of physical anthropology, particularly regarding the concept of race and its associations with racist science. See, for example, Stephen Jay Gould on craniometry, *The Mismeasure of Man*, rev. ed. (1981; repr., New York: Norton, 1996); and James H. Mielke, Lyle W. Konigsberg, and John H. Relethford, *Human Biological Variation* (New York: Oxford University Press), 3–22. For an overview of the concept of race in forensic anthropology and its medico-legal application, see Sabrina C. Ta'ala, "A Brief History of the Race Concept in Physical Anthropology," in Greg E. Berg and Sabrina C. Ta'ala, eds., *Biological Affinity in Forensic Identifications of Human Skeletal Remains* (Boca Raton, FL: CRC Press, 2015), 1–15; Kenneth A. R. Kennedy, "But Professor, Why Teach Race Identification if Races Don't Exist?" *Journal of Forensic Sciences* 40, no. 5 (1995): 797–800; Norm J. Sauer, "Forensic Anthropology and the Concept of Race: If Races Don't Exist, Why Are Forensic Anthropologists So Good at Identifying Them?" *Social Science & Medicine* 34, no. 2 (1992): 107–11; and Stephen Ousley, Richard Jantz, and Donna Freid, "Understanding Race and Human Variation: Why Forensic Anthropologists Are Good at Identifying Race," *American Journal of Physical Anthropology* 139, no. 1 (2009): 68–76.

32. Ismail Kadare, *The General of the Dead Army*, trans. Derek Coltman (New York: Arcade, 2011), 23.

33. Thomas Laqueur, *The Work of the Dead: A Cultural History of Mortal Remains* (Princeton, NJ: Princeton University Press, 2015), 3.

34. See, for example, Jay Aronson, *Who Owns the Dead: The Science and Politics of Death at Ground Zero* (Cambridge, MA: Harvard University Press, 2016); Sarah Wagner, *To Know Where He Lies: DNA Technology and the Search for Srebrenica's Missing* (Berkeley: University of California Press, 2008); Iosif Kovras, *Grassroots Activism and the Evolution of Transitional Justice: The Families of the Disappeared* (Cambridge, UK: Cambridge University Press, 2017), 99–104; Victor Toom, "Whose Body Is It? Technolegal Materialization of Victims' Bodies and Remains after the World Trade Center Terrorist Attacks," *Science, Technology, & Human Values* 41, no. 4 (2017): 686–708; and Lindsay Smith, "The Missing, the Martyred and the Disappeared: Global Networks, Technical Intensification and the End of Human Rights Genetics," *Social Studies of Science* 47, no. 3 (2017): 398–441.

35. Since 1991, all active-duty, reserve, and National Guard service members are required to give a DNA blood card. The card is collected for medical use, specifically for the identification of service members who have died in current theaters of operations. The samples are stored at the Armed Forces Repository of Specimen Samples for the Identification of Remains in Delaware, and the card is only pulled (and DNA genotyped) when needed. There is no DNA database for US service members.

36. The US military's dental records are comprehensive, though not consistently so. For example, records date back to World War I, with a small number even earlier, and have been the basis for multiple WWI identifications at the laboratory. Radiographic films, however, have been less effective. Whereas they are used extensively in Vietnam War cases, for World War II and Korean War cases, ex-

tant films were not culled and set aside as an independent collection for postmortem comparative use.

37. Radiographic matches can be as definitive as DNA testing, as in the example of two identical twins. Genetic profiles would reveal them as identical, thus indistinguishable, but their dental charts and radiographs would be different.

38. Timothy McMahon, director of the DNA Registry (Armed Forces DNA Identification Laboratory and Armed Forces Medical System), explained, "We use a dental bur to cut around the crown to maintain the integrity of the dental probative nature. The crown is removed and then we drill out the dentin from the inside. The tooth is then returned to the DPAA so that something is returned to the family." Email to author, January 3, 2018.

39. Lynch et al., *Truth Machine*, xi. Explaining how DNA typing supplanted conventional fingerprinting as the "ultimate identification scheme," Amâde M'charek describes the scientific practice of forensic genetics as "a number-generating machinery that produces facts out of human tissue" in "Technologies of Population," 137. In the case of the World Trade Center attacks, scientists at the Office of the Chief Medical Examiner faced a similar obstacle in families' and the public's preconceived notion of DNA's infallibility. Aronson, *Who Owns the Dead?*, 81.

40. The Armed Forces DNA Identification Laboratory pioneered the protocol in 2006, validating a "new demineralization technique" that enabled this significant reduction in the "input of skeletal material." Suni M. Edson et al., "Flexibility in Testing Skeletonized Remains for DNA Analysis Can Lead to Increased Success: Suggestions and Case Studies," in *New Perspectives in Forensic Human Skeletal Identification,* eds. Krista E. Latham, Eric J. Bartelink, and Michael Finnegan (Amsterdam: Academic Press, 2018), 142. See also Odile M. Lorielle at al., "High Efficiency DNA Extraction from Bone by Total Demineralization," *Forensic Science International Genetics* 1, no. 2 (2007): 191–95.

41. S. M. Edson et al., "Naming the Dead—Confronting the Realities of Rapid Identification of Degraded Skeletal Remains," *Forensic Science Review* 16, no. 1 (2004): 77. Notably, AFDIL has maintained over a 90 percent success rate for obtaining mtDNA sequence from non-chemically treated samples submitted by the CIL (now the Scientific Analysis Directorate under the Defense POW/MIA Accounting Agency), and over a 50 percent success rate for obtaining auSTR and Y-STR results from non-chemically treated samples.

42. Prior to its relocation to Dover Air Force Base in 2011, AFDIL was based in Rockville, Maryland.

43. For an excellent explanation of the science and practice of DNA testing used to identify victims of a mass fatality incident (in this case the World Trade Center attacks), see Aronson, *Who Owns the Dead?*, 81–89.

44. The use of "family reference samples" dates back to the First Gulf War. In 1991, the Armed Forces Medical Examiner System (which AFDIL falls under) had to utilize DNA to assist with the identification of service members from the conflict. This required obtaining references from the deceased service members' immediate family. In 1991–92, the Department of Defense was mandated to set up the DNA Registry, which included the Armed Forces Repository of Specimen

Samples for the Identification of Remains (AFRSSIR) and the Family Reference Specimen database. My thanks to Timothy McMahon for providing this information on historical and contemporary practice at AFDIL.

45. "A higher success rate is achieved with mtDNA compared with nuclear DNA, from old bones, severely decomposed or charred remains, or single hair shafts." A. Carracedo et. al., "DNA Commission of the International Society for Forensic Genetics: Guidelines for Mitochondrial DNA Typing," *Forensic Science International* 110, no. 2 (2000): 80.

46. AFIDL currently can use grandchildren as well, but due to the fact that they only share 25 percent of the DNA with the missing service member, more of those samples are required.

47. In 2006, AFDIL also began prioritizing the collection of paternal (Y-chromosomal STR [Short Tandem Repeat]) and nuclear (auSTR) family references. All samples are initially processed for mtDNA "to gauge the quality of the sample and to allow AFMES-AFDIL and DPAA scientists to segregate samples by mtDNA control region sequence. Once mtDNA profiles are obtained, and if paternal and/or nuclear references are available, Y-STR and auSTR testing is performed to help segregate samples with common mtDNA sequences or to aid further statistical relevance to the initial mtDNA results." Defense POW/MIA Accounting Agency, Armed Forces Medical Examiner System, DNA Identification Laboratory, "DNA FAQs," accessed April 27, 2019, http:/www.dpaa.mil/Resources/Fact-Sheets/Article-View/Article/590581/dna/#Question8.

48. Timothy McMahon. Email to author, January 3, 2018.

49. In the Vietnam War, loss incidents—cases of unrecovered or unaccounted for service members—were given "reference numbers," or REFNOs. The REFNO for the helicopter crash that killed Lance Corporal Merlin Raye Allen in June 1967 was 0746, meaning that it was the 746th incident of MIA/KIA/BNR at that point in the war; in this case, Cdr. Green's loss incident was the 1,895th.

50. Unless otherwise noted, the case summary, including direct quotations, comes from the Memorandum for the Record, "Identification of CIL 2009-156-I-01," Thomas D. Holland, November 1, 2010, Joint POW/MIA Accounting Command.

51. Sean D. Tallman, "Final Search and Recovery Report CIL 2009-156, an A-4F Crash Site Associated with REFNO 1895, in the Vicinity of Quang Son Village, Tam Diep District, Ninh Binh Province, Socialist Republic of Vietnam, 31 October Through 25 November 2009," January 11, 2010, Joint POW/MIA Accounting Command Central Identification Laboratory.

52. Laurel Freas, "Forensic Anthropology Report CIL 2009-156-I-01," October 6, 2010, Joint POW/MIA Accounting Command Central Identification Laboratory.

53. The case summary, including direct quotations, comes from the Memorandum for the Record, "Identification of CIL 2010-185-I-01," Thomas D. Holland, January 5, 2011, Joint POW/MIA Accounting Command.

54. I caught the very end of this practice, as by early 2012, the Department of Defense had phased out the funding that subsidized families' travel to the island for this purpose. Privately funded family visits still take place at the new DPAA

facility, and occasionally relatives who are current service members act as the official military escort for the remains. These visits follow a format similar to what I witnessed in 2011 and 2012, with a Public Affairs Office photographer present to document each stage, including a more formal "final salute" ceremony when the hearse departs the grounds.

55. Each branch of the military has its own casualty office (army, navy, air force, and marine corps), and the service casualty officers are the ones responsible for communicating directly with the families of the unaccounted for.

3. Trust, Expectations, and the Ethics of Certainty

1. Ismail Kadare, *The General of the Dead Army,* trans. Derek Coltman (New York: Arcade, 2011), 126.

2. Thomas Gibbons-Neff and Eric Schmitt, "U.S. Soldiers Were Separated From Unit in Niger Ambush, Officials Say," *New York Times,* October 26, 2017, https://www.nytimes.com/2017/10/26/world/africa/niger-soldiers-killed-ambush.html.

3. The controversy stemmed from conflicting accounts about the conversation President Trump had with Sgt. Johnson's wife while she was en route to receive her husband's remains. Ms. Johnson alleged that President Trump did not seem to know her husband's name and told her that "he knew what he signed up for." Yamiche Alcindor and Julie Hirschfeld Davis, "Soldier's Widow Says Trump Struggled to Remember Sgt. La David Johnson's Name," *New York Times*, October 23, 2017, https://www.nytimes.com/2017/10/23/us/politics/soldiers-widow-says-trump-struggled-to-remember-sgt-la-david-johnsons-name.html.

4. On November 21, 2017, the Department of Defense announced that a US Africa Command investigation team had recovered "additional remains" for Sgt. Johnson, but they provided few details to the family or the media. Alex Horton, "More Remains Belonging to Sgt. La David Johnson Found in Niger, Military Says," *Washington Post,* November 21, 2017, https://www.washingtonpost.com/news/checkpoint/wp/2017/11/21/more-remains-belonging-to-sgt-la-david-johnson-found-in-niger-military-says/. On May 10, 2018, the Department of Defense issued an unclassified report detailing how the four US troops "gave their last full measure of devotion to our country and died with honor while actively engaging the enemy." "Oct 2017 Niger Ambush, Summary of Investigation," May 10, 2018, https://www.defense.gov/portals/1/features/2018/0418_niger/img/Oct-2017-Niger-Ambush-Summary-of-Investigation.pdf.

5. "Transcript: Widow of Fallen Soldier La David Johnson Speaks Out," *ABC News,* October 23, 2017, http://abcnews.go.com/US/transcript-widow-fallen-soldier-la-david-johnson-speaks/story?id=50655055.

6. From 2009 to 2014, the Department of Defense's Prisoner of War / Missing Personnel Affairs Program annual spending, which included the Defense Prisoner of War / Missing Personnel Office (DPMO), Joint POW / MIA Accounting Command (JPAC), Armed Forces DNA Identification Laboratory (AFDIL), and Life Sciences Equipment Laboratory (LSEL), was approximately $110 million. The

annual budget for the Defense POW/MIA Accounting Agency (DPAA), which combined all but AFDIL into the same entity, was $127 million in 2015; $128 million in 2016; $112 million in 2017; and $131 million in 2018. It is important to note that the DPAA annual budget does not include markups (e.g., $15 million additional funds allocated in fiscal year 2018), nor does it capture the associated budgets of either AFDIL or the service casualty offices, or additional military pay, military airlift costs, etc.

7. Sheila Jasanoff and Sang-Hyun Kim define such concerns and assumptions as "sociotechnical imaginaries," which are "collectively held, institutionally stabilized, and publicly performed visions of desirable futures," animated by advances in science and technology. Sheila Jasanoff, "Future Imperfect: Science, Technology, and the Imaginations of Modernity," in *Dreamscapes of Modernity: Sociotechnical Imaginaries and the Fabrications of Power,* eds. Sheila Jasanoff and Sang-Hyun Kim (Chicago: Chicago University Press, 2017), 4.

8. Likewise, historical analyses of the Vietnam War POW/MIA movement have understandably focused on the archival record, on opinions and actions of those most politically active, and on popular cultural representations—all important sources, but by no means exhaustive or entirely representative of Vietnam War MIA families and veterans' experiences. For example, see Michael Allen, *Until the Last Man Comes Home: POWs, MIAs, and the Unending Vietnam War* (Chapel Hill: University of North Carolina Press, 2009); Thomas Hawley, *The Remains of War: Bodies, Politics, and the Search for American Soldiers Unaccounted For in Southeast Asia* (Durham, NC: Duke University Press, 2005); and H. Bruce Franklin's *M.I.A. or Mythmaking in America* (Brooklyn: Lawrence Hill Books, 1992).

9. Ann Mills-Griffiths, interview with author, November 17, 2017.

10. Josh Getlin, "Unfriendly Fire: POW-MIA Activist Ann Mills Griffiths Is a Power Player in Washington," *Los Angeles Times,* August 11, 1991, http://articles .latimes.com/1991-08-11/news/vw-931_1_ann-mills-griffiths.

11. Michael Allen, quoted in Jay Price, "Having Changed America, The League of POW/MIA Families Fades," October 19, 2017, NPR, *All Things Considered,* https://www.npr.org/2017/10/19/558137698/having-changed-america-the-league -of-pow-mia-families-fades. Allen describes Mills-Griffiths's "hardscrabble roots" and the confrontational style she cultivated in the early years, painting a portrait of an unlikely but "sophisticated political operative and bureaucratic infighter." Allen, *Until the Last Man Comes Home,* 193, 194.

12. National Defense Authorization Act for Fiscal Year 2010, Pub. L. No. 111-84, §541 (2009), https://www.govtrack.us/congress/bills/111/hr2647/text.

13. Of those eighty-two thousand, over forty-one thousand are presumed lost at sea, for example with ship losses, known aircraft water losses, etc., and therefore considered non-recoverable. For the Persian Gulf War, two service members are missing from the 1991 Operation Desert Storm.

14. Brenda S. Farrell, "DOD's POW/MIA Mission: Capability and Capacity to Account for Missing Persons Undermined by Leadership Weaknesses and Fragmented Organizational Structure," Testimony before the Subcommittee on Military Personnel, Committee on Armed Services, US House of Representatives, Au-

gust 1, 2013, United States Government Accountability Office, https://www.gao
.gov/assets/660/656479.pdf.

15. 10 U.S.C. § 1513, accessed December 18, 2018, https://www.law.cornell
.edu/uscode/text/10/1513.

16. Thomas Holland, interview with author, July 25, 2012.

17. National Defense Authorization Act for Fiscal Year 2010. In its 2018 assessment report, the Department of Defense inspector general reinforced this point, noting that "in order for an identification made by DPAA to count toward their goal of 200, DPAA must recover and identify that person's biological remains." Inspector General, US Department of Defense, Report No. DODIG-2018-138, "DoD's Organizational Changes to the Past Conflict Personnel Accounting Community," July 18, 2018, https://media.defense.gov/2018/Jul/20/2001945039/-1/-1
/1/DODIG-2018-138.PDF, 29.

18. Not included here is the Life Sciences Equipment Laboratory (LSEL). Though part of the DOD agencies tasked with MIA accounting, LSEL deals with military equipment artifacts rather than with human remains, and unlike the other two laboratories (Central Identification Laboratory, now Scientific Analysis Directorate, and the Armed Forces DNA Identification Laboratory), LSEL is neither accredited nor does it employ any scientists.

19. John Byrd, interview with author, July 24, 2012.

20. Claire McCaskill, "Mismanagement of POW/MIA Accounting," Hearing before the Subcommittee on Financial and Contracting Oversight, Committee on Homeland Security and Governmental Affairs, Washington, DC, August 1, 2013, https://www.hsgac.senate.gov/subcommittees/fco/hearings/mismanagement-of
-pow/mia-accounting.

21. United States Government Accountability Office, "POW/MIA Affairs: Issues Related to the Identification of Human Remains from the Vietnam Conflict," Report to the Chairman and Vice Chairman, Select Committee on POW/MIA Affairs, US Senate, October 1992, https://www.gao.gov/assets/160/152704.pdf.

22. In addition to assessing the mission according to the benchmarks set by the NDAA 2010, the 2013 GAO study also addressed allegations of inefficiency and waste set out by Oak Ridge Institute for Science and Education fellow Paul Cole in his draft "Information Value Chain Study," commissioned by the Joint POW/MIA Accounting Command. See Cole's August 1, 2013, statement before the House Armed Services Committee, Military Personnel Subcommittee: http://
docs.house.gov/meetings/AS/AS02/20130801/101212/HHRG-113-AS02-TTF
-ColeP-20130801.pdf. For the GOA report, see the United States Government Accountability Office, "DOD's POW/MIA Mission: Top-Level Leadership Attention Needed to Resolve Longstanding Challenges in Accounting for Missing Persons from Past Conflicts," Report to Congressional Committees, July 2013, https://www.gao.gov/assets/660/655916.pdf.

23. Opening Statement of Chairman Claire McCaskill, "Mismanagement of POW/MIA Accounting," August 1, 2013, https://www.hsgac.senate.gov/imo
/media/doc/Opening%20Statement-McCaskill-2013-08-01.pdf.

24. McCaskill, "Mismanagement of POW/MIA Accounting." Senator McCaskill said that during her preparation for the hearing, "echoes of Arlington

began resonating with me." On the Arlington National Cemetery scandal, see Micki McElya, *The Politics of Mourning: Death and Honor in Arlington National Cemetery* (Cambridge, MA: Harvard University Press, 2016), 307–9.

25. Requested by Congress and the Department of Defense, the inspector general also undertook an assessment of the MIA accounting community in 2014 and issued a report that found, among other obstacles, a lack of coordination among agencies and "duplication of personnel and functions." Inspector General, US Department of Defense, "Assessment of the Department of Defense Prisoner of War / Missing In Action Accounting Community," Report No. DODIG-2015-001, October 17, 2014, https://media.defense.gov/2014/Oct/17/2001713415/-1/-1/1/DODIG-2015-001.pdf. This report similarly addressed allegations of inefficiency and waste documented by Paul Cole in his "Information Value Chain Study."

26. Ayotte, "Mismanagement of POW/MIA Accounting."

27. "The War's Not Over Until the Last Man Comes Home," was the advertising slogan for Chuck Norris's film, *Missing in Action*. Franklin, *M.I.A. or Mythmaking in America,* 142.

28. The 2018 Inspector General Report notes that "as of August 2017, DPAA records showed that the DoD considered nearly 60 percent of the 82,500 missing persons from past conflicts as non-recoverable." "DoD's Organizational Changes to the Past Conflict Personnel Accounting Community," 29. This figure, however, remains somewhat fluid, given the potential for scientific and technological advances, collaborations with third-party entities, including universities, developed by the agency's Strategic Partnerships Directorate, and ongoing internal DOD discussions regarding the policy for burial at sea. On this final point, see "DoD's Organizational Changes to the Past Conflict Personnel Accounting Community," 58.

29. On the early postwar demands made of Vietnam to account for US service members missing in action, see Franklin, *M.I.A. or Mythmaking in America,* 129–30; and Edwin A. Martini, *Invisible Enemies: The American War on Vietnam, 1975–2000* (Amherst: University of Massachusetts Press, 2007), 22–24. On the "mercurial nature of North Korean–US relations," Michael Dolski notes that "the negotiations of field missions were often tense and subject to mutual recriminations, and in 2005 this activity halted entirely." Dolski, "When *X* Doesn't Mark the Spot: Historical Investigation and Identifying Remains from the Korean War," in *Missing Persons: Multidisciplinary Perspectives on the Disappeared,* ed. Derek Congram (Toronto: Canadian Scholars Press, 2016), 153.

30. Nick Simeone, "Hagel Orders Overhaul of POW/MIA Identification Agencies," DoD News, US Department of Defense, March 31, 2014, http://archive.defense.gov/news/newsarticle.aspx?id=121939.

31. The final bill for the consulting firm ended up significantly larger: the Clearing was paid a total of $9,207,754 for services rendered between September 30, 2013, and February 26, 2015, through three separate awards under the parent award GS10F0065X. These data are available at usaspending.gov.

32. Megan Towey, "Families Frustrated by Changes to POW/MIA System," *CBS News,* October 15, 2014, https://www.cbsnews.com/news/families-frustrated-by-changes-to-pow-mia-system/.

33. Alan Brochstein, "How Alisa Stack Jumped from the Department of Defense into the Cannabis Industry," *New Cannabis Ventures,* July 18, 2017, https://www.newcannabisventures.com/how-alisa-stack-jumped-from-the-department-of-defense-into-the-cannabis-industry/.

34. Michael Lumpkin, "Government Accountability Office Review of the Prisoner of War / Missing In Action (POW/MIA) Community and the Restructuring of These Agencies as Proposed by the Department of Defense," Hearing before the Subcommittee on Military Personnel of the Committee on Armed Services, House of Representatives [H.A.S.C. No. 113-117], July 15, 2014, https://www.gpo.gov/fdsys/pkg/CHRG-113hhrg89510/html/CHRG-113hhrg89510.htm.

35. Michael Lumpkin, "Government Accountability Office Review."

36. Like CIL, AFDIL is accredited by an independent institution, the American National Standards Institute—American Society of Quality Control National Accreditation Board. In 2018, it received zero findings of non-conformance during their quadrennial quality assessment.

37. Odile M. Lorielle et al., "High Efficiency DNA Extraction from Bone by Total Demineralization," *Forensic Science International Genetics* 1, no. 2 (2007): 191–95.

38. Under the National Institute of Standards and Technology, the group eventually became the Anthropology Subcommittee of the Organization of Scientific Area Committees. National Institute for Standards and Technology, "Scientific Working Groups," accessed December 18, 2018, https://www.nist.gov/oles/scientific-working-groups.

39. For example, Robert Burns, "AP Impact: MIA Accounting 'Acutely Dysfunctional,'" July 7, 2013, *San Diego Union Tribune,* http://www.sandiegouniontribune.com/sdut-ap-impact-mia-work-acutely-dysfunctional-2013jul07-story.html; Matthew M. Burke, "Families Express Frustration with JPAC's Efforts to Recover War Missing," *Stars & Stripes,* October 23, 2013, https://www.stripes.com/news/families-express-frustration-with-jpac-s-efforts-to-recover-war-missing-1.242757; and Bill Dedman, "Pentagon Agency under Fire for Refusing to ID Unknown World War II Soldiers," *NBC News,* August 1, 2013, http://investigations.nbcnews.com/_news/2013/08/01/19796976-pentagon-agency-under-fire-for-refusing-to-id-unknown-world-war-ii-soldiers.

40. NPR, "Grave Science," March 6, 2014, https://apps.npr.org/grave-science/; and ProPublica, "The Military Is Leaving the Missing Behind," March 6, 2014, https://www.propublica.org/article/missing-in-action-us-military-slow-to-identify-service-members.

41. "Dated Methods Mean Slow Return for Fallen Soldiers—Or None At All," NPR, *All Things Considered,* March 6, 2014, https://www.npr.org/templates/transcript/transcript.php?storyId=286886081.

42. ProPublica, "The Military Is Leaving the Missing Behind."

43. NPR, "Grave Science."

44. Lindsay Smith demonstrates how the NPR/ProPublica critique fit within an emerging field of security-focused forensic genetics, marked by an "increasing precedence" of the DNA-led (rather than a "holistic, investigatory") approach.

"The Missing, the Martyred and the Disappeared: Global Networks, Technical Intensification and the End of Human Rights Genetics," *Social Studies of Science* 47, no. 3 (2017): 412, 414n9.

45. NPR, "Grave Science."

46. On Bode and US congressional funding of missing person identification efforts in Latin America, see Smith, "The Missing, the Martyred and the Disappeared," 404–7.

47. "Bode Technology Uses DNA to Help Identify Missing World War II Soldier," *PRWeb*, April 7, 2014, http://www.prweb.com/releases/2014/04/prweb11741264.htm.

48. Sarah Wagner, *To Know Where He Lies: DNA Technology and the Search for Srebrenica's Missing* (Berkeley: University of California Press, 2008), 82–122.

49. In its 1995 report, the Department of Defense Science Board confirmed that mtDNA testing offered the best means to identify skeletal remains that cannot be identified through traditional methods. It also noted that "bone samples from Southeast Asia," in contrast to remains recovered from North Korea, "have demonstrated that they harbor only small amounts of mtDNA, and that it is severely fragmented." Report of the Department of Defense Science Board Task Force, "Use of DNA Technology for Identification of Ancient Remains," July 1995, 15. On the effectiveness of mtDNA testing in its early application by ADFIL, see Mitchell M. Holland et al., "Mitochondrial Sequence Analysis of Human Skeletal Remains: Identification of Remains from The Vietnam War," *Journal of Forensic Sciences* 38, no. 3 (1993): 542–53.

50. Because the remains are older and the DNA extracted of lower quality than in a modern case, there is a greater possibility for a modern contaminant to get amplified over the low-quality authentic DNA profile. Defense POW/MIA Accounting Agency, Armed Forces Medical Examiner System, DNA Identification Laboratory, "DNA FAQs," June 25, 2018, http://www.dpaa.mil/Resources/Fact-Sheets/Article-View/Article/590581/armed-forces-medical-examiner-system-dna-identification-laboratory/.

51. Defense POW/MIA Accounting Agency, "DNA FAQs."

52. On NGS and its implications for forensic genetics and human identification, see Jennifer Templeton et al., "DNA Capture and Next-Generation Sequencing Can Recover Whole Mitochondrial Genomes from Highly Degraded Samples for Human Identification," *Investigative Genetics* 4, no. 1 (2013): 26; Claus Børsting and Niels Morling, "Next Generation Sequencing and Its Applications in Forensic Genetics," *Forensic Science International: Genetics* 18 (2015): 78–89; and Terry Melton, "Digging Deep: Next Generation Sequencing for Mitochondrial DNA Forensics," *Forensic Magazine,* January 4, 2014, https://www.forensicmag.com/article/2014/01/digging-deep-next-generation-sequencing-mitochondrial-dna-forensics.

53. NPR, "Grave Science."

54. NPR, "Grave Science."

55. One of the few exceptions ran in the *Honolulu Star-Advertiser.* The article quoted a group of scientists, including former JPAC staff, who argued in a letter to Secretary of Defense Chuck Hagel that JPAC "was the gold standard of scien-

tific rigor and excellence that all other laboratories that undertake the identification of skeletonized human remains strive to achieve." William Cole, "JPAC Leadership Changes Criticized," *Honolulu Star-Advertiser,* October 19, 2014.

56. Smith, "The Missing, the Martyred and the Disappeared," 414n9. The same group of scientists writing to Secretary Hagel decried plans to remove Holland and install a medical examiner at the helm of the scientific process: "To replace him with a medical examiner—a (medical doctor) whose science and experience evolves around fleshed bodies—is inconceivable." Cole, "JPAC Leadership Changes Criticized."

57. Statement of Honorable Michael D. Lumpkin, Assistant Secretary of Defense, Special Operations / Low-Intensity Conflict, Performing the Duties of Undersecretary of Defense for Policy, Department of Defense, "GAO Review of the POW / MIA Community and the Restructuring of These Agencies."

58. Franklin, *M.I.A. or Mythmaking in America.*

59. Franklin, *M.I.A. or Mythmaking in America,* 145.

60. McKeague, "Mismanagement of POW / MIA Accounting."

61. Layla Renshaw describes that imaginary as a "forensic gaze" adopted by the layperson from crime fiction, film, and television. "The Forensic Gaze: Reconstituting Bodies and Objects as Evidence," in *Mapping the "Forensic Turn": Engagements with Materialities of Mass Death in Holocaust Studies and Beyond,* ed. Zuzanna Dziuban (Vienna: New Academic Press, 2017), 219. The notion of a "CSI effect"—that is, the impact of fictitious depictions of forensic science in the *CSI* television series and related programs—has been widely debated in academic and mainstream media, particularly regarding whether its effect on public perception influences criminal justice proceedings. See, for example, N. J. Schweitzer and Michael J. Saks, "The CSI Effect: Popular Fiction about Forensic Science Affects the Public's Expectations about Real Forensic Science," *Jurimetrics* 47, no. 3 (2007): 357–64; Simon Cole and Rachel Dioso-Villa, "*CSI* and Its Effects: Media, Juries, and the Burden of Proof," *New England Law Review* 41, no. 3 (2007): 435–69; and Corinna Kruse, "Producing Absolute Truth: CSI Science as Wishful Thinking," *American Anthropologist* 112, no. 1 (2010): 79–91.

62. Extending a Joint POW / MIA Accounting Command initiative, the Defense POW / MIA Accounting Agency has set aside a chest radiograph collection of several million (an estimated eight to thirteen million) images but has not been able to process them to date. Those radiographs are from 1941 to 1955, and they belong to service members from the US Marine Corps and US Navy.

63. Kate Webber, "Forensic Technique Developed by Brisbane Researcher Helps Identify Missing Soldiers," *ABC News,* May 2, 2016, http://www.abc.net.au /news/2016-05-03/forensic-anthropologist-dr-carl-stephan-pioneers-identification /7334668.

64. Carl N. Stephan et al., "Skeletal Identification by Radiographic Comparison: Blind Tests of a Morphoscopic Method Using Antemortem Chest Radiographs," *Journal of Forensic Sciences* 56, no. 2 (2011): 320–32; and Carl N. Stephan and Pierre Guyomarc'h, "Quantification of Perspective-Induced Shape Change of Clavicles at Radiography and 3D Scanning to Assist Human Identification,"

Journal of Forensic Sciences 59, no. 2 (2014): 447–53. Stephan won the Ellis R. Kerley Research Award in 2013, presented at the American Academy of Forensic Sciences annual meeting, for his research on the radiographic comparison technique. The ProPublica report briefly mentions the technique but dismisses its import.

65. Ian Burney and Neil Pemberton, *Murder and the Making of English CSI* (Baltimore, MD: Johns Hopkins University Press, 2016), 1.

66. David A. Kirby, "Forensic Fictions: Science, Television Production, and Modern Storytelling," *Studies in History and Philosophy of Biological and Biomedical Sciences,* 44 (2013): 94.

67. Kirby, "Forensic Fictions," 94–95; see also, Zoë Crossland, "Writing Forensic Anthropology: Transgressive Representations," in *Disturbing Bodies: Perspectives on Forensic Anthropology,* eds. Zoë Crossland and Rosemary A. Joyce (Santa Fe, NM: School for Advanced Research Press, 2015); and Kruse, "Producing Absolute Truth."

68. Sheila Jasanoff and Hilton R. Simmet, "No Funeral Bells: Public Reason in a 'Post-truth' Age," *Social Studies of Science* 47, no. 5 (2017): 757.

69. Steven Epstein, *Impure Science: AIDS, Activism, and the Politics of Knowledge* (Berkeley: University of California Press, 1996), 6.

70. Jasanoff and Simmet, "No Funeral Bells," 756.

71. ProPublica, "The Military Is Leaving the Missing Behind."

72. Jay Winter, *War beyond Words: Languages of Remembrance from the Great War to the Present* (Cambridge, UK: Cambridge University Press, 2017), 67.

73. Dave Philipps, "War Hero's Family Suing in Its Decades-Long Fight to Identify Remains," *New York Times,* May 29, 2017, https://www.nytimes.com/2017/05/29/us/veterans-graves-alexander-nininger.html.

74. Andrew J. Bacevich, *The New American Militarism* (New York: Oxford University Press, 2005), 2.

75. Bacevich, *The New American Militarism,* 21.

76. Rosa Brooks, *How Everything Became War and the Military Became Everything: Tales from the Pentagon* (New York: Simon & Schuster, 2016), 131–34. See also, Hugh Gusterson, *Drones: Remote Control Warfare* (Cambridge, MA: MIT Press, 2016).

1967

1. Mary included part of that letter in a note she left at the Vietnam Veterans Memorial, dated August 22, 2015.

2. From Mary Defoe's August 22, 2015, letter to the Department of Veterans Affairs.

3. Mary Defoe, interview with the author, Red Cliff, Wisconsin, July 28, 2017.

4. Alan "Butch" Kuepfer, interview with the author, Red Cliff, Wisconsin, July 30, 2017.

5. The Iwo Jima image was a stock photograph used by the Taylor Publishing Company, which was one of the leading publishers of yearbooks in the United

States. The company had made a name for itself during World War II publishing "memory books to the military" before expanding into the school yearbook market. "Taylor Publishing Company," International Directory of Company Histories, *Encyclopedia.com*, accessed December 18, 2018, http://www.encyclopedia .com/books/politics-and-business-magazines/taylor-publishing-company.

6. In mapping proportionate losses across different types of communities (e.g., urban, suburban, rural), Christian Appy notes that "In the 1960s only about 2 percent of Americans lived in towns with fewer than 1,000 people. Among those who died in Vietnam, however, roughly four times that portion, 8 percent, came from American hamlets of that size." Christian G. Appy, *Working-Class War: American Combat Soldiers and Vietnam* (Chapel Hill: University of North Carolina Press, 1993), 14. So too in his chronicle of the "Morenci Nine" (the nine marines who served in the Vietnam War from Morenci, Arizona, six of whom died in it), Kyle Longley argues that "the blood sacrifice made in Vietnam was uneven for small towns and working-class and lower-class communities. They experienced death on a much greater scale compared to areas of affluence or communities with strong anti-war cultures." Longley, *The Morenci Marines: A Tale of Small-Town American and the Vietnam War* (Lawrence: University of Kansas Press, 2013), 5.

7. For a discussion of this more expansive notion of dispossession, see Angela Garcia, *The Pastoral Clinic: Addiction and Dispossession along the Rio Grande* (Berkeley: University of California Press, 2010), 83–84.

8. For a detailed history of the national park's creation, see Harold C. Jordahl Jr. and Annie Booth, *Environmental Politics and the Creation of a Dream: Establishing the Apostle Islands National Lakeshore* (Madison: University of Wisconsin Press, 2011).

9. See Alan Solomon, "After 6 Weeks, 8,000 Miles and 139 Towns, This Is the Place," *Chicago Tribune*, August 3, 1997, http://www.chicagotribune.com /lifestyles/travel/chi-bayfield97jul14-story.html; and "A Decade Later, 'The Best Little Town' Still Fits Bayfield, Wisconsin," *Los Angeles Times*, July 15, 2007, http://www.latimes.com/travel/la-trw-bayfield-wisconsin-best-little -town30aug07-story.html; and Bess Lovejoy, "The 20 Best Small Towns to Visit in 2015," *Smithsonian.com*, April 16, 2015, http://www.smithsonianmag.com /travel/best-small-towns-2015-180954993/.

10. Bayfield Chamber of Commerce and Visitor Bureau, accessed December 18, 2018, http://bayfield.org/.

11. On the anti-war demonstrations at the University of Wisconsin Madison, including the October 18, 1967, "Dow riots," see David Maraniss, *They Marched into Sunlight: War and Peace, Vietnam and America, October 1967* (New York: Simon & Schuster, 2003).

12. James W. Feldman, *A Storied Wilderness: Rewilding the Apostle Islands* (Seattle: University of Washington Press, 2011), 21.

13. Jordahl and Booth, *Environmental Politics and the Creation of a Dream*, 79–85; Feldman, *A Storied Wilderness*, 176.

14. The US House of Representatives and the Senate held two sets of hearings respectively between 1967 and 1970. Feldman, *A Storied Wilderness*, 179.

15. Hearings before the Subcommittee on Parks and Recreation of the Committee on Interior and Insular Affairs, United States Senate, Ninetieth Congress, First Session on S. 778, "A Bill to Provide for the Establishment of the Apostle Islands National Lakeshore in the State of Wisconsin, and for Other Purposes," May 9, June 1 and 2, 1967 (US Government Printing Office, Washington, DC: 1967), 229–30.

16. "A Bill to Provide for the Establishment of the Apostle Islands National Lakeshore," 230.

17. From the "massive buildup"—15,000 in 1964 to 550,000 in 1968—to the "gradual withdrawal of ground troops" beginning in 1969, the "bell curve of escalation and withdrawal spread the commitment into a decade-long chain of one-year long tours of duty." Appy, *Working-Class War,* 17–18.

18. "A Bill to Provide for the Establishment of the Apostle Islands National Lakeshore," 148.

19. Feldman notes that as the movement to create the park gained momentum in the 1960s, "only the people most directly affected by the park proposal—property owners and residents of the Red Cliff and Bad River reservations—maintained their opposition." *A Storied Wilderness,* 175.

20. "A Bill to Provide for the Establishment of the Apostle Islands National Lakeshore," 246.

21. "A Bill to Provide for the Establishment of the Apostle Islands National Lakeshore," 242.

22. "A Bill to Provide for the Establishment of the Apostle Islands National Lakeshore," 241–42.

23. Ronald N. Satz, *Chippewa Treaty Rights: The Reserved Rights of Wisconsin's Chippewa Indians in Historical Perspective* (Madison: The Wisconsin Academy of Sciences, Art and letters, 1991), 51–82. See also, Chantal Norrgard, *Seasons of Change: Labor, Treaty Rights, and Ojibwe Nationhood* (Chapel Hill: University of North Carolina Press, 2014).

24. Red Cliff Band of Lake Superior Chippewa, "Origins and History," accessed December 18, 2018, http://redcliff-nsn.gov/divisions/TNRD/H.htm.

25. Red Cliff Band of Lake Superior Chippewa, "Origins and History." Moningwanikoning means "home of the yellow-breasted woodpecker."

26. Andy Gokee, "Tribal Histories Q&A: Andy Gokee," Wisconsin Public Television, WPT blog, November 22, 2016, https://wptblog.org/2016/11/tribal-histories-qa-andy-gokee-red-cliff-ojibwe/. During the negotiations, Chief Buffalo insisted on a Chippewa-appointed (rather than US government) interpreter, explaining, "We do not want to be deceived any more as we have in the past" (quoted in Satz, *Chippewa Treaty Rights,* 68–69).

27. On the "century-old pattern of Native American land loss" and historical significance of the Red Cliff and Bad River Band's victory in keeping reservation land out of the national park plan, see Feldman, *A Storied Wilderness,* 185–89.

28. On June 2, 1924, through the Indian Citizenship Act, the United States Congress granted full citizenship to all Native Americans born in the United States.

29. Feldman, *A Storied Wilderness,* 193.

4. A Recovery Mission

1. In this chapter and its map, the spelling of Vietnamese names, including place names, correspond to either how they appear in US military documents or as they are written—with diacritics—in the Vietnamese language.

2. Jeff Savelkoul, "Team Striker Story," (unpublished document), shared with the author, September 15, 2016.

3. "Socialist Republic of Vietnam Recovery Assessment: Case 0746," March 20, 2006. Case file, REFNO 0746, Joint POW/MIA Accounting Command, Joint Base Pearl Harbor-Hickam, Hawaii.

4. Savelkoul, "Team Striker Story," and interview with author, September 17, 2016.

5. Savelkoul, "Team Striker Story." Lawrence C. Vetter Jr. provides a similar account in *Never without Heroes: Marine Third Reconnaissance Battalion in Vietnam, 1965–70* (New York: Ivy Books, 1996). See also the details and chronicle provided by the Alpha Reconn Association, "Search and Recovery, a CH-46A Crash Site Associated with REFNO 0746, Phu Loc District, Thua Thien-Hue Province, Socialist Republic of Vietnam," accessed October 24, 2017, http://www.alphareconassociation.org/striker.htm.

6. Savelkoul, "Team Striker Story."

7. Jay Winter, "Forms of Kinship and Remembrance in the Aftermath of the Great War," in *War and Remembrance in the Twentieth Century*, eds. Jay Winter and Emmanuel Sivan (Cambridge, UK: Cambridge University Press, 1999), 40–60.

8. Winter, "Forms of Kinship and Remembrance," 40, 41.

9. Winter, "Forms of Kinship and Remembrance," 41.

10. Viet Thanh Nguyen, *Nothing Ever Dies: Vietnam and the Memory of War* (Cambridge, MA: Harvard University Press, 2016), 19.

11. Nguyen, *Nothing Ever Dies*, 10.

12. Nguyen, *Nothing Ever Dies*, 19.

13. In 2006, a Joint POW/MIA Accounting Command investigative team documented "the purported recovery scene has been extensively scavenged leaving only tiny fragments of wreckage." "Detailed Report of Investigation of Case 0746 (VM-01464) Conducted during the 83rd Joint Field Activity in the Socialist Republic of Vietnam," September 7, 2006. Case file, REFNO 0746, Joint POW/MIA Accounting Command, Joint Base Pearl Harbor-Hickam, Hawaii.

14. Although there were no visible examples of the CH-46 wreckage used on private property along the route traveled by JPAC and VNO teams to and from the excavation site, photographs of such practice can be found in JPAC archives, including images of machetes cut from airplane propeller blades and sandals made of rubber tires. An MIA daughter described traveling to the site where her father's plane crashed and local villagers showing her a cooking pot that had been fashioned from the metal of the downed plane. On the "vigorous trade in war scrap metal" that "emerged in the informal economies" of Laos, Cambodia, and Vietnam (her focus), see Christina Schwenkel, "War Debris in a Postwar Society: Managing Risk and Uncertainty in the DMZ," in *Interactions with a Violent Past: Reading*

Post-conflict Landscapes in Cambodia, Laos, and Vietnam, eds. Vatthana Pholsena and Oliver Tappe (Singapore: NUS Press, 2013), 135–56.

15. For example, see "Telegram From JCRC Liaison Bangkok TH To CDR JCRC Barbers Pt. HI—re: JCRC Report M85-118; Dog Tag of Allen and House (REFNO 0746)," February 13, 1986, 11270804038, Garnett Bell Collection, The Vietnam Center and Archive, Texas Tech University; and "Telegram From JCRC Liaison Bangkok TH To CDR JCRC Barbers Pt. HI—re: JCRC Prt. S86-012, Dale A. Pearce (REFNO 1747) and G. L. Runnels (REFNO 0746)," October 6, 1986, 11270823019, Garnett Bell Collection, The Vietnam Center and Archive, Texas Tech University.

16. James W. Wold, Deputy Assistant Secretary of Defense, Letter to Mrs. Amy House, December 11, 1995. Case file, REFNO 0746, Joint POW/MIA Accounting Command, Joint Base Pearl Harbor-Hickam, Hawaii.

17. Sarah Wagner, "A Curious Trade: The Recovery and Repatriation of Vietnam MIAs," *Comparative Studies in Society and History* 57, no. 1 (2015): 161–90; and Michael J. Allen, *Until the Last Man Comes Home: POWs, MIAs, and the Unending Vietnam War* (Chapel Hill: University of North Carolina Press, 2009), 227. On forensic traces of remains trading, see Robert Mann et al., "A Blue Encrustation Found on Skeletal Remains of Americans Missing in Action in Vietnam," *Forensic Science International* 97, no. 2 (1998): 79–86.

18. "Socialist Republic of Vietnam Recovery Assessment: Case 0746," March 20, 2006. Case file, REFNO 0746, Joint POW/MIA Accounting Command, Joint Base Pearl Harbor-Hickam, Hawaii. On the artifacts, see "Memorandum for J2212," Subject: Case 0746 Research, April 19, 2005. Case file, REFNO 0746, Joint POW/MIA Accounting Command, Joint Base Pearl Harbor-Hickam, Hawaii.

19. "Detailed Report of Investigation of Case 0746 (VM-01464) Conducted during the 83rd Joint Field Activity in the Socialist Republic of Vietnam," September 7, 2006.

20. Just north of Thừa Thiên–Huế Province, where the excavation site was located, and abutting the former demilitarization zone (DMZ), Quảng Trị Province in Central Vietnam is considered to have "the highest density of explosive remnants of war" in the country. Christina Schwenkel, "War Debris in a Postwar Society," 135.

21. "Contamination Situation," Technology Centre for Bomb and Mine Disposal Engineering Command, accessed December 19, 2018, http://www.bomicen.vn/?lang=en&category=63. This source lists a total of fifteen million tons of bombs, mines and munitions used by US forces in Vietnam during the war. In neighboring Laos, the US military dropped 2.1 million tons of ordnance, making it the "most heavily bombed country in history." Elaine Russell, "Laos—Living with Unexploded Ordnance: Past Memories and Present Realities," in *Interactions with a Violent Past: Reading Post-conflict Landscapes in Cambodia, Laos, and Vietnam,* eds. Vatthana Pholsena and Oliver Tappe (Singapore: NUS Press, 2013), 96–134. The first US President to visit Laos, on his trip to Vientiane in 2016, President Barack Obama pledged $90 million to assist in UXO cleaning operations and victim rehabilitation.

22. Christina Schwenkel writes powerfully about the disconnect between US veterans' experiences of reckoning with the war by returning to Vietnam, sometimes for humanitarian projects, and that of Vietnamese MIA families and veterans, cautioning against narratives of shared suffering and loss that minimize or neglect the "tremendous discrepancies in wartime and postwar trauma and dislocation." *The American War in Contemporary Vietnam: Transnational Remembrance and Representation* (Bloomington: Indiana University Press, 2009), 47.

23. Included in the first Detailed Report of Investigation, from May 1993, is testimony from a local "witness" who came across the site in 1991 while he was searching for wood. The man explained that "the site [had] been heavily scavenged and all large metal pieces [had] been removed." "Detailed Report of Investigation of Case 0746," 23rd Joint Field Activity, May 28, 1993. Case file, REFNO 0746, Joint POW/MIA Accounting Command, Joint Base Pearl Harbor-Hickam, Hawaii.

24. My thanks go to Tâm Ngô for locating this information in the Thừa Thiên–Huế provincial report, dated May 14, 2013. She noted that the GDP increased to $2,020 by 2016.

25. Thomas M. Hawley, *The Remains of War: Bodies, Politics, and the Search for American Soldiers Unaccounted for in Southeast Asia* (Durham, NC: Duke University Press, 2005), 92.

26. "Collectively, Southeast Asia represented 48 percent (90 of 187) of the number of planned missions for FYs 2017 and 2018, and nearly 70 percent ($70.2 million of $101.8 million) of the total mission budget for those 2 years." Inspector General, US Department of Defense, Report No. DODIG-2018-138, "DoD's Organizational Changes to the Past Conflict Personnel Accounting Community," July 18, 2018, https://media.defense.gov/2018/Jul/20/2001945039/-1/-1/1/DODIG-2018-138.PDF, 49.

27. Mark Bryant, interview with the author, June 14, 2012.

28. Hau Le, interview with the author, June 19, 2012.

29. Nicole McMinamin, interview with author, June 15, 2012.

30. Andrew Childs, interview with the author, June 15, 2012.

31. The site was officially closed in August 2014, a little over two years after our recovery team had opened it.

32. Victor Turner, *The Ritual Process: Structure and Anti-Structure*, rev. ed. (1969; repr., New Brunswick: AldineTransaction, 2011), 95.

33. Arnold Van Gennep, *The Rites of Passage*, rev. ed. (1960; repr., New York: Routledge, 2004), 12.

34. Van Gennep defined rites of passage as "rites which accompany every change of place, state, social position and age" (quoted in Turner, *The Ritual Process*, 94).

5. The Time in Between

1. Thomas Laqueur, *The Work of the Dead: A Cultural History of Mortal Remains* (Princeton, NJ: Princeton University Press, 2015), 10.

2. Mark Brunswick, "After 44 Years, Browns Valley Will Bury One of Its Own," *Minneapolis-St. Paul Star Tribune*, June 8, 2011, 1B.

3. Dwayne Spinler, "Bringing Dad Home," United States Military Historical Collection, accessed December 19, 2018, http://www.usmhc.org/biographies /BRINGING_DAD_HOME.pdf.

4. Spinler, "Bringing Dad Home."

5. This and the following two excerpts are taken from the author's interview with Dwayne Spinler, October 24, 2017.

6. Spinler, "Bringing Dad Home."

7. Jeff Savelkoul, "Team Striker Story," (unpublished document), shared with the author, September 15, 2016. For an account of Merl's service, his friendship with Jeff Savelkoul, and his eventual homecoming, see also Erin Miller, *Wisconsin's 37: The Lives of Those Missing in Action in the Vietnam War* (Jefferson, NC: McFarland, 2018), 53–57.

8. Louise Olesen, "American Heroes Outdoors Partners with Wounded Warriors," *Devils Lake Journal,* May 25, 2015, http://www.devilslakejournal.com /article/20150525/NEWS/150529405.

9. Savelkoul, "Team Striker Story."

10. Savelkoul, "Team Striker Story."

11. US troops left the ace of spades, a psychological warfare "calling card" that warned of death and, in some versions, urged the North Vietnamese to defect, at the entrances and exits of villages they "cleared" and on the bodies of dead NVA soldiers. Charles Brown, "How the Ace of Spades Became One of the Enduring Legends of Vietnam Psychological Warfare," *Vietnam* 20, no. 3 (2007): 13–15.

12. Savelkoul, "Team Striker Story."

13. Savelkoul, "Team Striker Story."

14. According to the Vietnam Conflict Extract Data File of the Defense Casualty Analysis System (DCAS) Extract Files, there were 11,363 deaths in 1967; 16,899 in 1968; and 11,780 in 1969. Vietnam War US Military Fatal Casualty Statistics, Electronic Records Reference Report, National Archives, accessed December 19, 2018, https://www.archives.gov/research/military/vietnam-war /casualty-statistics.

15. Laura McCallum, "Minnesota Marine Receives Bronze Star for Heroism in Vietnam," Minnesota Public Radio, August 19, 2004, http://news.minnesota .publicradio.org/features/2004/08/19_ap_bronzestar/.

16. Dineshe Ramde, "Wisconsin: 46 Years after Marine Died in Vietnam, Remains Coming Home to Be Buried," *Pioneer Press,* June 24, 2013, https://www .twincities.com/2013/06/24/wisconsin-46-years-after-marine-died-in-vietnam -remains-coming-home-to-be-buried/.

17. Jeff Savelkoul, email to the author with attached copy of the letter, March 24, 2018.

18. Jeff Savelkoul, email to the author, March 24, 2018.

19. Patriot Guard Riders, "Thread: LCpl Merlin Raye 'Merl' Allen, USMC, KIA Vietnam, Minneapolis-St. Paul, MN/Washburn, WI, 26, 28, 29 JUN 13," accessed February 16, 2018, https://www.patriotguard.org/showthread.php ?379247-LCpl-Merlin-Raye-Merl-Allen-USMC-KIA-Vietnam-Minneapolis-St -Paul-MN-Washburn-WI-26-28-29-JUN-13.

20. Holding up placards with the slogan "Thank God for Dead Soldiers," the Westboro Baptist Church views military deaths as the just reward for a nation and its armed forces that "condone homosexuality." Alan Feuer, "Revving Their Engines, Remembering a War's Toll," *New York Times,* May 29, 2006, http://www.nytimes.com/2006/05/29/nyregion/29patriot.html.

21. Patriot Guard Riders, "Our Vision," accessed December 19, 2018, https://www.patriotguard.org/about-us/.

22. Scott Walker, Office of the Governor, the State of Wisconsin, Executive Order #106, "Relating to a Proclamation that the Flag of the United States and the Flag of the State of Wisconsin be Flown at Half-Staff as a Mark of Respect for Lance Corporal Merlin Raye Allen of the United States Marines Corps Who Lost His Life While Serving His Country During the Vietnam War," June 25, 2013, https://walker.wi.gov/sites/default/files/executive-orders/EO_2013_106.pdf.

23. Jay Winter, *Sites of Memory, Sites of Mourning: The Great War in European Cultural History* (Cambridge, UK: Cambridge University Press, 1995), 29.

24. Spinler, "Bringing Dad Home."

25. G. Kurt Piehler, *Remembering War the American Way* (Washington, DC: Smithsonian Institution Press, 1995), 186.

26. Ramde, "Wisconsin: 46 Years after Marine Died in Vietnam."

27. Meg Jones, "46 years after His Death in Vietnam, Marine Returns Home for Funeral," *Milwaukee Journal Sentinel,* June 29, 2013, http://archive.jsonline.com/news/wisconsin/46-years-after-his-death-in-vietnam-soldier-returns-home-for-funeral-b9943895z1-213713351.html/.

28. Meg Jones, "46 years after His Death in Vietnam, Marine Returns Home for Funeral." See also Ramde, "Wisconsin: 46 Years after Marine Died in Vietnam"; David C. Kennedy, "Bayfield Community Honors Fallen Marine Merlin Allen: Final Goodbye Comes 46 Years after His Death in Vietnam," *Ashland Daily Press,* June 30, 2013, http://www.apg-wi.com/ashland_daily_press/news/bayfield-community-honors-fallen-marine-merlin-allen-final-goodbye-comes/article_66e84c65-59e9-55b2-98d9-10028835561f.html; Meg Jones, "Vietnam War-era Veteran Keeps Solemn Vow to His Lost Brother in Arms," *Milwaukee Journal Sentinel,* April 30, 2013, http://archive.jsonline.com/news/wisconsin/vietnam-warera-veteran-keeps-solemn-vow-to-his-lost-brother-in-arms-tf9op0o-205500991.html/.

29. Viet Thanh Nyugen, *Nothing Ever Dies: Vietnam and the Memory of War* (Cambridge, MA: Harvard University Press, 2016), 231.

30. Marilyn Neff, email to the author, February 19, 2018.

31. Georges Perec, *Species of Spaces and Other Pieces,* ed. and trans. John Sturrock (New York: Penguin Classics, 2008), 91–92.

32. The PBS show *History Detectives* profiled the vessel in an episode, tracing its history from storming the beaches of France in August 1944 to its present-day role in dredging, construction, and transport on Lake Superior. "Episode 3 2004—LCT 103—Bayfield, Wisconsin," accessed December 19, 2018, http://www-tc

.pbs.org/opb/historydetectives/static/media/transcripts/2011-04-20/203_LCT
.pdf.

33. Casey Alden Allen, email to the author, February 18, 2018.

34. Casey Alden Allen, email to the author, February 18, 2018.

35. Spinler, "Bringing Dad Home."

1970

1. "Florence V. Hessing | 1916–2015 | Obituary," Bratley Family Funeral Homes, accessed December 19, 2018, http://www.bratleyfamilyfuneralhomes.com /obituary/3193256.

2. Vietnam War US Military Fatal Casualty Statistics, Electronic Records Reference Report, National Archives, accessed December 19, 2018, https://www .archives.gov/research/military/vietnam-war/casualty-statistics.

3. "James William Hessing," the Wall of Faces, Vietnam Veterans Memorial Fund, accessed December 19, 2018, http://www.vvmf.org/Wall-of-Faces/22902 /JAMES-W-HESSING.

6. In Absentia

1. *Pioneer Press,* "Red Cliff/Little VFW Post Comes Back to Life in a Big Way," June 12, 2010, https://www.twincities.com/2010/06/12/red-cliff-little-vfw-post -comes-back-to-life-in-a-big-way/. See also Erin Miller, *Wisconsin's 37: The Lives of Those Missing in Action in the Vietnam War* (Jefferson, NC: McFarland, 2018), 45.

2. Randy Bresette, interview with author, July 30, 2017.

3. Jay Winter, *Sites of Memory, Sites of Mourning: The Great War in European Cultural History* (Cambridge, UK: Cambridge University Press, 1995), 97.

4. Alan "Butch" Kuepfer, interview with author, July 30, 2017.

5. David C. Kennedy, "Bayfield Community Honors Fallen Marine Merlin Allen: Final Goodbye Comes 46 Years after His Death in Vietnam," *Ashland Daily Press,* June 30, 2013, http://www.apg-wi.com/ashland_daily_press/news/bayfield -community-honors-fallen-marine-merlin-allen-final-goodbye-comes/article _66e84c65-59e9-55b2-98d9-10028835561f.html.

6. Randy Bresette, interview with author, July 30, 2017.

7. Randy explained that he got the idea from a veterans display at the Bad River casino in Odanah, Wisconsin, and that it quickly took off among the post members in Red Cliff. "A lot of [them] starting out bringing pictures of their own, and letting other people know. Soon, members were saying, 'I gotta get mine up there, I gotta get mine up there.'" Interview with author, July 30, 2017.

8. Tom Holm, *Strong Hearts, Wounded Souls: Native American Veterans of the Vietnam War* (Austin: University of Texas, 1996), 10, 123. See also John A. Little, "Between Cultures: Sioux Warriors and the Vietnam War," *Great Plains Quarterly* 35, no. 4 (2015): 357–58; and Theresa D. O'Nell, "'Coming Home'

among Northern Plains Vietnam Veterans: Psychological Transformations in Pragmatic Perspective," *Ethos* 27, no. 4 (1999), 445.

9. In an official letter to Mrs. Caroline Newago, Wotsy's mother, Lieutenant Colonel W. N. Clelland, US Marine Corps, wrote that "at approximately 8:00 p.m. Duwayne was being medically evacuated for a fever of unknown origin when the helicopter he was in had an engine failure and went down at sea. To this date [May 5, 1967] his body has not been recovered. A Requiem Mass was held in Duwayne's honor on 4 May 1967." LtCol W. N. Clelland, Headquarters, Seventh Communications Battalion, First Marine Division, May 5, 1967. Stan Pace's account, however, aligns with the American Legion Auxiliary "Wisconsin" POW/MIA Profile on Duwyane Soulier, which reports that Soulier "had been wounded during a combat operation and transported to the hospital at Chu Lai, Quang Tin Province, South Vietnam, for medical treatment." The profile is among the VFW post's archival material, displayed near Soulier's photograph. See also Miller, *Wisconsin's 37,* 44.

10. Vietnam Veterans Memorial Fund, "Father's Day 2012 at the Vietnam Wall with Pam Cain," YouTube video, 1:06, June 19, 2012, https://www.youtube.com/watch?v=7GwpO0r2KOs.

11. In her study of the ambiguity of presence and absence, Pauline Boss touches on the Vietnam War MIA families' experience (particularly that of MIA wives), noting that "families could not complete their mourning when their loss remained so uncertain." Boss, *Ambiguous Loss: Learning to Live with Unresolved Grief* (Cambridge, MA: Harvard University Press, 1999), 27.

12. Department of the Air Force, "Continuance of Missing in Action Status Beyond 12 Months—Case #53," February 14, 1967, USAFMPC, Randolph AFB Texas, accessed December 19, 2018, https://cdn.loc.gov/master/frd/pwmia/198/58171.pdf.

13. This and the following two excerpts, as well as the other quotations in this section of the chapter, are taken from the author's interview with Pam Cain, December 2, 2017.

14. Historian Christian Appy explores the "baby-killer" rhetoric associated with the antiwar movement as an "essential way of getting at one of the central moral legacies of military service in Vietnam," interrogating the "axiomatic" notion that the antiwar movement considered veterans "immoral killers." Appy, *Working-Class War: American Combat Soldiers and Vietnam* (Chapel Hill: University of North Carolina Press, 1993), 303–5. See also Jerry Lembcke's discussion of the "baby-killer" epithet in *The Spitting Image: Myth, Memory, and the Legacy of Vietnam* (New York: New York University Press), 83; and Michael A. Messner, *Guys Like Me: Five Wars, Five Veterans for Peace* (New Brunswick, NJ: Rutgers University Press, 2018), 18–19, 122–23.

15. According to Ann Mills-Griffiths, "presumptive findings of death were made on those listed as MIA and POW" as a "matter of law and administration" based on a "lapse of time without information to prove the man is still living." Interview with author, November 17, 2017.

16. Pauline Boss and Donna Carnes, "The Myth of Closure," *Family Process* 51, no. 4 (2012): 457.

17. Boss argues that while "religious rituals for mourning loss are reserved for the clearly dead," families experiencing ambiguous loss "are left on their own to figure out how to cope." *Ambiguous Loss, 50.*

18. A Vietnam War veteran and strong supporter of the Vietnam Veterans Memorial Foundation, Tom Carhart had also decried Lin's design as a "trench" and a "scar" and asked, "Can America truly mean that we are to be honored by a black pit?" Patrick Hagopian, *The Vietnam War in American Memory: Veterans, Memorials, and the Politics of Healing* (Amherst: University of Massachusetts Press, 2011), 102–3.

19. Maya Lin, Address before the Veterans Day Ceremony at the Vietnam Veterans Memorial, November 11, 2017, https://www.c-span.org/video/?c4691456 /maya-lin. On Lin's "conception of mourning," see James Tatum, *The Mourner's Song: War and Remembrance from the Iliad to Vietnam* (Chicago: University of Chicago Press, 2003), 3–9; and on the "double consciousness" of its reflective mode of remembrance, see Viet Thanh Nguyen, *Nothing Ever Dies: Vietnam and the Memory of War* (Cambridge, MA: Harvard University Press, 2016), 53–56.

20. Christian Appy invites us to imagine a memorial like the Wall dedicated "to the Indochinese who died in what they call the American, not the Vietnam, War": "If similar to the Vietnam Memorial, with every name etched in granite, it would have to be forty times larger than the wall in Washington." For Appy, "to insist that we recognize the disparity in causalities between the United States and Indochina is not to diminish the tragedy or significance of American losses, nor does it deflect attention from our effort to understand American soldiers. Without some awareness of the war's full destructiveness we cannot begin to understand their experience." *Working-Class War,* 17.

21. Michael Allen and H. Bruce Franklin have argued that eliding the two categories raised the profile of the MIA issue and thus the political pressure to resolve it. Allen, *Until the Last Man Comes Home,* 209. H. Bruce Frankin, *M.I.A. or Mythmaking in America,* 11–13, 96–99. Indeed, Allen notes that the decision in 1980 to collapse the distinction among POWs, MIAs, and KIA/BNRs into the "unaccounted for" label reflected "league worries that MIA ranks were nearing zero as the missing were presumed dead." *Until the Last Man Comes Home,* 211. On debates within the league and some members' early opposition to plans to bury an Unknown Soldier for the Vietnam War, see Allen, *Until the Last Man Comes Home,* 237–39.

22. Hagopian, *The Vietnam War in American Memory,* 147.

23. Ann Mills-Griffiths, interview with author, November 17, 2017. Mills-Griffiths specifies the objection to "missing men" identified as killed in action, but it is worth noting that not all the dead were men. There are eight women, all nurses, listed on the Wall; all eight are accounted for. On women's military service in Vietnam and their presence as civilian contractors, see Heather Marie Stur, *Beyond Combat: Women and Gender in the Vietnam War Era* (New York: Cambridge University Press, 2011).

24. Ann Mills-Griffiths, interview with author, November 17, 2017.

25. Hagopian, *The Vietnam War in American Memory,* 147.

26. Kristin Ann Hass, *Carried to the Wall: American Memory and the Vietnam Veterans Memorial* (Berkeley: University of California Press, 1998), 2. Hass sees the "gifts Americans bring to the Wall as part of a continuing public negotiation about patriotism and nationalism." *Carried to the Wall,* 3. While such negotiations invariably take place, gifts left may also entail private reckonings and intimate gestures of sociality between the living and dead apart from, or at least not exclusively defined by, patriotic or national sensibilities.

27. Deanna Klenda, interview with author, June 21, 2017.

28. Dean Klenda's REFNO was 0147, meaning that his was the 147th MIA/KIA/BNR case of the war.

29. Roy Wenzl, "A Sister's Efforts to Find Her Missing Brother Finally Pay Off," *The Wichita Eagle,* September 9, 2016, http://www.kansas.com/news/local /article100957232.html.

30. Ashley M. Wright, "Airman Laid to Rest after Being Shot Down in 1965," Twenty-Second Air Refueling Wing Public Affairs, Eighteenth Air Force, September 20, 2016, http://www.18af.amc.af.mil/News/Article-Display/Article /953962/airman-laid-to-rest-after-being-shot-down-in-1965/.

31. Tom Holland, email to author, March 28, 2018.

32. Maya Lin, Address before the Veterans Day Ceremony at the Vietnam Veterans Memorial.

33. Bob "Hogman" Thompson, interview with author, July 24, 2017. In contrast to WWII veterans, who came home together after two-year periods, with "virtually the whole generation" having served in the conflict, "the men who returned from Vietnam drifted home in isolation, one at a time. . . . Old friends from the neighborhood who had gone to Vietnam might well have moved or never returned." Appy, *Working-Class War,* 308.

34. G. Kurt Piehler, *Remembering War the American Way* (Washington, DC: Smithsonian Institution Press, 1995), 186.

35. Wisconsin Public Television, "The Origins of LZ Lambeau," YouTube video, 14:10, June 9, 2011, https://www.youtube.com/watch?v=EEXMS01YtGM.

36. LZ Lambeau was sponsored by the state's Department of Veterans Affairs, the Wisconsin Historical Society, and Wisconsin Public Television.

37. Michael Messner argues that this kind of "manly silence" reflects "an all-too-common tendency for veterans to stuff inside and cordon off their memories of war," which robs them of "emotional and moral healing" and deprives future generations the opportunity to hear the voices of veterans, including those who testify to the "inglorious realities of war." *Guys Like Me: Five Wars, Five Veterans for Peace* (New Brunswick, NJ: Rutgers University Press, 2019), xvii.

38. Eliza Decorah, "LZ Lambeau: Long Overdue but Never Too Late," *Hocak Worak* 24, no. 10, May 28, 2010, 1.

39. The Fond du Lac Band is part of the Lake Superior Band of Minnesota Chippewa.

40. The "born storyteller," Jim Northrup died on August 1, 2016, in Sawyer, Minnesota. Sam Robert, "Jim Northrup, Vietnam Veteran Who Wrote About Res-

ervation Life, Dies at 73," *New York Times,* August 3, 2016, https://www.nytimes
.com/2016/08/04/books/jim-northrup-vietnam-veteran-who-wrote-about-life-on
-the-reservation-dies-at-73.html.

41. Wisconsin Public Television, "LZ Lambeau: Jim Northrup," YouTube
video, 6:55, August 2, 2016, https://www.youtube.com/watch?v=URastjiT2is.

42. Jim Northrup, *Walking the Rez Road* (Golden, CO: Fulcrum, 2013), 9.

43. On the psychological and cultural responses to memories of combat among
Native American veterans and challenges they faced in seeking treatment at the
Department of Veterans Affairs, see O'Nell, "'Coming Home' among Northern
Plains Vietnam Veterans," 441–65.

44. Mary Defoe, letter shared with the author, dated August 22, 2015.

2018

1. Defense POW/MIA Accounting Agency, New Releases, "Funeral Announcement For Marines Killed During Vietnam War (House, J., Killen, J., Runnels,
G.)," September 21, 2018, https://www.dpaa.mil/News-Stories/News-Releases
/Article/1641568/funeral-announcement-for-marines-killed-during-vietnam-war
-house-j-killen-j-run/.

2. US Department of Defense, FY2019 Defense Budget, "Videos: End of a
Mournful Tale," accessed January 29, 2019, https://dod.defense.gov/News/Special
-Reports/0218_Budget/?videoid=628938&dvpTag=fallen&dvpcc=false.

Conclusion

1. The building was named after decorated World War II veteran and Medal
of Honor recipient Daniel Inouye, who served in the US Senate, representing his
home state of Hawaii from 1963 until his death in 2012. Formerly the Defense
Prisoner of War/Missing Personnel Office, DPAA East is headquartered in Crystal
City, Virginia.

2. Following the fiscal year calendar, identifications are tracked October 1
through September 30; thus, April 2018 is almost three-quarters into the year. In
the end, DPAA accounted for a total of 203 individuals for FY2018, including ten
from the Vietnam War.

3. The final quarter push, especially in September, reflects the annual cycle (and
episodic delays during the winter) that forces a catch-up beginning in spring and
running through the end of the final quarter. John Byrd, email to the author, January 11, 2018.

4. "In FY 2017, DPAA accounted for 183 missing personnel (131-WWII,
42-Korean War, 10-Vietnam War). Additionally, we individually identified the remains of 18 personnel who were previously accounted for in a group (12-WWII,
6-Vietnam War), bringing DPAA's identification total for FY 2017 to 201." Fami-
lies/VSO/MSO and Partners DPAA Quarterly In Person/Teleconference Update
Notes, October 6, 2017, Defense POW/MIA Accounting Agency, http://www

.dpaa.mil/News-Stories/Recent-News-Stories/Article/1362758/familiesvsomso
-and-partners-dpaa-quarterly-in-personteleconference-update-notes/.

The 2018 Inspector General Report notes that "DPAA's operational budget estimates for FYs 2017 and 2018 were heavily weighted toward missions in Southeast Asia (related to the Vietnam War), a conflict with just over 1,600 (2 percent) of more than 83,000 total unaccounted-for service members. Collectively, Southeast Asia represented 48 percent (90 of 187) of the number of planned missions for FYs 2017 and 2018, and nearly 70 percent ($70.2 million of $101.8 million) of the total mission budget for those 2 years." Inspector General, US Department of Defense, Report No. DODIG-2018-138, "DoD's Organizational Changes to the Past Conflict Personnel Accounting Community," July 18, 2018, https://media.defense.gov/2018/Jul/20/2001945039/-1/-1/1/DODIG-2018-138 .PDF, 49.

5. The first group (commingled) disinterment project, that of the unknowns from the USS *Oklahoma,* was begun in 2015. After undergoing initial accession and dental analysis at DPAA's Hawaii facility, the remains were transported to DPAA's satellite laboratory at Offutt Air Force Base in Omaha, Nebraska, for anthropological examination and DNA sampling. Katherine Dodd, "USS Oklahoma Disinterments Complete," Defense POW/MIA Accounting Agency, November 9 and 10, 2015, http://www.dpaa.mil/News-Stories/Recent-News-Stories /Article/628567/uss-oklahoma-disinterments-complete/. Regarding the July 2018 unilateral turnover, as of February 15, 2019, three individual service members have been identified and "it is likely there may be more than 55 separate individuals represented [among the sets of returned remains]." "Progress on Korean War Accounting," Defense POW/MIA Accounting Agency, https://www.dpaa.mil /Resources/Fact-Sheets/Article-View/Article/569610/progress-on-korean-war -personnel-accounting/.

6. Jay Price, "Having Changed America, The League Of POW/MIA Families Fades," NPR, October 19, 2017, https://www.npr.org/2017/10/19/558137698/ having-changed-america-the-league-of-pow-mia-families-fades.

7. Benedict Anderson, *Imagined Communities: Reflections on the Origin and Spread of Nationalism,* rev. ed. (1983; repr., New York: Verso, 2006), 7.

8. Viet Thanh Nguyen, *Nothing Ever Dies: Vietnam and the Memory of War* (Cambridge, MA: Harvard University Press, 2016), 26.

9. Thomas Laqueur, *The Work of the Dead: A Cultural History of Mortal Remains* (Princeton, NJ: Princeton University Press, 2015), 10.

10. US Department of Defense, News Transcript, Press Briefing, Tuesday, June 30, 1998, http://archive.defense.gov/Transcripts/Transcript.aspx?Transcript ID=1625.

11. There are two service members missing from Desert Storm (January 17, 1991–February 28, 1991) in the First Gulf War, and the Department of Defense "continues to pursue the fullest possible accounting of one serviceman lost in 1986 during Operation El Dorado Canyon in Libya." Defense POW/MIA Accounting Agency, "Conflicts: Iraq Theater & Other Conflicts," accessed December 19, 2018, http://www.dpaa.mil/Our-Missing/Iraq-Other-Conflicts/. The most high-profile MIA case from the First Gulf War was that of Captain Scott Speicher, a navy pilot

shot down on January 17, 1991, the first evening of Operation Desert Storm. His status underwent multiple reviews and changes over the next two decades: after the first four months listed as MIA, on May 22, 1991, his status was changed to KIA/BNR; in January 2001, reverted to MIA; changed to "Missing/Captured" on October 11, 2002; and changed back to MIA on March 10, 2009. His remains were finally recovered, eighteen years after he was shot down, on August 2, 2009.

    12. Viet Thanh Nguyen, *Nothing Ever Dies*, 50.

Acknowledgments

On my desk there are two bracelets, one nested in the other, off to the side but within ready view. One is for the "Wisconsin 37"—a copper band bearing the names of the thirty-seven original unaccounted-for from the state of Wisconsin that Larry "Bootin" Soulier gave me the first time we met in 2014. The other is a slimmer, green-colored aluminum POW/MIA bracelet for Colonel Oscar Mauterer, father to Pam Cain. She presented it to me recently, explaining that I shouldn't feel compelled to wear it but that she wanted me to have it. I cherish them both.

This book is born of myriad gifts, acts of generosity big and small stretched across a decade of research and writing. It's not just that it's richer for them; this book could not exist without them. And so I have many gifts to acknowledge, and yet I acknowledge from the onset that words of gratitude and recognition can only convey so much.

To the families of the missing and unaccounted for who shared their stories with me, welcomed me into their homes, spoke with me over meals or coffee, over the phone and through emails, I am profoundly grateful for your trust. Many of you I met through formal functions such as the jointly held National League of POW/MIA Families annual meeting and government briefing, smaller regional family updates, and tours of the Joint POW/MIA Accounting Command facilities. Others I encountered along more serendipitous routes. The conversations and exchanges, no matter how brief, built the foundation for my reflections on what accounting means to surviving kin.

And yet upon that foundation rest the specific stories of several individual service members, whose lives infuse this book with meaning. I wish to thank in particular the Allen family, for all your patience and for sharing your memories of your brother, both his loss and his homecoming—Marilyn Neff, Casey (Alden) Allen, Cindy Hawkins, Sheila Kelly, Sean Allen, and Jeff Savelkoul. Thank you as well, Boot and Rose Soulier and Jimmy Heipel, for your generous hospitality and for including me in Wotsy's remembrance gathering; that invitation meant more than you can imagine. Thank you, Dwayne Spinler, for your extraordinary candor and grace in telling your family's story and for your encouragement along the way. Thank you, Deanna Klenda, for your metaphors, sunsets, and bundles of wheat. And thank you, Pam Cain, for your courage and your friendship. To all of you: through your willingness to share your experiences, you let me glimpse your loved one and helped me understand how his absence and memory have forever shaped your lives. I cannot thank you enough.

To the veterans of the Duwayne Soulier Memorial VFW Post 8239 in Red Cliff, Wisconsin, most especially Randy Bresette and Butch Kuepfer, and to Diane Fizell of the Ladies Auxiliary, please know how much I value the support you have given me over the past few years. From the moment I stepped through that screen door, you welcomed a stranger—a particularly talkative one at that—into your community and taught me about its history. Mary Defoe, thank you for your poetry and your conversations, including those you shared with me of your late husband Ken. Joanna Hessing Rothermund and Bill Hessing, thank you for helping me get to know Jimmy and, through her careful clippings, photographs, and mementos, his loving mother, Florence. To Vietnam War veterans Ken "Polack" Pezewski and Bob "Hogman" Thompson, thank you for telling me the story of the MIA bike.

Alongside the families of the unaccounted for are those who seek to find them and bring them home: the personnel, civilian and military, of what was formerly the Joint POW/MIA Accounting Command (JPAC), now part of the Defense POW/MIA Accounting Agency (DPAA), and the Armed Forces DNA Identification Laboratory (AFDIL). I am deeply indebted to a whole slew of people in these agencies. First and foremost, the forensic scientists and staff at the (former) Central Identification Laboratory—this book depended on their willingness to host me, to allow me to shadow them as they went about their daily tasks, explaining the science and fielding my questions, no matter how rudimentary. Some have retired or gone on to work elsewhere, while others continue at the lab. I'm grateful to the entire staff, especially Greg Fox, John Byrd, Bill Belcher, Laurel Freas, Hugh Tuller, Derek Congram, Denise To, Greg Berg, Paul Emanovski, Marin Pilloud, Joe Hefner, Carl Stephan, Pierre Guyomarc'h, Carrie Brown, Chris Pink, Jennie Jin, Ashley Burch, Mary Megyesi, Owen O'Leary, Cullen Black, Sean Tallman, Cal Shiroma, Vince Sava, and Ben Sorensen. My appreciation also goes to Bob Maves at JPAC (now DPAA), Larry Greer of the Defense Prisoner of War / Missing Personnel Office, and Hattie Johnson, Head of the US Marine Corps POW / MIA Section. At AFDIL, Tim McMahon helped me translate the complex science of genetic testing into lay terms; thank you as well to Jim Canik and Suni Edson. In May 2012, I had the extraordinary opportunity to take part in a JPAC recovery mission in central Vietnam. My fellow team members made sure that I learned the work, stayed safe, and, above all, felt welcome among their ranks. To all twelve of 12-3VM (aka Team Knee Sweat), it was an honor to dig and screen alongside you. My particular thanks go to Laurel Freas, Nicole McMinamin, Jimmy Gasaway, Mark Bryant, Hau Le, Seth Barker, and my dig partner, Andrew Childs. And on behalf of the team, to the Vietnamese workers on the site, I extend a heartfelt *cảm ơn*.

But none of that—my fieldwork at the lab or the opportunity to participate in a recovery mission—would have been possible without the support of Tom Holland, one of the finest people I know and my mentor throughout this project. He believed in the value of this research and in me. Of all the gifts this book has given me, his friendship is among the most treasured.

In one of my favorite passages of the seminal text, *The Collective Memory*, Maurice Halbwachs explains that memories are always collective because, though individuals, we are each social beings. "In reality, we are never alone. Other[s] need not be physically present, since we always carry with us and in us a number of distinct persons." By this he means that other people, the people who fill our lives, have taught us to see, experience, and know the world in different ways. That intellectual sociality is especially true—and critical—in academic endeavors. I was never alone in this project because I had constant companions, both brilliant and thoughtful, helping to steer my ethnographic gaze and tease out deeper social meanings. First and foremost, thank you to my principal interlocutor, the historian who never let me off easy, Michael Dolski. This book is so much stronger for your engagements along the way and your close readings, down to the final draft. I am similarly grateful for conversations, feedback, and support from Sarah Daynes, Arthur Murphy, Joan Paluzzi,

Tom Matyók, Eric Jones, Adam Rosenblatt, Luis Fondebrider, Paco Fer-rándiz, Natan Sznaider, Sabrina Perić, Admir Jugo, Robin Reneike, Andy Bickford, Gerard Toal, Marilyn London, Amy Mundorff, and Dawnie Steadman. Through her subtle prompting, Tâm Ngô helped me recognize and address gaps in my analysis. Students in my War and Memory semi-nars at the University of North Carolina at Greensboro and at George Washington University have helped push my thinking in important ways, as did the students in my Forensic Science and Technology of Truth sem-inar in fall 2018. At GWU, I had the great fortune to work through ideas and to fine tune passages from this book with several graduate students: thank you, Görkem Aydemir, Devin Proctor, Evy Vourlides, Scott Ross, Emma Backe, and Shweta Krishnan for your insights. Sarah Richardson, thank you for your exacting eye and eleventh-hour encouragement.

From the early stages of fieldwork to the final writing-up process, this project has received generous funding, including support from the John Simon Guggenheim Memorial Foundation, the National Science Founda-tion (#1027457), the National Institutes of Health (#R01HG0057020), the Oak Ridge Institute for Science and Education, and the National Endow-ment for the Humanities, both a Summer Stipend grant and a Public Scholar Program award (FZ-256468-17); please note, any views, findings, conclu-sions, or recommendations expressed in this publication do not necessarily reflect those of the National Endowment for the Humanities. At critical points in the project, I benefited from two workshops, the first funded by the Wenner-Gren Foundation that explored the theme "The Gift of Death," and the second, a "book incubator" supported by GWU's Institute for Eu-ropean, Russian, and Eurasian Studies, the Sigur Center for Asian Studies, and the Institute for Ethnographic Research. This second workshop con-vened several colleagues who read drafts of the manuscript and provided invaluable comments. Leading the charge in urging more clarity and force at key moments in the analysis was Jay Winter, whose own writing has served as an inspiration and model for me since my research in Bosnia and Herzegovina. To the other participants, my attentive, generous readers Richard Grinker, Ruth Toulson, Andy Bickford, and Tom Holland, I hope there will be the chance to repay you for the care you showed this work. In the past year, I had the opportunity to present—and thus try out—some of the book's central claims to a range of different audiences. Thank you to Paco Ferrándiz for including me in the illustrious "Las políticas de memoria" research team and for the invitation to participate in the 2018 conference organized by the Center for Human and Social Sciences

(CCHS), Spanish National Research Council (CSIC); the same goes to Tâm Ngô for including me in her workshop, "The Sociopolitical Lives of the Dead," at Radboud University in the Netherlands; Alice Kelly and the CultCommWar Workshop Four: American Wars, American Memory, at the Rothemere American Institute, University of Oxford; Barbara Heath and the University of Tennessee 2018 graduate seminar; Josh Rivers at the University of Wisconsin-Milwaukee; and Jelena Subotić at Georgia State University.

"Only in appearance did I take a walk alone." The collective intellectual work behind this book extends as well into the final strides of refining its argument and polishing its prose. Here, I reaped the benefits of my external reviewers' keen assessments, including those of Thomas Laqueur. I am deeply appreciative for his incisive and honest comments; the book is better for his readings. Though he wasn't directly part of this project, classicist James Tatum long ago taught me the creative possibilities of interdisciplinarity; his lessons and example are never far away, and I hope he will recognize their traces among the pages of this book.

At Harvard University Press, Andrew Kinney's light but deft editorial hand helped the text take its final shape, both in structure and voice. With his gift for language, Richard Feit smoothed off this work's rough edges and caught my errors; any that remain are mine alone. Thank you as well to Kate Brick and Olivia Woods for their careful attention to detail. Isabelle Lewis created the maps, and Amanda Wilmot generously allowed me to include images from her stirring chronicle of Merlin Allen's homecoming. This project spanned a decade, and thus many of its concepts have been percolating for a while, finding slivers of daylight in earlier publications. Chapter 1 builds on ideas first discussed in "Monumental Change: The Shifting Politics of Obligation at the Tomb of the Unknowns," an article I coauthored with Thomas Matyók and published in *History & Memory* 30, no. 1 (Spring/Summer 2018): 40–74. Chapters 1 and 4 continue lines of inquiry first discussed in "A Curious Trade: The Recovery and Repatriation of U.S. Missing in Action from the Vietnam War," *Comparative Studies in Society and History* 57, no. 1 (January 2015): 161–90. Portions of Chapter 1 were first published in "The Making and Unmaking of an Unknown Soldier," *Social Studies of Science* 43, no. 5: 631–56 and are reprinted here with permission of Sage Publications. Jim Northrup's poem "wahbegan" is reprinted from *Walking the Rez Road*, 20th anniversary ed. (Golden, CO: Fulcrum Publishing, 2013) by kind permission of Fulcrum, Inc.

I have researched and written this book warmed by the sunlight of my family's love. To my mother, Shannon McCune Wagner, I marvel at your courage and am grateful each day for what you have always given me—your love, support, and guidance. To Wallace Watson and Johanna McCune Wagner, thank you for every page you read and idea you heard out, and for your abiding understanding—of me and this project. To Jonathan Wagner, Nat and Christy Wagner, Rob Wagner, and Carin and Sue Ruff, please know how much I appreciate your encouragement and care over these past several years.

Alejandro and Emilio Pérez, you have brought such joy to my life—the effervescent, wondrous kind but also that deep, everyday, grounding kind. And you've been so very patient with me writing this book, word by word, page by page. Thank you, Emilio, *y gracias poochon.*

Illustration Credits

p. 190   Lawrence "Bootin" Soulier with his lake trout catch. Photograph by the author.

p. 193   Then Major Oscar Mauterer, Bien Hoa Air Base, Vietnam, 1965. Photograph courtesy of Pam Cain.

p. 194   Pam Cain with her father. Photograph courtesy of Pam Cain.

p. 201   Deanna Klenda's annual tribute to her brother at the Vietnam Veterans Memorial. Photograph courtesy of Deanna Klenda.

p. 202   Major Dean Albert Klenda. Photograph courtesy of Deanna Klenda.

p. 204   Siblings Deanna and Dean Klenda with the bouquet of weeds. Photograph courtesy of Deanna Klenda.

Index

273